Mr. Lincoln's Bridge Builders
The Right Hand of American Genius

Phillip M. Thienel

WHITE MANE BOOKS

This White Mane Books publication
was printed by
Beidel Printing House, Inc.
63 West Burd Street
Shippensburg, PA 17257-0152 USA

In respect for the scholarship contained herein, the acid-free paper used in this book meets the guidelines for permanence and durability of the Committee on Production Guidelines for Book Longevity of the Council on Library Resources.

For a complete list of available publications
please write
White Mane Books
Division of White Mane Publishing Company, Inc.
P.O. Box 152
Shippensburg, PA 17257-0152 USA

Library of Congress Cataloging-in-Publication Data

Thienel, Phillip M.
    Mr. Lincoln's bridge builders : the right hand of American genius / Phillip M. Thienel.
        p. cm.
    Includes bibliographical references and index.
    ISBN 1-57249-198-1 (alk. paper)
    1. United States--History--Civil War, 1861-1865--Engineering and construction. 2. Military bridges--United States--History--19th century. 3. Military engineering--United States--History--19th century. I. Title.

E468.9 .T455 2000
973.7'3--dc21

                                                                00-020385

PRINTED IN THE UNITED STATES OF AMERICA

For My Schoolteachers

Contents

Illustrations and Maps

Introduction

This book is a history of the Civil War bridge-building handiwork of the army's engineer and pioneer officers, soldiers, and civilian craftsmen on the building of a selected number of bridges.

Engineers were members of designated engineer staffs or units. Pioneers were members of infantry regiments who were assigned to pioneer corps. Military doctrine prescribed the engineers and pioneers areas of responsibilities and duties.

The wartime terrain formed a difficult obstacle in the marches to battle of the infantry, cavalry, and artillery, and the movement of the wagon trains that delivered their food and military necessities. The engineers and pioneers, propelled by the technology of the time, constructed innovative bridges to assure mobility for the combat and supply troops to reach the battlefields.

At the outbreak of the war, the army's Corps of Engineers provided a source of highly skilled engineer officers. They had pursued their education at the United States Military Academy, one of the country's principal engineering institutions. The Corps of Engineers administered the academy until July 1866.

A Congressional Act of March 16, 1802, established the Corps of Engineers and prescribed such responsibilities and duties as planning, constructing, and repairing all fortifications, and constructing of civil works projects authorized by Congress.

The corps' wartime duties included preparing plans for the attack and defense of military works, laying out and constructing field defenses, redoubts, entrenchments, roads, and military bridges. On the terrain the corps built obstacles to deter the enemy or destroyed them to enhance the friendly army's mobility.

For fifty-nine years the Corps of Engineers achieved a notable record on the construction of civil and military projects.

To provide engineering services in 1861, the corps commanded a limited staff of engineer officers, and a skeleton organization of a company of engineer soldiers, authorized by congressional legislation, manned by three officers and one hundred enlisted men.

The corps' leadership assessing the incredible physical efforts required for mandated engineering tasks, hastily recognized that the terrain the war would be fought on would require many additional engineer officers and engineer units manned by enlisted men with mechanical aptitudes and skills. The additional personnel would perform the physical tasks to build roads and bridges, and battlefield construction projects. They would be called upon to build bridges over formidable rivers, creeks, and streams to cross soldiers, animals, animal-drawn wagon trains, artillery pieces, and ambulances to carry away the sick and wounded. They would also face the task to build and reconstruct railroad bridges.

The resources available to the corps at the outbreak of the war were insufficient to handle the anticipated expanded workload of engineer duties. To build bridges, roads, and other construction projects, a requirement existed for many new units. The Congress vetoed requests to authorize additional engineer units, but, alternatively, authorized additional companies to join the active company to form an engineer battalion.

With the authorization of volunteer forces in the states, foresighted engineer officers recognized the need to take the initiative to encourage state citizens to recruit and organize engineer units, and the Congress to authorize such units to be designated engineer units with responsibilities and pay and benefits equal to the regular engineer battalion.

Steps were taken by citizens to organize engineer companies in Kentucky, Missouri, and Pennsylvania, and regiments in Michigan, Missouri, and New York. In the volunteer units engineers with experience on construction projects throughout the country were recruited to fill the officer positions. The occupations of enlisted engineer soldiers were such to fill the ranks with experienced carpenters, woodsmen, masons, wagon makers, blacksmiths, farm hands, railroad artificers, and laborers.

The volunteer engineers filled the positions of regimental and company commanders, staff officers, and company officers.

As the war progressed, the advancement of technology in the railroad industry increased the role of the railroads in the mobility of the army and the transport of military personnel and equipment. Thus, when the secretary of war established the United States

Military Railroads Service, an additional need arose for railroad construction engineers and technically qualified railroad construction mechanics.

In essence, the duties and responsibilities of railroad construction and reconstruction of destroyed tracks, stations, depots, and repair facilities existed as a decentralized function in the army. The duties were performed by army staff officers, engineer units, and the United States Military Railroads Service.

Early in the war, Brigadier General Herman Haupt served as a staff officer for Major General Irvin McDowell's Army of Northeastern Virginia. Haupt personally supervised the planning, construction, reconstruction, and maintenance and operations of the railroads in northern Virginia. He employed, and trained, soldiers of the line regiments and contrabands to build railroad bridges and tracks. He performed the same function for Major General John Pope when he succeeded McDowell as army commander.

In the Peninsular Campaign of 1862, the 50th New York Volunteer Engineers reconstructed the Richmond and York River Railroad on Black Creek. In the follow-up Antietam campaign, the engineer battalion worked on the reconstruction of the Confederate-burned railroad suspension bridge at Harpers Ferry.

In the Midwest, the Michigan and Missouri engineer regiments, in addition to their battlefield engineering tasks, spent a large portion of their engineering labors on railroad work. Their work, though, was supplemented by civilian artisans and the cooperative labors of the United States Military Railroads Service.

Major General William T. Sherman, as commander of the Military Division of the Mississippi, retained to himself control of the construction-reconstruction, and operations and maintenance of the railroads in his division's geographic area. He employed the Michigan and Missouri engineer regiments, United States Military Railroads Service, civilian artisans, and contrabands.

This story omits the achievements of the United States Military Railroads Service because the subject merits a separate history. Mentioned in this story are instances where army engineers and the above mentioned organization worked on joint railroad construction projects.

There is no intent in this story to downplay the fact that the engineers also employed their imaginative and innovative skills on corduroying primitive roads, paths, and trails to enable soldiers to march to the battlefields. They designed and constructed fixed and hasty-field fortifications for defensive tactics, and they built canals for army units to deploy on flanking operations. In essence, they labored at "dirty hands, boots, and clothes engineering tasks."

   The wartime mission of the engineers also called upon them to build siege works at Yorktown, New Madrid, Vicksburg, Petersburg, Chattanooga, and Atlanta. They were also called upon to destroy the railroad bridges, tracks, and depots behind enemy lines to disrupt the supply system. With the advent of the policy to destroy totally the enemy's war-making technology, the engineers supervised the total destruction of such resources in Jackson, Mississippi; Atlanta, Georgia; and Richmond, Virginia. On General Sherman's march from Atlanta to Savannah to Goldsborough, they supervised the implementation of the total-war policy to destroy bridges, railroads, factories, arsenals, armories, and any other asset of technology contributing to the continuance of the war. At the same time they ravaged the earth of agricultural and animal products for food and fodder.

   This book emphasizes the engineers' bridge-building feats. Bridge building ranked high as a major task, and the task engineers earned by their mind-propelled energy and their mark for creative and innovative technology.

   The engineers' innovativeness provided the field armies with heavy-duty ponton bridges for record-length bridges to cross soldiers over rivers, creeks, and streams with their artillery pieces and wagon trains, and lightweight canvas ponton bridges for cavalrymen to cross water obstacles to conduct reconnaissance or battle missions. To facilitate the increasing use of railroads in the army's logistical system, the army's engineers on occasion designed and built unique railroad trestle bridges, and rebuilt destroyed railroad trestle bridges.

   The bridges were also highly visible monuments that triggered the instincts of artists and photographers to capture their impressions of the engineers' *savoir-faire* in visual representations. Unfortunately, because of the pace of battlefield activities they could only capture a limited amount of the engineers' work.

   When the war erupted, the army's engineers undertook a hasty program, with the technology available, to develop and fabricate pontons for portable bridge trains, and to replace the untested India rubber ponton bridge train fabricated in the Mexican War.

   In a short time, the engineer units were equipped with effective portable bridge trains. When an immediate need arose in battle they built a number of ponton bridge expedients that earned the description "spectacular."

   Instances of critical situations arose on the battlefields where an engineer or pioneer office stood on a riverbank with orders from a commanding general to build a bridge *tout de suite.*

Quickly, the engineer or pioneer officer, mindful of his duty, with the energy of his mind, and confidence, analyzed the challenge confronting him. Through systematic steps the officer followed a series of tasks to conceptualize an outline of a bridge; form a construction plan; and conduct an analysis of the stresses. He then set to work his engineer or pioneer soldiers to tasks by work parties to collect materials in the area, and then supervised the ongoing construction of the planned floating or fixed bridge.

The bridges the engineers and pioneers built on the battlefields provided expedients to maintain the army's mobility. They were not intended to be permanent structures. Some bridges, as President Lincoln remarked, looked miraculous and some looked fragile. A number provided artful sights in their own way of wonder as to their construction and ability to carry heavy loads.

There were a number of examples during the war (which in themselves seem ordinary expedients), that bear out that notable American skill of applied mechanics to the building of unique bridges. Examples were: (1) forming a bridge by placing the tongue, of successively lined-up wagons, under the body of another, taking out the two end gates and teamster's seat, with the beds of the wagons for a pathway; (2) weaving wild grape vines to form the cable to build a suspension bridge over a creek; and (3) employing bales of cotton for pontons to build a floating bridge.

The bridge-building phenomenon of the Civil War demonstrated an impressive example of technology by the engineers and their artificers and craftsmen, military and civilian, in a critical event in our country's history, and one that today inspires admiration for a prideful historical achievement.

Acknowledgments

I am frank to write, as an author preparing a manuscript, I needed many human resources to complete my work. I had the good fortune to meet many knowledgeable persons, librarians, archivists, writers, readers, who generously helped me in locating, or in suggesting materials, and others who expressed interest, and offered encouragement and inspiration, thus contributing to and becoming a part of this book.

I especially express my thanks to the staffs at the archives and libraries who assisted me on technical questions and on locating source materials: Alderman Library, the University of Virginia, Charlottesville; the George Peabody Library of the Johns Hopkins University, Baltimore; the John Pace Library of the University of West Florida, Pensacola; Enoch Pratt Free Library, Baltimore; Library of Congress, Washington, D.C.; National Archives and Records Administration, Washington, D.C.; U.S. Army Engineer Center and School Library (then at Fort Belvoir, Virginia); State of Kentucky Archives, Frankfort; Records Management and Archives, Missouri State Government, Jefferson City.

I would especially like to thank Pauline Page, Copy Center Division, Alderman Library, University of Virginia, and Barbara Natanson, Prints and Photographs Reading Room, Library of Congress for their assistance in obtaining photographs. Heather A. Packard, Science and Engineering Libraries, University of Virginia, and Dean DeBolt and Katrina King, Special Collections, John Pace Library, University of West Florida, for assisting me in obtaining source materials. Erma Lookabough, West Florida Regional Library System, for obtaining materials through interlibrary loan service.

Donald Purcell, faculty of Clarkson University, Potsdam, New York and Emma Ferguson, faculty of University of West Florida, who gave of their time to read my writing and provided to me the benefits of their writing skills and helpful review comments.

I am especially thankful to my family for their continuous interest in my writing, and the many ways they extended a helping hand with the tasks assigned on the job description of a researcher-writer. I am grateful to my son, Norman L. Thienel, for making available to me his computer expertise, and guiding me through the intricacies and rewards of creating a manuscript by computer.

Chapter 1

1861
Volunteers Join the Engineers

Amidst the atmosphere of impending sectional strife, Lieutenant Cyrus B. Comstock, an instructor at the United States Military Academy, West Point, New York, on January 6, 1861, recorded in his diary, "excitement in the air."

Colonel Richard Delafield, the academy's superintendent, aroused the excitement with his issuance of an alert order to the Engineer Company, the only Corps of Engineers' company of approximately one hundred engineer soldiers, "to be ready at a moment's warning for war service." If the prospect of service in the impending civil war excited the officers, soldiers, and cadets at the academy, the Engineer Company could record in its records its presence at the war's beginning.[1]

On January 20 a detachment of the Engineer Company, under command of Lieutenant James C. Duane and company officer Lieutenant Godfrey Weitzel, received orders to proceed to Washington, D.C. Upon arrival at the capital city rife with tension fearful of the outbreak of armed rebellion, the detachment performed duties protecting public buildings, stores, and arsenals. The engineer soldiers drilled frequently, and were only permitted to leave their armory quarters in groups of three and for one hour. They also served as an escort for President Abraham Lincoln's inauguration.[2]

On April 3 the Engineer Company's detachment received sealed orders to proceed from Washington to Fort Hamilton, Brooklyn, New York. The soldiers, ready to embark on the steamer *Atlantis*, remained excited about their adventure, but speculated about their destination. On April 7, the detachment embarked from Fort Hamilton.

1

The engineer detachment arrived at Santa Rosa Island, on the Gulf Coast, on April 16, four days after the outbreak of civil war precipitated by the Confederate soldiers' bombardment of Fort Sumter.

The next day the engineer detachment disembarked at Fort Pickens, which guarded the ships' pass to Pensacola Bay. At the fort the engineer detachment's soldiers set to work at tasks to improve the works' readiness for defense and built traverses, and placed lateral parapets, bombproofs, and exterior batteries. The engineer soldiers reported the duty hard and unremitting. They endured the lack of fresh rations, scarce food, and the deterioration of their health. They completed their work to reinforce Fort Pickens, which insured the fort's remaining in the possession of Union soldiers. Under orders to leave the fort, the engineer detachment embarked on September 17, and on September 30 arrived at their quarters at the military academy at West Point.[3]

The Engineer Company performed well limited tasks on the alert during heated up secession fever, but the impending strife that exploded into civil war forced the Corps of Engineers, with a roster of forty-three officers, to expand in officers, troops, engineer organizations, and materiel to provide widespread service to support the army's war mission. Also, there was a Corps of Topographical Engineers, the surveyors and map makers, with a roster of forty-two officers. In 1863 the topographical engineers were merged with the Corps of Engineers.

The Corps of Engineers' mission statement prescribed, among its diverse duties, to provide:

(1) the field armies with engineer organizations. To accomplish that task, in the absence of congressional legislation to increase the strength of Corps of Engineers' troop units, a must would be mobilization of state volunteer units to share the heavy workload of battlefield support.

(2) fixed and floating bridges to assure the field armies mobility. Fixed bridges met the requirements for railroad and wagon trains, ambulances, and soldiers and animals to cross rivers, creeks, swamps, and other obstacles. They could be built by engineers from timber resources near the bridge sites.

(3) portable floating bridge trains filled the need for rapid river crossings by infantry, artillery, cavalry, and their wagon trains.

For floating bridge purposes, the Corps of Engineers possessed a portable India rubber ponton bridge train. The pontons consisted of air-filled cylinders (pontoons) fabricated with duck and coated with India rubber. The equipment dated in manufacture from the Mexican War. Colonel Delafield assigned Captain George W. Cullum to direct the project to design and procure the ponton bridge train. Cullum became the corps' expert on floating bridge equipment. The equipment he procured, when authorized by Congress on May 13, 1846, arrived too late to enable General Zachary Taylor's expeditionary force to cross the Rio Grande River in November 1846. From that belated experience Cullum's ponton-bridge train failed to be tested as military bridge equipment. His innovations, though, on the India rubber pontons became recognized as a contribution to technology, and a "creditable instance of that mechanical ingenuity that left Americans in a proud state of mind."[4]

Bull Run

Engineers, First on the Battlefield

At the outset of the July 21 battle of Bull Run, seven Corps of Engineers' officers and two Topographical Engineers' officers, on duty with Major General Irvin McDowell's army, experienced their initiation into battlefield duties.

The usual duties of the engineers to facilitate the army's battlefield mobility, bridge building, bypassed the nine officers because McDowell's force lacked a bridge train and an organization of bridge builders.

The officers present at Bull Run filled an important role. In the absence of a bridge train, or creeks and runs not requiring bridges, they provided expedients of gathered-up timber to cross creeks and runs or reconnoitered for fords for the soldiers to wade across.

As it related to the topographical engineers, McDowell also lacked current maps to particularize any roads, paths, or trails on the primitive terrain where he proposed to fight a battle.

On July 18, McDowell assigned Major John G. Barnard, his staff engineer officer, and Captain Barton S. Alexander, engineer officer of Colonel Daniel Tyler's First Division, the task to conduct a reconnaissance of a prospective ford, such as Blackburn's Ford on Bull Run, south of Centreville. The two engineer officers were to determine the feasibility of soldiers wading the ford. Upon their completion of their tasks at Blackburn's Ford, Barnard and Alexander noted the Confederate soldiers were already posted in the thick woods on the south side of the ford. They also observed east of their location Confederate soldiers were marching from Manassas Junction to Blackburn's Ford. They reported to McDowell their belief of the unsuitability of the ford as a site for soldiers to wade across to begin an attack.[5]

Barnard also reconnoitered the most prominent crossing over Bull Run, the stone bridge on the Warrenton Turnpike. He concluded from his observations that the bridge was guarded by a large force of Confederate soldiers and there were already in place cannon and abatis. As a bar to McDowell's force's mobility, he also surmised the Confederates had mined the bridge, as a standing order, to blow it up in the face of a Union attack. He hesitated though to show himself to the enemy and walk to the bridge to examine it.

In his report to McDowell, Barnard suggested, as an alternative to Blackburn's Ford and the turnpike bridge, an attempt be made to turn the enemy's left flank at the ford at Sudley Springs, two to three miles to the west from the turnpike bridge. At Sudley Springs, he believed, soldiers could wade the ford. Barnard, though, lacked knowledge of the approach roads to Sudley Springs, but stated he would conduct a reconnaissance.

On a reconnaissance to seek information about Sudley Springs, Major Barnard and Captain Daniel P. Woodbury, engineer officer of Colonel David Hunter's Second Division, and a spearhead cavalry company, proceeded northwest up the valley of Cub Run, on the dirt roads approximately four miles from Centreville and reached a road they believed led to a ford at Sudley Springs. After arriving at and making a preliminary survey at the ford, Barnard concluded it would be practicable at the ford's location to wade the stream. He reported his findings to McDowell.

On the next day, Captain Horatio G. Wright and First Lieutenant George W. Snyder, engineer officer of Colonel Andrew Porter's Third Division, also made a reconnaissance to Sudley Springs. First Lieutenant Frederick E. Prime, engineer officer of Colonel Dixon S. Miles' Fifth Division, and Captain Amiel W. Whipple of the Topographical Engineers attempted to conduct a reconnaissance of a dirt road and ford at Cub Run, west of the Warrenton Turnpike, but failed in the effort because the Confederate soldiers appeared to be occupying the wooded land on the Union-held side of the ford.

McDowell then decided his engineer and topographical officers provided him with enough information on the terrain to form a decision. He decided to cross three divisions at the Sudley Springs ford and to force a battle to turn the enemy's left flank. He expected his troop deployment to surprise the Confederates and to delay their abandonment of their position at Blackburn's Ford, and then march west to meet the Union attack.[6]

McDowell issued orders to his division commanders to march out at 2:30 a.m., Sunday, July 21.

Colonel Tyler's First Division received orders to make an attack on the turnpike bridge, and if successful to march to the ford at Sudley Springs.

Colonel Hunter's Second Division and Colonel Porter's Third Division, with engineer officers Captain Woodbury, Captain Wright, and Lieutenant Snyder leading them on the march route, were to march to the ford at Sudley Springs. Captain Woodbury, who led the Second Division on its march route, failed to stay on the assigned road. To avoid enemy batteries he marched the division on a circuitous road which inordinately delayed the division's reaching its destination.

Colonel Porter reported the delay of the Third Division at its march out and the follow-up two and one-half-hour delay when it turned off the Warrenton Turnpike for the march to Sudley Springs. "A slow and intermittent movement," he reported, "through woods for four hours brought the head of the division to Bull Run and Sudley Springs." He halted the division for a half hour to refresh and water the soldiers and the animals. He observed the enemy, he reported, in the distance marching to confront the Union line.

The three divisions failed to follow the assigned scheduled times to march out of their camps to seek battle. Because of their dalliance they fell behind in their assignments. Tyler's First Division marched out two hours late. As a consequence the other divisions in succession were delayed in their departures to take up the line of march to their designated positions.

McDowell reported, when he reached Sudley Springs ford, "I found the leading brigade of Hunter's Second Division had crossed, but the men were slow in getting over because they were stopping to drink water." He also wrote the delay in starting the march in the morning, as it turned out, became a "great misfortune."[7]

In response to the battlefield situation at the ford at Sudley Springs, McDowell sent orders to Tyler's First Division to force its crossing at the Warrenton Turnpike bridge. The division attacked and captured the bridge intact and marched west to the battlefield. Captain Alexander, with foresight, had earlier assembled timber there to construct a trestle bridge in the event the Confederates destroyed it on their withdrawal. In actuality, the Confederates fooled Barnard on his earlier surmise; they chose not to mine the bridge.

Barnard, as the staff engineer officer completing his role to see the soldiers across the ford and taking up battlefield positions, made the interesting comment in his report: "I remained an anxious spectator and for the first time beginning to anticipate a possible defeat."[8]

What Barnard had astutely anticipated became reality.

After finally reaching the battlefield, McDowell's ill-trained troops, fighting their first battle, determinedly attacked the enemy. They routed them from their hilltop in a hapless event.[9]

The early success did not herald the outcome of the battle. The battlefield contestants traded attacks and counterattacks throughout the afternoon, but in the final attack, General Pierre G.T. Beauregard's newly arrived train-transported reinforcements made an all-out attack and drove McDowell's panic-stricken troops in *sauve qui peut* from the battlefield.

Captain Alexander sent a message to the War Department: "General McDowell's army in full retreat through Centreville. The day is lost. Save Washington and the remnants of this army. The routed troops will not reform." The contents of the message were made known to President Lincoln.[10]

Colonel Hunter wrote in his after battle report, "Captain Woodbury fearlessly exposed himself in front of the skirmishers during our whole advance, and determined with great judgment the route of the division."

General McDowell wrote few words in the record on the role of his engineer and topographical officers, but he wrote of his staff engineer officer, "Barnard gave me most important aid."[11]

At Bull Run engineer officers performed limited tasks in their roles. In comparison, the large group of Regular Army and Volunteer engineer officers who were called upon in the progress of the war performed a wide range of complex and innovative and imaginative tasks. The records will verify they demonstrated their leadership and immense number of engineering skills on the dynamic battlefields.

The President's Choice

The incredible defeat at Bull Run shocked President Lincoln. He experienced his own and the public's pressure for a quick victory. He journeyed out to the banks of the Potomac River where he observed McDowell's army cowering in its sprawling camp along the river's banks. In his first act to counter disaster, he removed McDowell from command of the Department of Northeastern Virginia. He sought to have the soldiers in that department imbued with the fighting spirit and military discipline sufficient to put down quickly the rebellion. To Washington he ordered a replacement commander, Major General George Brinton McClellan. A month earlier McClellan earned a reputation for himself when a militia force of his Department of the Ohio cleared the lower part of western Virginia of all Confederate troops. His success brought him to the attention of President Lincoln.[12]

Upon taking over command from McDowell, McClellan renamed the department's field army the Army of the Potomac. Diligently, McClellan set about to organize his army to his own design. He reputedly possessed rare executive ability and, as a former Corps of Engineers' officer, an engineer's aptitude for systematic building. He "worked hard" to build a fine army from the bottom up. Also, the army's logistic arrangements, armaments, and individual and unit training had to be completed before McClellan would lead his army into battle.

McClellan's soldiers sensed his devotion to their readiness for combat. They seemingly accepted him with affection. McClellan was firm in his intention not to commit his soldiers to battle until they had been completely equipped and thoroughly trained. Allied to that intention was his grasp of General Winfield Scott's doctrine on the preparation of an army, and the strategic plan to put down the "unnatural and unjust rebellion."[13] There were at the time vocalists who thought an army could fight just as soon as it was organized with soldiers gathered into its ranks. McClellan shrugged off their clamor.

McClellan Organizes His Engineers

McClellan also turned his attention to organizing his staff of engineer officers and engineer units to perform their battlefield duties. He retained Major Barnard as chief engineer, Army of the Potomac. Barnard received an appointment as brigadier general, United States Volunteers, September 23, 1861. In his past career in the Corps of Engineers he supervised throughout the country the construction of many public buildings. To protect the national capital city at the outbreak of the rebellion he planned and supervised the initiation of the construction of 68 forts in a fourteen-mile ring around Washington, D.C. He also acquired initial battlefield experience as an engineer officer on McDowell's staff in the battle of Bull Run.[14]

The Obsolete Bridge Train

When McClellan turned his attention to the need for a portable bridge train, he declared, "I was satisfied that the India rubber ponton bridge train was entirely useless for general purposes of campaign. He made his decision based on his experience as an engineer officer in the Engineer Company in the war with Mexico.[15]

Based on his recollected Mexican War experiences as an officer in the Engineer Company, and conclusions on military impedimenta, McClellan, as commander of the Army of the Potomac, ordered Barnard to procure the new model, French bateau ponton for the bridge train, and engineer tools and wagon trains.

Barnard assigned the newly promoted Lieutenant Colonel Alexander the task to organize engineer soldiers into units and to

Top, India Rubber Pontoon. *Bottom,* Engineer Soldiers Inflating India Rubber Pontoon.

Mottelay and Copeland, *The Soldier in Our Civil War*

French Ponton

Photographic File, U.S. Army Engineer School

prepare the portable bridge equipment for the Army of the Potomac. Alexander was reported to be a man of massive build and of a brusque manner, and to be a "doer." When a special engineer job had to be done he was the officer assigned to do it. Barnard remarked that Alexander had acquired an "enviable reputation" as a construction engineer and possessed great practical ingenuity. Barnard offered additional remarks on the tasks assigned to Alexander, "prudence demands that the safety of an army shall not be jeopardized by giving it a bridge which experiment has not fully tested. American genius is fertile in this as in all other expedients, but no genius can provide for an object which is not understood. The numerous proposers of flying bridges forget that if a military bridge is intended to be carried with an army it is also intended to carry an army, its columns of men, its cavalry, its countless heavy wagons, and its ponderous artillery. It must carry all these, and it must do it with certainty and safety, even though a demoralized corps should rush upon it in throngs. No make-shift expedient, no ingenious inventions not tested by severe experiment, nor light affair, of which the chief merit alleged is that it is light, will be likely to do what is required, and what the French ponton has so often done."[16]

Colonel Alexander's Expectancy

An engineer officer in his daily duties lived with an expectancy. An expectancy that out of the clear blue he would be confronted with a task to perform. The task would require him to assess it, and to conceptualize quickly in his imaginative mind a response in either a written plan or a physical expediency. When Colonel Alexander received the assignment from Barnard he faced an expectancy. An expectancy to spell out the role of the non-present engineers in the Army of the Potomac and their means to acquire their requirements in men and equipment.

Alexander responded to Barnard on October 13 in a brilliant conceptualization of engineer tactics and requirements for officers, men, and equipment necessary to support McClellan's strategic battle plan.

Alexander stressed the point that if the Army of the Potomac, in the implementation of the national strategy and the engineers' support tactics, moved south of Washington, it would be an army of invasion. As such the army would have to (1) cross numerous rivers and streams; (2) overcome obstructions on the march route; (3) reduce fortifications; and (4) construct siege works.

He believed to march an army forward without engineer officers and soldiers, bridge equipment, and engineer trains, would invite defeat.

As an army would not go forward without infantry, he wrote, likewise it should not go forward without engineers. "Such a course against an enemy as we have to meet, we know would result in disgrace and disaster, in whatever numbers we may move."[17]

There were, Alexander emphasized, no engineer troops, no bridge equipment, and no train of tool wagons. There was, he reported, an untried ponton bridge [India rubber], and one company of engineer soldiers, but they were a drop in the bucket when the engineers contemplated their future requirements. "The country," he declared, "must secure the services of its practical bridge builders. We do not have time to spend a year training a brigade of engineer troops.

"What then are we to do? This becomes a grave question, and I could wish that it had been committed to wiser heads than mine.

"The answer must be, however, we must make them. Our country is full of practical bridge builders. We must secure their services. It is full of instructed labor of a kind so nearly akin to that which we require in engineer troops, that we must, if possible, embark in that channel.

"If I were the general commanding, and possessed no more light on the subject than I do at present, I would in the first place direct that the four companies of engineer soldiers now authorized by law be filled up to the maximum. This, I believe, may be done by transfers from the volunteer forces now assembled near the city.

"Let us limit the force here to one hundred regiments, and say we want 500 men. This will call for five men from each regiment on average. If the order inviting or authorizing such transfers should limit the number to ten to be taken from each regiment without the consent of the colonel, I believe the four engineer companies may at once be filled, and after an explanation of the absolute necessity for such troops all opposition on the part of the regimental commanders would be silenced, or at least could be met by silence. These men should not be taken at random. Only such as are qualified by previous pursuits to make engineer soldiers should be transferred.

"This would soon give us a small body of men, but by no means the number the emergency requires. Without the authority of law to raise such troops, and without the power to raise the pay so as to command the services of good mechanics, I see no other way to supply them than by taking two or three of our best volunteer regiments, detaching them from the line of the army, and instructing them as best we may with the limited number of officers who have made this a specialty in the duties of engineer troops. I understand that there have been several volunteer regiments organized with a view of being converted to engineer troops. These will probably be the regiments to be selected.

"We shall have roads and railroads to build and repair; telegraph lines to put up; bridges to construct and destroy; and fortifications to build, to defend, and reduce. Except in the construction of military bridges, and the investment and reduction of fortified places, it may be hoped with some degree of confidence that after a little experience our engineer troops so obtained will soon become proficient. These two subjects require study. Each of them is a specialty, and I confess that my ideas are not sufficiently matured to enable me to give clear and distinct views on the subject, or to direct your attention to something that is fixed and will not require alteration hereafter.

"I made the canvas boats [Russian model], that Lieutenant Joseph C. Ives, of the Topographical Engineers, used in his expedition on the Colorado River. Before letting them go out of my hands I used them on several occasions. I was much pleased with them, and Lieutenant Ives afterwards informed me that they answered his purpose admirably. I confess myself favorably impressed with this boat. A bridge train with these boats for pontons could be very rapidly made.

"It should not be forgotten that in any advance of our army we ought to avail ourselves of the mechanical skill of our soldiers and the timber of the country to replace all such bridges, where it is possible, by more permanent structures. In many cases ferry-boats may be made to take the place of bridges if we carry the necessary tools in the engineer trains with such to construct them and the necessary rigging with which to maneuver them."[18]

Russian Ponton

Official Records (O.R.),   Atlas, Plate CVI

Alexander was not understating the difficulty of the American obstacle-laden terrain as a battlefield. In an army's march to battle, the engineers would have to hack and build roads through the wilderness, build bridges over creeks and rivers, and remove felled trees and abatis and other obstacles the enemy would put in the route of march to impede an attack.

On October 14, General McClellan addressed a letter to Thomas A. Scott, assistant secretary of war, in reference to a letter he sent a few days previously relative to a request for authority to construct from ten to fifteen Barrago (French) bridge trains.

"A more full consideration of the subject has convinced me," he continued, "that we may not have time enough to construct the necessary number of bridge trains of that particular pattern, although it is the best now in use in Europe. As the exigency of the case admits no delay, I would respectfully suggest to be immediately empowered to have bridge trains constructed in such numbers and kinds as may prove to be best adapted to our wants. It is necessary to avail ourselves at once of all the resources which the mechanical skill and ingenuity of the country can furnish in this matter. As much time is necessary to prepare these trains, I would respectfully request an immediate answer to this communication, as well as to the other requests embodied in my letter Friday.

"As the four regular companies of engineer troops authorized by the late law of Congress are not yet organized, and when filled will prove totally insufficient for our purposes, I respectfully request authority to detail for this service such regiments of volunteers or such portions of regiments as may prove best adapted to the duty.

"Although I have full authority to detail them on that service, it would be well to have the special authority of the War Department as an additional security for their obtaining from Congress at its next session some increase of pay commensurate with the arduous and difficult nature of their duties."[19]

In its response to the outbreak of the Civil War, the United States Congress authorized the Regular Army ten additional regiments of infantry, cavalry, and artillery, but failed to authorize the Corps of Engineers any additional officers or engineer soldiers. In a letter to Colonel Joseph G. Totten, the Chief of Engineers, Major General Henry W. Halleck, commander of an army force in Saint Louis, and a former Corps of Engineers officer, said the failure of Congress to allot the engineers additional soldiers was a "most unaccountable error." Totten continued to prod Congress for an increased troop strength. The Congress responded to authorize the Corps of Engineers three additional companies of engineer soldiers.

Engineer Battalion Organized

The Chief of Engineers took steps to hasten an organizing of an engineer battalion.

On October 21, the Engineer Company was redesignated Company A of the engineer battalion, under command of Second Lieutenant Chauncey B. Reese, and transferred from the United States Military Academy at West Point, New York, to the vicinity of the Washington Navy Yard where Colonel Alexander operated his engineer training camp.

With congressional authorization for three additional companies, engineer officers started a recruiting campaign.

Captain Thomas Lincoln Casey traveled to Portland, Maine to organize, and recruit for, Company B. He signed up his first engineer soldier, Neil Clerk. Casey also opened a branch recruiting office at Saco, Maine.

Captain James B. McPherson traveled to Boston to organize, and recruit for, Company C. He signed up his first engineer soldier, John W. Hansen.

On December 2, Companies B and C left Boston by train for Washington. At New London, Connecticut, the two companies transferred to a steamer. Two days later they arrived at the engineer training camp in Washington, D.C. Second Lieutenant Charles E. Cross then assumed command of Company B and First Lieutenant Orville E. Babcock assumed command of Company C. Efforts to recruit Company D were canceled. Recruiting for Company A enlisted one hundred men; for Company B, sixty-five men; and Company C, one hundred men.

Each Engineer Company was authorized 4 officers and 150 enlisted men. Their grades were 10 sergeants, 10 corporals, 2 musicians (fifer and drummer), 64 privates first class or artificers, and 64 privates second class.

The three companies were formed into an engineer battalion under command of Captain James C. Duane.

Volunteer Engineers

From his experience in the Mexican War, McClellan was in complete accord with Barnard and Alexander on the army's need for engineer soldiers and portable bridge equipment. In his earlier request to the secretary of war on the troop units needed for his army, he requested five volunteer infantry regiments to be detailed to engineer duties. The secretary of war approved the detailing of two regiments for the Army of the Potomac: the 15th and 50th New York Volunteer Infantry regiments.

Each engineer regiment was authorized 12 companies, and each company's organization was to adhere to the table of organization of a company of the engineer battalion.

On October 25 the two infantry regiments were redesignated, respectively, the 15th New York Volunteer Engineer Regiment and the 50th New York Volunteer Engineer Regiment.

To the dismay of the engineer officers organizing the engineer brigade, the War Department Paymaster ruled the 15th and 50th New York Volunteer Engineer regiments' new duty assignments did not entitle them to extra pay of engineer soldiers, a compensation for their special skills. The extra pay required congressional approval. The paymaster's ruling precipitated a running feud with the secretary of war and the engineer officers working to build up an engineer organization. The soldiers in the volunteer engineer regiments were particularly perturbed by the ruling. They exclaimed they believed they volunteered as engineer soldiers, not as infantrymen. They expected to receive the additional pay that was disbursed to the engineer soldiers in the engineer battalion. At times the attitude of the volunteer engineer soldiers became rancorous, with such actions as their refusal to turn out for work.

A soldier of the 15th New York Volunteer Engineers wrote in his diary soon after his regiment's redesignation that Colonel John MacL. Murphy, the regimental commander, "was frequently absent because he was up at the Capitol lobbying to have his regiment redesignated an engineer regiment by an Act of Congress."[20]

The 15th New York Volunteer Engineers' records state the regiment was organized as sappers and miners at Bellevue Garden, New York City and Camp Morgan, Willets Point, Long Island, during the months of April–June 1861. The regiment advertised for members in New York City newspapers and opened a recruiting office at 63 Spring Street. It also recruited some members from Newark, New Jersey, which caused an inordinate amount of red tape on assigning them to an out-of-state regiment. Because the governor of New York failed to obtain recognition of the regiment as an engineer regiment, it was mustered into Federal service as an infantry regiment on June 17 under the command of Colonel John MacL. Murphy. He received orders from the secretary of war to report with his regiment to the Army of the Potomac.

On June 29 the regiment left by steamer from Willets Point, sailed to Elizabeth, New Jersey where the soldiers debarked and boarded the Camden-Amboy Railroad for the trip to Washington. Arriving at Washington on June 30, at 6 p.m., the soldiers marched to their encampment on the grounds of the Virginia Theological Seminary near the western boundary of Alexandria. In addition to its training duties the regiment performed picket duty between Falls Church and Bailey's Crossroads, and the slashing of timber to construct fortifications in the area.

Within two months the regiment's 1,600 soldiers and 12 officers were busily engaged in building entrenchments, and frequently put on alert for an enemy attack.

On August 1, Colonel Murphy issued an order that the regiment's camp should be known as "Camp Saint John." According to the regiment's records he also established a rigorous daily regimen:

General Order 32 - Camp Saint John - August 1, 1861

2:30 a.m. Reveille - roll call - tents and arms inspection under supervision of First Sergeant; same at guardhouse.

5:00 a.m. Morning drill, 1 hour.

6:00 a.m. Officer drill, 1 hour.

7:00 a.m. Drum of guard will sound "pea on the trencher" (food on the plate).

7:30 a.m. Sick Call.

8:00 a.m. Guard mounting.

9:00 a.m. Battalion drill - target practice - company officers to supervise.

12:00 a.m. Drum of guard will sound "roast beef" after dinner (immediately) men put arms and accoutrements in perfect order under supervision of company sergeants.

2:00 p.m. Inspection quarters by officer of the day and surgeon - grounds to be perfectly policed - tents and quarters in good order, men fall-in in complete uniform.

4:30 p.m.	Assembly for company drills - manual of arms - officers inspect arms.
5:30 p.m.	Evening parade, consist in part of review and battalion drill.
7:00 p.m.	Supper.
9:00 p.m.	Tattoo will be dispensed with - in place of which 3 taps will be sounded on drum for immediate extinguishment of lights throughout camp of officers and men - rigid enforcement - departure cause for court martial charges. No officer is allowed to sleep out of camp or garrison or to be absent for one moment without leave from Commanding Officer. Colonel Murphy[21]

The 50th New York Volunteer Engineers were organized August 15 at Elmira, New York and mustered into Federal service on September 18. The regiment enlisted its members from cities and towns of upstate New York and eastern Pennsylvania. Under command of Colonel Charles B. Stuart the regiment left for Virginia on September 20. On its arrival there the regiment was assigned to Colonel Andrew Porter's Third Division, Army of the Potomac, and performed picket duty at Hall's Mill.[22]

Engineers' Training Camp

With the redesignation of the 15th and 50th Regiments as engineer regiments, Colonel Alexander moved the two regiments to his training camp near the Washington Navy Yard. When the training of the engineer soldiers became an established and ongoing activity, Alexander directed his attention to the need to construct the ponton bridge trains the regiment would need to build bridges on the battlefield.

The pontons in the bridge trains Alexander's engineer soldiers built were wooden, French type, and canvas, Russian type. They supported a wooden-plank roadway for the use of marching troops, horse-drawn (or mule) wagon trains, and artillery carriages to cross rivers, streams and other bodies of water. Engineer soldiers were expected to construct, or, in their jargon, "throw across a river," a bridge whenever in battle the infantry, artillery, or cavalry, and wagon trains or herds of cattle needed to make a river crossing.

To build a floating bridge, engineer soldiers placed pontons in the water, floated them into a position of side-by-side, 20 feet apart, and anchored them, in sections. Balk or girders were placed longitudinally across gunwales of pontons and fastened, and chess or planks laid across (transversely) on balk for flooring. The flooring usually extended one foot in width and thirteen feet in length. Successive sections were built until the bridge reached the far shore of the bridged body of water.

The bridge, which taxed the engineers' skill to the utmost, was the most important avenue of approach for the strategic movements of the army. Bridges leading across rivers and other bodies of water, and especially railroad bridges, were destroyed whenever possible by the retreating enemy in order to retard the progress of the pursuers. Such bridges required effective and prompt repair, and at times entirely new construction.

With the engineers' decision to adopt the new type of ponton, Alexander immediately put the engineer brigade's carpenters and artificers to work building the pontons, and the accessories, balk and chess, in large numbers. They built wooden pontons to the dimensions of 31 feet long, 2 feet and $9^1/_2$ inches wide at the bow, and 4 feet, 8 inches wide at the stern.

Wagons, with horse, mule, oxen teams, to transport the bridge trains to the battlefield, were assembled at the engineer brigade's camp.

When the first wooden ponton trains were completed, the engineer soldiers uttered many humorous comments about what they called their "tubs," because of their likeness in appearance to big wooden tubs.

Builders of the Engines of War

A semblance of an engineering corps in a military organization dates back to ancient history.

The Romans with their advanced civilization and system of warfare organized the rudiments of such a corps.

In the Roman army system there was a special corps of carpenters *(fabri)* and diggers or sappers *(fabri geraril)* who with their skills built roads, hasty field fortifications, trenches, bridges, and performed all other work for the advance of the march of the army.

The Roman army is also credited with the early development of siegecraft to overcome fortifications.

Advances in siegecraft weapons continued in the 100 years of war (1337–1453) between Great Britain and France. The designers and builders of such weapons were given the designation "engineers," and the weapons were designated "engines of war."

Engines of war in medieval warfare included: fortifications, bastions, moats, catapults that threw missiles, crossbows that shot spears, slingshots that threw stones, pots of boiling oil, and greek fire, and battering rams.

The engineers also built high movable towers to fire weapons at 30 to 40-foot walls of the enemy's fortifications. They also dug saps up to and under fortifications to plant mines.

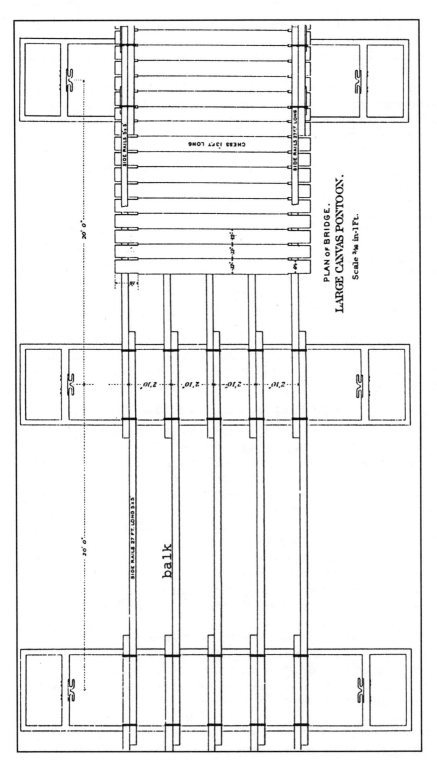

PLAN of BRIDGE.
LARGE CANVAS PONTOON.
Scale 3/16 in=1 Ft.

SIDE RAILS 5x3

CHESS 13 FT LONG

SIDE RAILS 27 FT LONG

SIDE RAILS 27 FT. LONG 5 x 5

balk

20' 0"

2' 10" 2' 10" 2' 10" 2' 10"

O.R., Atlas, Plate 56(1)

Balk and Chess for Floating Bridge

Engines of war were employed offensively and defensively.

In the fifteenth century, with the development of projectile firing guns, they too became the engineers' engines of war because the gun's action functioned in a similar manner to the engineers' weapons that threw missiles.

In the Thirty Years War (1618–1648), the illustrious French engineer, Sebastine le

Engineers' Castle Insignia

Photographic File, U.S. Army Engineer School

Prestre Marquis de Vauban, developed further fortifications and siege methods. His methods were employed for centuries. He also improved the system of parallel trenches and the laying of underground mines. He is particularly noted for his recognition of the need for, and organizing of, a corps of military engineers.[23]

In the early nineteenth century, United States military engineers built the seacoast fortifications that protected the country's coastline against hostile attack. Their uniform insignia, a pinned-on metal turreted castle-like fortification, depicted their line of work.

Engineer Soldier's Uniform

In addition to wearing an identifying castle insignia, the United States Army engineer soldier also wore a distinctive uniform. Like other soldiers, he wore a single-breasted frock coat of dark blue cloth with a skirt extending halfway between the top of the hip and knees. The coat had a stand-up collar and nine buttons evenly spaced down the front. To distinguish him as an engineer soldier, the edge of his collar and cuffs was trimmed with a yellow cord, the color designation for the Corps of Engineers. The trousers were also a dark blue cloth. Sergeants and corporals were permitted to fasten a yellow stripe one and one-half inches wide down and over the outer seam of their trousers. A black belt was worn with the coat around the waist. A black tie, a pair of boots, and felt hat completed the uniform. On the right side of the felt hat the brim was folded up and held in place with a pin fastened to an eagle. On the left side of his hat the soldier placed a black ostrich feather. A yellow cord circled the hat three times at the brim seam, and at each end of the cord a tassel was affixed. On the front of the hat the engineer soldier fastened a pompon, a ball of yellow wool and a turreted-castle pin, made out of brass, with the letter designation of his company affixed to its top edge, both visual evidence that the wearer was a member of the Corps of Engineers. When out on work detail, the engineer soldier wore a one-piece white-cotton canvas coverall that covered the body to his shoulders, and a dark blue forage cap. Above the visor of his cap on the soft cloth he fastened the turreted-castle pin with the affixed letter designation of his company.

Because of his special skills the engineer soldier, except privates second class, received additional recognition in the form of extra pay:

	Monthly Pay	
	Infantry	Engineers
Sergeant	$ 17.00	34.00
Corporal	15.00	20.00
Privates first class	14.00	17.00
Privates second class	13.00	13.00

Officer Corps

As the size of the Union army increased, many of the officers of the Corps of Engineers were reassigned or withdrew from the corps to accept command or staff positions of volunteer non-engineer units, organized and mustered by the states, because of the need for experienced officers to command volunteer units and the opening up of opportunities for higher command and rank. Fortunately, the situation of the loss of those officers to the volunteers was ameliorated by the many engineers who entered the service as officers with the volunteer units. The volunteer engineer officers were able to assume leadership of the battlefield armies' engineer work, and their *éclat* achieved records that are the envy of their profession. To this date some of their feats remain unexcelled.

Pioneers

Although the Civil War engineers and pioneers performed military engineering tasks requiring the practical application of knowledge of battlefield construction, a line of distinction existed in their organizational status.

An Act of Congress defined the engineers' status, which included officers, engineer soldiers, troop units, and mission.

Orders of assignment issued by field commanders at corps, division, or regiment level to officers and soldiers of the line to pioneer units defined their status.

As to battlefield duties, both engineers and pioneers were capable of performing the tasks of military engineering. On the major task of building floating and fixed bridges for the strategic deployments of corps or armies, the engineer units were equipped with portable bridge trains to perform that mission. There were, though, exceptions of pioneer units equipped with portable bridge trains. In the campaign for Atlanta, Savannah, and the Carolinas, the 58th Indiana Volunteer Infantry Regiment was assigned to pioneer duty and equipped with a portable bridge train, and assigned the mission to build floating bridges for the army's strategic river crossings. In the Vicksburg campaign, Company I, 35th Missouri Volunteer Infantry Regiment, was assigned to pioneer duty and equipped with the India rubber ponton bridge train, and assigned the mission to build a floating ponton bridge.

Pioneers (also at times called pontoniers, sappers and miners, or engineers), like the engineers, achieved a distinguished record throughout the history of warfare.

The technical tasks of the pioneer officers and soldiers have been important in warfare since early historical times. They performed their duties in the wars of the oldest warring nations. Their duties evolved into new tasks as new technologies evolved in military technical services and impedimenta.

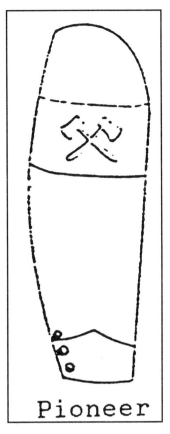

Pioneer Soldiers' Badge

O.R., Atlas, Plate CLXXII

By definition the pioneers were soldiers of the line who marched ahead of a marching force to prepare the march route and the site of the battle ground. They built roads, hasty breastworks, and small bridges. They performed their tasks because they possessed mechanical skills and aptitudes with hand tools particularly adaptable to such a pioneer's assignment. They were equipped with common axes, mattocks, picks, spades, and shovels. A patch of crossed axes sewn on their uniform coat sleeve identified their duty assignment with the pioneers.

For the Union army, one description of the organization of the pioneers was defined by Brigadier General Rufus Ingalls, chief quartermaster, Army of the Potomac. He suggested ten infantrymen from each regiment in a division be assigned to a division pioneer corps. With the strength of the division, the strength of the pioneer corps varied from approximately 100 to 150 pioneers. Half of the pioneers carried common axes, the other half carried spades, shovels, picks and mattocks. They also carried arms.

Their duties were to serve as pioneers to wagon trains to secure them against delays and losses by bad roads or attacks of the enemy. They were under orders of the quartermaster who led the wagon train. Ingalls also recommended a party of thirty pioneers from a corps were to go in advance of wagon trains or to distant points to repair roads. He perceived of pioneers "to be of great service on marches."[24]

In the Confederate States Army, General Robert E. Lee believed the pioneer companies should be organized in each division to be employed on marches or on battlefields to construct and repair bridges and roads, and to demolish fences. He also assigned them the duty to fill up ditches to facilitate the passage of troops. He further stated the pioneers had to habitually operate in each division, and engineer soldiers were not to be transferred from the engineer regiment to the division pioneer companies.[25]

A pioneer officer, of the 59th Illinois Volunteer Infantry Regiment, reported his pioneer company performed such duties as: built roads, dug entrenchments in advance of main body, cleared brush, built *chevaux-de-frise*, opened field works to move artillery pieces, and built defensive breastworks.[26]

A Record Right-Off-the-Bat in Kentucky

Captain Cullum, who participated in the design and manufacture of the India rubber ponton bridge equipment, stated that in the context of the bridge's employment in the Mexican War, "We only need to look in the composition of our portable floating bridge train to passage of streams of medium width, not exceeding the Rio Grande, 600 feet."[27]

The Civil War nullified Captain Cullum's prophecy. The outbreak of the war forced the engineers, in the absence of prescience, to face the requirement for portable ponton bridge equipment to cross rivers much wider than 600 feet.

There was further irony.

Colonel Alexander busily engaged his engineer soldiers in building and testing ponton bridge equipment.

At Paducah, Kentucky on the Ohio River, five months into the war, an engineer officer and his Missouri company of pioneers arrived to construct a floating bridge across the river. The pioneers faced what seemed an unbelievable feat. They built one of the army's earliest ponton bridges, and to add more unbelief, built a bridge of record length.

On September 6, after Confederate forces violated the neutrality of Kentucky, General Ulysses S. Grant marched a force into Kentucky as a countermeasure and occupied Paducah. With the Union forces in control of the town, the Tennessee and Cumberland Rivers became accessible to gunboats of the Union navy. General John C. Fremont, commander of the Department of Missouri, ordered Grant to have constructed a bridge across the Ohio River, connecting Ohio and Illinois. The bridge was intended to establish Paducah as a supply base for further Union operations in Kentucky and Tennessee.

Grant in turn ordered Captain E. B. Pike and his company of Missouri sappers and miners to build the bridge across the Ohio River.

Captain Pike confronted an engineer officer's expectancy. He responded to the challenge. He conceptualized quickly in his creative mind an image of the required bridge, hurried to the task to collect materials, and to start building the bridge.

An artist of *Frank Leslie's Illustrated Newspaper* wrote the following description of the construction of the bridge:

"For some time past it has been known to the select few that a bridge was in contemplation, which would span the Ohio or Mississippi rivers but the exact locality was known to the engineers. A quantity of barges [were] purchased with considerable secrecy at points along the Ohio River and after being collected at Cincinnati were towed as a fleet accompanied by a detachment of the Cincinnati Independent Regiment, under command of Captain Peter Rudolf Neff. Those in charge of the expedition were apprehensive of opposition, but the fleet arrived safely at Paducah on September 19. The steamer *N. W. Thomas* was chartered as flagship, while others followed with coal barges in tow. Captain E. B. Pike and Radnitz, staff engineer officer on General Fremont's staff, commanded the expedition.[28]

"At Evansville, Indiana, they were warned of dangers at Paducah, but as the place ten days previous had been occupied by Federal troops under General Grant no fears were entertained as to the success of the undertaking.

"About a half mile below the city is situated the camps of the 9th and 12th Illinois regiments. Here it was decided to construct the proposed bridge where the river is nearly 5,000 feet from shore to shore.

"The coal barges were 22 x 100 feet. These are anchored side by side eight feet apart; in the center of each barge is erected a heavy tressel [sic] work 20 feet in width over which 12-inch timbers

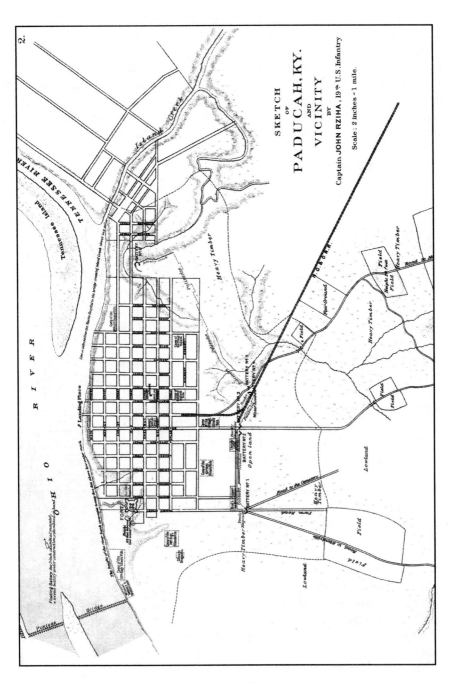

SKETCH
OF
PADUCAH, KY.
AND
VICINITY
BY
Captain JOHN RZIHA, 19ᵗʰ U.S. Infantry

Scale : 2 inches - 1 mile.

Paducah and Vicinity

are thrown across; these are covered with 3-inch oak plank. The whole is fastened together by wooden pegs which can be taken out if necessary. Across the bridge at intervals of 50 feet are telegraph posts over which in a few days wire will be put.

"The structure crosses the island called in steamboat parlance the Low Head an entire reach of nearly a mile in length, comparing favorably with the Long Bridge at Washington City. The distance between the Kentucky shore and the island is nearly double that on the opposite side of the island. About halfway on the other side of the island and between either shore is a draw, which consists of two barges so arranged that in a very few minutes they can be removed and brought back.

"The time employed in the construction of the bridge was nearly four days and a great deal of credit is due the engineers for the energy and the expedition with which the whole was accomplished."

The article concluded, "the bridge [is] an example of military engineering unprecedented in the history of this country."[29]

A news story appeared in *Harper's Weekly* on October 26, 1861, with a sketch by J. C. Beard and Bill Travis.

"The sketches I send are drawn on the spot from nature," Beard wrote. "The bridge at Paducah surpassed anything of the kind ever before attempted in the United States. The river at the bridge is 3,600 feet. It is spanned by 100 coal barges strongly braced together, 12 feet apart, connected by trestle work, and planked over. The planking is 20 feet wide. The bridge is constructed to carry the heaviest ordnance."[30]

The reports on the Paducah bridge vary as to its exact length. In essence, the figures are estimates. As written above by the correspondent of *Harper's* the length was 3,600 feet across the river. The correspondent for *Leslie's* stated the distance to be approximately 5,000 feet. The sketch in the *Atlas of the Official Records* indicates the river was approximately 4,260 feet wide. The official sketch indicates the section of the bridge on the Kentucky side of the island was approximately 2,310 feet and the section of the bridge on the Illinois side was approximately 1,650 feet long. The approximate length of the floating bridge was 3,960 feet long, but still a record length.

Other Engineer Units

While Grant moved against Confederate forces in western Kentucky, Major General George H. Thomas' Union army took up arms against the Confederate forces threatening to march through Cumberland Gap into the eastern part of the state. There on September 25, General Thomas recruited Captain William F. Patterson's

Ponton Bridge across Ohio River at Paducah

Harper's Weekly, October 26, 1861

Kentucky Company of Mechanics and Engineers with two officers and 41 engineer soldiers. Throughout the war his company would exemplify imaginative and innovative skills in bridge building.

On October 11, Colonel Edward W. Serrell and his 1st New York Volunteer Engineer Regiment's soldiers were mustered into service. The next day the regiment boarded a steamer and sailed for Fort Monroe, Virginia, where it arrived three days later. On November 8 the regiment received its initiation into battle when it participated in Brigadier General Thomas W. Sherman's South Carolina Expeditionary Corps' amphibious operation with the navy to capture Port Royal, South Carolina. Upon success of the operation, Colonel Serrell deployed his regiment to a camp on Hilton Head Island.

Michigan Engineers and Mechanics Regiment

On October 7, Colonel William P. Innes reported 700 men had enlisted in his newly formed regiment. He observed the men felt better about their decision, and there seemed a good prospect the regiment would be up to full strength in a few days. It actually took more time for the regiment to reach full strength and to be mustered into Federal service.

He addressed a letter to the Ladies Soldiers' Aid Society on October 25 saying their "welcome gifts to gallant soldiers were each appreciated" by the regiment.

On October 28, Innes sent a message to the secretary of war announcing, "We are ready to march, and awaiting orders." He received orders to move his regiment to Louisville and to report to Major General Don Carlos Buell of the Department of the Ohio. The full-strength regiment was mustered on November 29, and began its movement to Louisville. On arrival there General Buell assigned the regiment to duty stations.

The regiment experienced its first war reality in the battle of Logan's Cross-Roads, Kentucky, on December 19. In addition to engineer duties, the regiment guarded the Union army camp and, after the battle, collected and buried the dead of both combatants and moved the wounded to battlefield hospitals.[31]

Missouri Engineer Regiment

Major General John C. Fremont of the Department of Missouri authorized Colonel Josiah W. Bissell to organize and recruit a volunteer Missouri Engineer Regiment. The regiment was also called 1st Missouri Engineer Regiment and the Engineer Regiment of the West. Between August and October 1861, ten companies of the regiment were recruited and mustered into the Federal service for three years at Camp Lafayette Park, Saint Louis. The enlisted men trained at building earthworks, repairing bridges and roads, and drilling and practicing for the required duties of engineer soldiers. The officers attended school conducted by Colonel Bissell.

Occupations of the newly enlisted soldiers were recorded in the regiment's descriptive book as former mason, carpenter, wagon maker, laborer, blacksmith, soldier, clerk, actor, and printer.

Colonel Bissell continued a strict regimen of training at Camp Julia for the remaining months of the year.[32]

General in Chief: A Step Down and a Step Up

On October 31, General Scott brought to a close his long army career with his retirement from active duty.

General McClellan assumed command of all the armies as general in chief. He assured President Lincoln he could fill the two command positions of general in chief and commanding general, Army of the Potomac. President Lincoln believed him. There were critics of McClellan who believed he would give little time to the leadership of the Army of the Potomac.

Also, winter weather began to cast its influence. The roads became impassable. General Joseph E. Johnston moved his Confederate army into quarters for the winter at Manassas and Centreville. General McClellan also moved the Army of the Potomac into winter quarters in northern Virginia.

The Year's Progress of the Strategy

As the first year of the war ended, progress had been made in the national strategy, and the building up, equipping, and training of the Union army, with special attention to engineer soldiers and units, and portable bridge-building equipment.

There were achievements the Union army could point to: (1) forces were in place and had a foothold on the southeast coast to implement the blockade; (2) the victories in Virginia, Kentucky, and Missouri denied the Confederacy the Ohio River as a defensive line; (3) the feats of Captain Pike building a 3,960-foot ponton bridge across the Ohio River, and (4) Colonel Alexander in training engineer soldiers to construct ponton bridge trains, epitomized the advance in technology, and skills Union engineer officers and soldiers brought to their wartime duties in meeting requirements to build bridges with individual imaginativeness and innovativeness combined with their body energy and hand tools.

Chapter 2

1862
The Engineers "Throw the Bridges"

The President Orders Action

The new year started with the continuing demands of Northern newspaper headlines for the Union army to start an attack. President Lincoln, too, wanted action. The immobility of the army irked him. Prompted by the public outcry and impatient himself for some battlefield activity by his generals, Lincoln issued his first general war order on January 27, 1862. He ordered that the 22nd day of February 1862 be the day for a general movement of the land and naval forces of the United States against the insurgent forces, especially that the Army of the Potomac be ready to move on that historic day. Lincoln included the admonition he would hold the general in chief responsible for the prompt execution of the presidential war order.[1]

To implement his general war order, four days later Lincoln issued his first special war order. He ordered all the soldiers of the Army of the Potomac who did not have an assignment in the force set up to defend Washington to be organized into an expedition to seize and occupy a point upon the railroad southwest of the place called Manassas Junction. By the order the expedition was to move before the anniversary of the birth of George Washington. Even with those prodding instructions General McClellan prolonged his soldiers' entry into combat. He busied himself preparing plans and training his officers and soldiers. Whereupon Lincoln, in a follow-up action, thinking he should give McClellan all his time to bring his army to a state of readiness, relieved McClellan from his duty as general in chief of the army. McClellan's sole job shifted to preparing the Army of the Potomac to march to battle.

Early in March, McClellan on horseback made a reconnaissance mission out to Centreville and Manassas to a point where he could observe the activities of the winter camp of General Johnston's Confederate army. To McClellan's chagrin, he failed to see any signs of the foe's army.

General Johnston had slipped away earlier with his army to the south bank of the Rapidan and Rappahannock Rivers because he had heard from women spies that McClellan had planned to move his army by water down the Chesapeake Bay to Fort Monroe, located on the tip of the peninsula between the York and James Rivers.

The Union army soldiers camped nearby did not report seeing their adversary depart.

Engineer Soldiers Train

The records report that Colonel Alexander continued the bridge-building training of the Engineer Brigade's soldiers throughout the winter.

An engineer soldier wrote that living conditions at the camp in Washington were difficult in the winter, and that several men died of disease and were buried in Washington's Congressional Cemetery. The company's log of activities reported one burial took place late at night during a heavy rain. The first sergeant, Fred Gerber, read the burial service from the *Episcopal Book of Common Prayer* by the light of a lantern "for a real soldier."[2] Pontons continued to be built at the engineers' camp. On January 2 the first bridge-building drill took place with a complete bridge train. On January 12 while the engineer soldiers were conducting their bridge-building drill with the pontons, President Lincoln paid a visit to the engineers' camp, and, reportedly, "showed an interest."[3]

Under Alexander's intensive training, the engineer soldiers were prepared to work for the mobility and success of the infantry, cavalry, artillery, and teamsters and animals of the wagon trains, in the suppression of the rebellion. They were trained too in the school of the soldiers; they had to be prepared for the time they would be called upon to lay aside an ax or shovel and shoulder their musket on the firing line. The events of the war made the firing line real for them on several occasions.

On February 24, the Engineer Battalion departed their Washington camp at 11 a.m. on the Baltimore and Ohio Railroad with a ponton train aboard for Sandy Hook, Maryland, on the north side of the Potomac River opposite Harpers Ferry. On arrival the battalion set up a Sibley tent camp at the east end of the railroad bridge crossing the Potomac River. Two days later, at two o'clock

Engineers' Bridge-Building Drill

Mottelay and Copeland, *The Soldier in Our Civil War*

Public Demonstration of Building Bridge

Mottelay and Copeland, *The Soldier in Our Civil War*

in the morning, Companies B and C turned out and unloaded the pontons from the railroad cars and hand carried them a mile to the Potomac River where a site had been selected to test their ability to build a bridge. At daylight, Company A started to build a ponton bridge across the river to Harpers Ferry. A report stated it was a cold and windy day; the river water was 15 feet above summer level and filled with driftwood and ice. With difficulty the engineer soldiers pulled the pontons into position in the water. It was necessary to make use of ships' anchors and chain cables to hold the pontons in place. Under difficult work conditions the bridge was completed in eight hours.

To build the 840-foot-long floating bridge, it required 60 pontons. McClellan accompanied the engineers to Harpers Ferry and closely followed the construction of the bridge. Upon its completion he led Major General Nathaniel P. Banks and his troops and wagon train over the bridge onto Virginia soil.

At day's end McClellan wrote a message to the secretary of war, reporting, "the bridge was splendidly thrown. It was one of the most difficult operations of the kind ever performed."[4]

The engineer soldiers maintained and guarded their bridge across the Potomac River, and regulated the flow of traffic across it.

The Engineer Battalion's bridge across the Potomac River was the first ponton bridge constructed for military operations by Regular Army engineers in the United States, according to their record. Some writers declared the bridge was the first for military operations. Actually, the ponton bridge the volunteer engineers built in Paducah, Kentucky, across the Ohio River the previous September holds the record for first for military operations.

The Engineer Battalion also constructed a "flying bridge" (ponton), over the Shenandoah River east of Harpers Ferry on March 1 for the crossing over of Pennsylvania volunteer soldiers.

On March 4 the battalion returned to its camp at Washington. The success of the engineer soldiers' mission to demonstrate, at Harpers Ferry, their skill to build a ponton bridge instilled in them a feeling of pride in their work and their outfit. The tubs, the adopted name for the pontons in army jargon, were now the subject of affectionate and respectful remarks. One engineer soldier wrote in his diary that the ponton excelled a gymnasium for the development of muscles; they sheltered engineers from the rain and sun; hid them from the foe; carried the wounded; and received the dead.[5]

Engineer Bridge Building Saves the Army

During the past winter McClellan mulled over the strategy and tactics to strike his first Union blow in the Eastern Theater of Operations. He decided to transport his army to Fort Monroe, Virginia. From that point it would march and fight its way up the peninsula between the York and James Rivers to engage and suppress General Johnston's Confederate army. McClellan thought his operation would take place as he envisioned it in his mind and laid it out on paper, but surprises awaited him. Spies, who prowled around army headquarters and encampments, ferreted out the information on his plan.

When McClellan approached President Lincoln with his battle plan early in March, and asked for authority to transport his army down the Chesapeake Bay, Lincoln refused to give his consent. If the Army of the Potomac left its camp on the Potomac River, weakening Washington's defenses, the advantage would pass to the Confederates in the tug-of-war to threaten each other's capital city. A loss of Washington would be a blow to the Union. Also, such a loss might bring the Confederacy recognition by foreign governments.[6]

While the idea prevailed about capturing the capital cities, President Lincoln had stated in his Mill Springs victory message, the Union army's mission in the war "is to attack, pursue, and destroy a rebellious enemy, and to deliver the country from danger menaced by traitors."[7]

Amidst much arguing between the civil and military leaders, McClellan insisted on the acceptance of his plan. Lincoln in an about-face, reconsidered his decision, reversed it, and gave his consent to avoid any charge that McClellan lacked presidential support and confidence. It was a strange about-face. The commander in chief did not believe McClellan's plan merited his approval. Still concerned about the deployment of the Army of the Potomac, the president issued General War Order Number 3* on March 8 stipulating that a change of base of the Army of the Potomac would not take place without leaving in and about Washington a force to protect the city.[8]

Lincoln preferred a direct road march south to seek out, engage, and destroy the Rebel army. Such a deployment kept the Union army facing the Confederate army, which adhered to Lincoln's conceptualization of the national strategy.

McClellan objected to an overland march; in the spring the roads turned to mud. Confederate cavalry raids would be able to cut the tracks of the Richmond, Fredericksburg, and Potomac Railroad carrying supplies from Washington to his army in the field.

By transporting his army by boats down the Chesapeake Bay, debarking at Fort Monroe, and marching it up the peninsula, McClellan believed his army would outflank Johnston's. His belief was based on the expectation he would move his army to the south

---

* General War Order Number 2, issued the same day, constituted a corps Army of the Potomac for active operations.

before Johnston moved overland. Unfortunately, McClellan lost what he perceived to be his advantage when Johnston's aides learned of his plans for the campaign. In a countermove Johnston quickly placed his army in front of McClellan's.

Finally, there was a response by McClellan to Lincoln's General War Order Number 1. On March 17 the Army of the Potomac started sailing from Annapolis, Maryland and Alexandria, Virginia.

Brigadier General Stewart Van Vliet, who managed the operation, reported the vessels used were:

> 71   sidewheel steamers (29,071 tons)
> 57   propeller ships (9,824 tons)
> 187 schooners, brigs, and barks (36,634 tons)
> 90   barges (10,749 tons)

A total of 405 vessels (86,278 tons).

Based on McClellan's figures the vessels transported approximately 130,000 men, 22,000 animals for cavalry, artillery, and unit wagon transportation, 3,600 wagons of depot trains with 14,400 animals, and 700 ambulances with 2,800 horses.[9]

The Engineer Brigade under its new commander, Brigadier General Daniel P. Woodbury, Corps of Engineers, sailed on the night of March 27 on the steamers *Herald* and *Maryland*. Rain hampered their embarkation. The engineer soldiers huddled below deck in soggy uniforms. One of them wrote home that the boats were "dirty little pent up crowded water bruisers, and only fit for cattle." After an uncomfortable two-day trip the Engineer Brigade disembarked at Fort Monroe.

A soldier in Company C of the Engineer Battalion died on April 1 from pleurisy that struck him on the boat trip. As a token of respect for him the company carpenters pulled boards off a nearby house to make him a coffin. The company then turned out to bury their deceased companion in the fort's cemetery.

While marching up the peninsula between the York and the James Rivers McClellan planned on navy support. That expectation turned out to be impossible in the early days of the march. The York River was blocked by Confederate coastal batteries at Yorktown and Gloucester Point. On the James River side Norfolk remained in possession of the Confederates; their gunboat *Merrimac* prowled the river. Only the long and roundabout way by road up the peninsula remained opened to McClellan's army.

McClellan planned his campaign on a three-pronged tactical attack, with all the prongs jabbing towards Johnston's army. The first prong would be McClellan's army's march up the peninsula; the second would be the smaller armies of Generals Nathaniel Banks, Robert H. Milroy, James Shields, and John C. Fremont marching up the Shenandoah Valley; and the third would be McDowell's corps of the Army of the Potomac, which Lincoln retained in northern Virginia for the security of Washington, marching down the turnpike to join McClellan.

From Fort Monroe to Richmond the distance required a march of 70 miles along mostly level terrain. The roads were dirt traces through thick woods. In the rainy season the roads turned into mudlands. Mosquitoes infested the area and caused many non-battle casualties, especially malaria.

A shining sun made April 4 a bright spring day; a day that, in spite of the drudgery, raised the spirits of the soldiers. They were sensitive to the natural beauty of the Virginia landscape spreading out around them. Buds on the trees were beginning to snap open into flowers and leaves. Fresh green plants and grasses folded over on the ground from the trampling soldiers' feet. The soldiers of the army spent a moderate day on their first march day from Fort Monroe heading up the peninsula. They marched silently along the dirt traces listening to the birds singing in the trees. The wagons with their loads rocking and their white canvas tops proudly announcing their U.S. origin stencilled in letters on the sides, rolled with squeaking, straining wheels through the soft-earth tracks. Late in the day a sudden and unexpected change occurred in the weather. Rain drenched the army. The wagons and the animals pushing them churned the earth and rain into mud. A dreary day lowered the soldiers' morale.

On its first day of marching the huge human and animal force dispersed in the wooded area covered nine miles. It bivouacked for the night at Big Bethel where the Confederate soldiers set the bridge on fire, on the Northwest Branch of the Back River, to delay the Union army. Before the fire could be put out at the bridge, darkness enveloped the countryside. The line soldiers camped, but not the engineer soldiers who underwent their initiation into battlefield duties; they worked throughout the night repairing the burned-out timber bridge.

After leaving Big Bethel early the next morning in the rain, the soldiers began to discard their extra baggage, overcoats, blankets, and shoes; it was difficult enough to lift one's feet out of the mud without the extra weight of impedimenta. The engineer soldiers frequently had to unload the tool and ponton wagons in order to reduce the burden of lifting them out of the mud.

On their second day of marching, April 5, a ten-mile march, the soldiers came to a halt before Yorktown. They learned Confederate guns surrounded the town. McClellan thought the Warwick River ran parallel to his march route. Without a map to verify his position, he discovered the Warwick River flowed across his march route. The river and Wormley's Creek placed an obstacle on the army's march route.

To remove the Wormley's Creek obstacle, Captain W. A. Ketchum with a detail from Company H, 15th New York Volunteer Engineers, supervised the construction of a trestle bridge across it and roads to the approach at each end. "This work accomplished to the entire satisfaction of McClellan," the records state, "who made a personal examination of the work and pronounced it a complete success."[10]

To protect themselves, and their wagon trains, Johnston's soldiers constructed a 13-mile defense line of artillery, redoubts, and rifle pits, and dammed the Warwick River to put a large lake in front of the Union invaders. Showing concern for the cost in casualties, McClellan decided to call a halt to the assault on Yorktown.

Fearful of the enemy's strength, McClellan decided to resort to a siege. The siege decision did not fit well with President Lincoln. It forfeited the army's mobility. On April 6 he sent a message to McClellan stating, "you better break the enemy's line."[11]

In the absence of a response by McClellan, three days later Lincoln sent another message with a stronger temper, "indispensable you strike a blow."[12]

The president's messages did not stir McClellan; he continued the siege operation. McClellan's decision left little time for idleness by the engineer soldiers. They started work on a laborious engineering job.

Continuous rain and mud made the engineers' work difficult. They corduroyed 5,000 yards of road. To cross the army over the many swamps and creeks around Yorktown and into siege positions, the Engineer Battalion constructed seven bridges, both trestle and ponton. The 15th and 50th New York Volunteer engineers built gun positions, parapets, fascines and gabions, and filled 113,550 bags with sand.

McClellan, inspecting the progress of the siege works, declared to the soldier work-details that when the guns started laying siege to Yorktown, the Confederates would surrender because of the "murderous assault" that would be poured down upon them. Even though the siege deprived McClellan of his advantage of mobility and of a surprise attack, he thought it prepared the way for a great victory.

On the morning of May 3 every siege gun positioned was ready to begin the "murderous assault" on Yorktown. An entire month had been spent constructing the elaborate siege works. When the Union soldiers went to bed on the night of May 2, they expected to wake up in the morning ready to begin action on the exciting job of bombarding the Confederate army, helplessly jailed inside the barricades around Yorktown, into submission. A reporter traveling with the army wrote with a tinge of sarcasm that the army's officers and men were not early risers! If they had been, they would have discovered early in the morning that Johnston with his army had once again slipped away.[13]

McClellan's army, seemingly, slept late on the morning of May 3. Because its members had not planned on marching anywhere, they did not think about a schedule. When they woke up to reality, they then had to spend time organizing themselves, their equipment, and animals. They hastily readied themselves to march after Johnston's soldiers.

The main body of the Army of the Potomac made a slow march through the mud to Williamsburg. Outside of the town at a fork where the roads from Yorktown and Lee's Mill joined, the Confederates built Fort Magruder to stop the Yankees. The two armies skirmished for two days in the rain, and their combat sparked and exploded like a string of firecrackers. On May 6 the Union soldiers breathed in again the freshness of a sunny spring day. The flowers were in bloom along the roads. To their surprise they learned Johnston had repeated himself and slipped away from Williamsburg. Denied battle, they marched into the deserted town.

Before the abandonment of Yorktown, McClellan had planned to have McDowell's corps land at Gloucester Point on the York River to open it to gunboats. The Confederate army would then be forced to withdraw. McClellan called off his plan when the president ordered McDowell's corps to remain in the Washington area.[14]

As an alternate force to McDowell's, the president sent Major General William B. Franklin's division of 11,000 soldiers to the peninsula. When Yorktown was cleared earlier than expected, McClellan decided to shift the landing of Franklin's division to West Point where the Mattapony and Pamunkey Rivers joined to form the York River. A landing in the rear of Johnston's army, if successful, would block its retreat route upon its evacuating Williamsburg.

In a masterful joint operation with the navy, supported by the construction of Colonel Alexander's innovative expedient to transfer soldiers from transports in the river to landing craft, an amphibious operation succeeded on the York River.

At 1:15 p.m. on May 6 General Franklin's division, on transports escorted by naval vessels, arrived at Brick House near the mouth of the Pamunkey River. At 4:15 p.m. the soldiers began to leave the transports and board the ponton boats. They were ferried to the shore. In successive trips throughout the evening the pontons ferried Franklin's complete division ashore.

Early in the morning, May 7, pickets of Franklin's division came in contact with Johnston's soldiers in the area of Barhamsville-Eltham's Landing. By 9 a.m. the combatants were engaged in serious fire, but in a short time Johnston's soldiers left the field.

With Franklin's division safely ashore, McClellan ordered that General John Sedgwick's division be transported up the York River and put ashore in a like amphibious operation. Sedgwick's division arrived at Brick House on the morning of May 7, and during the day ferried ashore in the same manner as Franklin's division. At 1 p.m. while Sedgwick's soldiers were marching through the landing site, Confederate artillery opened fire. The naval vessels in the river returned the fire; shortly thereafter the enemy ceased his artillery fire.

On the York River Colonel Alexander proceeded to build piers, wharves, and a supply depot for the army at White House.

The corps of the Army of the Potomac spent three days at Williamsburg waiting for supplies. Muddy roads delayed the supply wagons from Yorktown. As the army marched up the peninsula the engineers conducted reconnaissance and repaired roads and bridges. On May 11 the soldiers with McClellan reached Roper's Church and Barhamsville where they joined Franklin's and Sedgwick's troops. With his army joined in that area, an important decision faced McClellan. He would have to decide whether to cross the Chickahominy River and approach Johnston's encampment along the James River on the south side of the peninsula, or to continue up the York River side of the peninsula. He could then deploy towards Johnston's encampment when he reached the Richmond-York River Railroad, which he could then follow as a route to the battlefield.[15]

McClellan decided to issue orders for his army to march up the York River side of the peninsula. He based his decision primarily on the fact that the James River was open to navigation only to within seven or eight miles of the Confederate's capital city. A Confederate fort at Drewry's Bluff blocked entry to the city. The Union gunboat *Monitor* tried without success to reduce the fort with its gun so as to open the river to navigation.

The soldiers in the Army of the Potomac again had the pleasurable benefit of a picturesque march up the dirt roads and traces of the peninsula. A wealth of spring growth arrayed the countryside: magnolias, Virginia jessamines, azaleas, blue bonnets, green valleys, and wooded hills. They listened to the mocking birds and watched the humming and other birds flying about among the trees. They watched strange snakes wiggle along the ground. They gazed at stately river mansions and shabby slave cabins. The topographical engineers marched ahead of the army, making sketches of the terrain. In back of the main body of the army the ponton trains and supply and tool wagons stretched out in a line over an immense space. The soldiers marched an average of six miles a day and some of them recorded in diaries they enjoyed the marching. Through open spaces over on the York River they were able to view the supply boats sailing up the river. On the decks of the boats and in their holds the boats carried biscuits, salted meat, coffee, sugar, barley, hay, and corn. When the soldiers camped at night and a quiet settled over the terrain, they reported they could hear the mockingbirds. Upon leaving their campsites in the morning, the soldiers could look over a wide expanse of ground and see that by their marching, sleeping, and pushing their wagons along on it, they had deflowered and rutted the dirt surface.

On May 16 the marching army reached the area of White House on the Pamunkey River. Amidst the feverish activity of preparations for the campaign, the soldiers could see piles of supplies were accumulating at the supply base established there.

With McClellan's hostile army posted on the peninsula, Captain William W. Blackford, a Confederate engineer officer, quickly recognized the danger of the Union army making a rapid crossing of the Chickahominy River and marching west to the James River. Below Richmond the river flowed directly north and south. Blackford's mental topographical map projected Drewry's Bluff, seven miles below Richmond, an advantageous crossing point on the James for McClellan's army, and an opened and unopposed march route to the city.

Blackford also had thought out the enemy's options. Based on the intelligence collected, he learned McClellan had invaded the peninsula well equipped with ponton bridge trains to make the crossing of the James River.

He further deduced if McClellan crossed the James and marched on Richmond, and if General Lee decided to withdraw the army from its defense works at Richmond, pontons would not be available to accomplish a crossing of the river. He brought the situation to the attention of the staff at the Confederate engineer bureau, and suggested, as an alternate expedient, the building of a ponton bridge, utilizing canal and riverboats.

The engineer bureau responded that it lacked the resources to build a ponton bridge and sent an accompanying suggestion to Blackford, which in its content was an order, for him to build the bridge. The communication startled Blackford. He was apprehensive about the responsibility placed on him, but from the day he hit upon the idea of the bridge he had given thought and analysis to the bridge. The Rebels, like the Yankees, had entered the army with the same American trait of ingenuity in applied engineering tasks. He had conceptualized a bridge, and he was ready to take the initiative.

He first hired carpenters and purchased lumber in Richmond. Captain Alfred L. Rives, an engineer in the engineer bureau, located timber supplies and impressed four schooners. The provost marshal rounded up black and white laborers, who were divided up into two working parties of 500 men each. Captain Blackford set them to work at the bridge site building pontons. From his conceptualization of a plan for his bridge, abutments were built on the river's banks. The pontons and canal boats were one-by-one maneuvered into his planned position in the river. Carpenters connected them with spiked timber spans. The impressed schooners were positioned in the river as bridge center spans. The largest formed a mobile draw that could be floated out of the bridge to form an opening to permit passage between Drewry's Bluff and Richmond.

Blackford's working parties finished the bridge on May 25 and opened it to river traffic. General Joseph E. Johnston, whose attention and tactical importance was drawn to the newly constructed bridge, commended Blackford for his innovative home-built bridge.[16] It seems strange, with Captain Blackford's discerning the tactical importance of the crossing of the James, McClellan failed to perceive of the crossing of the James at Drewry's Bluff, but instead allowed his army to become bogged down on the Chickahominy River.

Engineers' First Phase of Bridge Building

McClellan, with his headquarters and supply depot established and in operation at White House, turned his attention to the preparation of march orders for his army.

On the nineteenth McClellan's headquarters and General Fitz John Porter's V Corps, and General William B. Franklin's VI Corps, relocated to Tunstall's Station, five miles from White House.

Rain hampered the army's march.

General Barnard, on orders of McClellan, started on a reconnaissance of Bottom's Bridge, on the army's left flank. He wrote in a report of his observations that he acquired a "perfect" knowledge of the character of the Chickahominy River.

The Stony River and Brook Run joined northwest of Richmond, at Meadow Bridge, to form the Chickahominy. The river continued to flow in a southeasterly direction around Richmond to join the James River.[17]

At Bottom's Bridge, Barnard said he reached a quick conclusion there would be no serious enemy resistance to McClellan's attempt to cross his soldiers.

Barnard continued his reconnaissance along the bank of the Chickahominy to New Bridge, on the army's right flank. He recorded at his springtime arrival on the river the army confronted one of the formidable obstacles an army could expect to face in an advance to battle. As a military obstacle the river's natural makeup consisted of a stream, a swamp, and a bottom land. The stream flowed through a belt of heavily timbered swamp, which averaged 300–400 yards in width.

A few yards below New Bridge

Major General John G. Barnard

Miller, *The Photographic History of the Civil War*

he noted a short length of stream without a margin of timbered swamp, but elsewhere between New Bridge and Bottom's Bridge the belt of timbered swamp was continuous and wide. The tops of the trees rose to the level of the crests of the highlands, thus screening from view the bottom lands and slopes of the highlands on the enemy's side. In some places Barnard gained a glimpse of the physical features of the enemy's side where the swamp was bare of timber.

Through the belt of swamp Barnard observed flowed the Chickahominy stream, some places in a single channel, but more frequently it divided into several channels. When the Chickahominy was above its summer level of one or two feet, the water flowed over the whole swamp. The bottom lands between the swamp and highlands were then minimally elevated at their margins above the swamp. A few feet of rise of the stream overflowed large areas of bottom lands. The cultivated bottom lands were intersected by deep ditches, and on their lower portions were spongy and made the movement of cavalry, artillery, and wagons impossible.

Barnard reported to McClellan that on the eight miles of land between Bottom's Bridge to New Bridge, there were two or three places with summer fords or footpaths in place soldiers could use to move through the swamp and stream. He also stated he believed the infantry would be able to march through the Chickahominy area, but (1) bridges would have to be provided for cavalry, artillery, and wagons, and (2) corduroy roads for certain lengths built through the banks and margins.

The bridges that Barnard visualized would be needed to cross the Chickahominy would have to be built by the engineer and pioneer soldiers, with the assistance of work parties from the infantry soldiers. They all faced arduous manual-labor tasks in the Chickahominy morass. Before the Union soldiers were to leave the formidable Chickahominy River, they were to leave a record of building or repairing 13 bridges in General McClellan's three tactical maneuvers to cross the river. They wrote in their record of events, "never did we see bridges so difficult to build."

When the army left the field of battle their tasks were to keep the bridges out of enemy hands by destroying the skillful accomplishments of their labor.[18]

On May 21 McClellan positioned his troops as follows:

General George Stoneman's cavalry's advance guard was posted one mile, and General Franklin's VI Corps was posted three miles from New Bridge. General Porter's V Corps was posted at a supporting distance in the rear of General Franklin's corps. General Erasmus Keyes' IV Corps was posted on New Kent Road, near Bottom's Bridge, with General Samuel P. Heintzelman's III Corps posted at a supporting distance in the rear of the IV Corps.

On May 22 McClellan moved his headquarters to Cold Harbor. Prompted by Barnard's reconnaissance report he ordered the start of the first phase of bridge building. He reported he was being pushed forward with great vigor in the daily rains that continued to fall, flooding the river valley, and raising the water to a greater height than had been known for twenty years.[19]

On May 25 President Lincoln sent a message to McClellan stating that he was disturbed by the Confederate movements in the Valley. He concluded his message with the notice he had a mind for the Army of the Potomac to move vigorously against Richmond or return to Washington.[20]

First Phase of Bridge Building

Bottom's Bridge. Captain Ira Spaulding with Companies C and E, 50th New York Volunteer Engineers, started work to build a trestle bridge at Bottom's Bridge. The completed bridge was 120 feet long, with corduroyed approaches.

General Samuel P. Heintzelman's III Corps and General Erasmus Keyes' IV Corps marched over the bridge to the south side of the Chickahominy, with orders from McClellan to march upstream to uncover crossing sites, which would permit the building of more bridges.

Building Corduroy Approaches to Grapevine Bridge

Battles and Leaders of the Civil War

Colonel Charles B. Stuart, commander of the 50th New York Engineers, reported the army made constant use of the bridge upon its completion. On one day bridge guards reported to him 79 regiments, 900 wagons, and 7 artillery batteries passed over the bridge between sunrise and sunset.

In a letter to President Lincoln, McClellan wrote, "I personally crossed the Chickahominy today at Bottom's Bridge and went a mile beyond, the enemy being about a half mile in front."[21]

Sumner's Lower and Upper Bridges. About three miles above the railroad bridge, at the crossing of the Williamsburg Road that led to Seven Pines, the division engineers and the pioneers of the divisions of General Edwin Sumner's corps, constructed two trestle bridges. They were called Sumner's lower bridge, replacing a bridge called *Sunderland's,* and Sumner's upper bridge, replacing a bridge called *Grapevine.* Long corduroy approaches to the two bridges were built through the swamps.

Pioneers and an infantrymen work force from the 1st Minnesota Infantry and the 5th New Hampshire Infantry worked on the bridge-building task. Other detailed infantrymen from the regiments collected timber in the woods and floated it to the work sites. The piers were assembled and then sunk into the mud, and then connected by stringers. A corduroy roadway connecting to the bridges

Reconstruction of Richmond and York River Railroad, Black Creek at Tunstall's Station, by 50th New York Volunteer Engineers

was built on stringers. Soldiers wrote, "They had to work in water waist deep all day." The channel of the Chickahominy at the bridges was 40 feet, but the bridges had to be much longer to provide roads over smaller channels and the bottom lands on both sides of the river. One bridge was completed by May 28 and the other by May 30.

Richmond and York River Railroad Bridge. Equally as important as the trestle bridges over the Chickahominy River for the soldiers and animals to cross over was the reconstruction of the railroad bridge for the movement of the railroad trains. To put the railroad back into operation, sections of the burned-out Chickahominy bridge were in need of reconstruction.

The first reconstruction job was a burned-out section of the bridge six miles from the Chickahominy River, over Black Creek at Tunstall's Station. To return the bridge to service, the engineers had to reconstruct a span fifty feet long with supporting trestle work rising twenty-one feet high.

On May 19 Major Frederick E. Embick and a work party of the 50th New York Volunteer Engineers started the repair job. Only a lack of machinery for bringing timber from the woods nearby delayed its early completion.

The engineers also repaired a stretch of track between the bridge and the White House depot.

Colonel Stuart, commander of the 50th New York Engineers, supervised the reconstruction of the second section of the railroad bridge. He reached the bridge site on May 23 with Companies I and

K of his regiment. He found three spans of the trestle, each eleven feet long and fifteen feet high, and one truss span forty-four feet long and fifteen feet high, entirely destroyed by fire. Two other spans were partially destroyed by fire. At a saw mill three miles east of the bridge he found a handcar and a quantity of timber, which he had hauled to the job site. Repair work started immediately. Colonel Stuart reported completion of the reconstruction of the three trestle spans three days later. He then started his work force on the reconstruction of the truss span.

The same day Engineer Charles McAlpine, United States Military Railroads, arrived with a crew of forty bridge builders and a carload of sawed timber and tools to assist in the repair of the truss span. With McAlpine's valuable aid, by the afternoon of May 27, his craftsmen completed the reconstruction work.

Lieutenant Daniel H. Andrus, of Colonel Stuart's staff, examined the bridge west of the destroyed section and also the track for four miles to Fair Oaks Station, and reported the bridge and track in safe condition. At 7 p.m. the first locomotive in the Union service crossed over the bridge and traveled three miles south of the Chickahominy. A few days later a train passed all the way to the Union soldiers who were deployed at Fair Oaks Station. Colonel Stuart advised General Woodbury a guard was needed at the bridge because it was a long and high one and the guard he posted was insufficient for its protection. Lieutenant William W. Folwell, who worked on the bridge, reported it to be a quarter mile long. "The rebs," he added, "fortunately for us, burnt only some 80 feet of the bridge over the channel. What fools the rebs were not to do their work better."[22]

New Bridge. The 15th New York Volunteer Engineers were ordered by General Woodbury to march to New Bridge to rebuild the burned-out trestle bridge.

On the march from White House to the bridge site Captain William H. Ketchum, facing the need to build bridges on the road to reach his work site, supervised the building of a 26-foot timber bridge over Black Creek, and a 38-foot timber bridge over Mill Creek.

On arrival at New Bridge, Captain Ketchum's engineer soldiers were prevented from approaching New Bridge because of the presence of enemy pickets. A day later he took possession of the bridge site and took the measurements of his construction job.

According to Ketchum's report, Colonel Murphy's engineer soldiers never found a meaner river over which to build a bridge. His report stated the task puzzled the wits of the engineers. With water up to their necks, the engineer soldiers waded, chopped, hewed, floated, and dragged logs to the bridge in the rain, sultry sun, and

under hostile fire. All day and night on May 27 the engineer soldiers cut logs in the forest, shaped them into bridge planks, and
then hauled them to the bridge. They completed a 7-span, 114-
foot-long trestle bridge a day later. They also cut timber that
corduroyed 1,000 feet of road, and cut new roads through the woods.
Colonel Murphy added in his report that his engineer soldiers
worked faithfully and cheerfully at whatever hour he called them
out for duty.

On May 27, amidst rain and mud, General Porter's corps
cleared Johnston's soldiers from the army's right flank and forced
them to retreat to Hanover Court House. General McClellan reported it was a "glorious victory."

General Woodbury reported the work completed by his engineer brigade up to May 29:

(1) Bridges built en route from White House to work sites on
Chickahominy River:

> Timber 1—26 feet
> Timber 1—20 feet
> Timber 1—18 feet
> Timber 3 @ 8 feet = 24 feet.

(2) Bottom's Bridge Chickahominy River:

> Trestle 1—120 feet

(3) New Bridge Chickahominy River:

> Trestle 1—114 feet

(4) Railroad Bridge:

> Span 1—51 feet in length, 21 feet in height
> Span 3—11 feet in length, 15 feet in height
> Truss Span 1—44 feet in length, 21 feet in height.

(Pioneers did not submit reports on length of bridges built.)[23]

General Barnard reported to General McClellan that the five
bridges were ready for the remainder of the army to cross to the
south side of the Chickahominy.

With his army formed in the shape of a V astride the river,
McClellan based his tactical plan upon the availability of the bridges.
The base of the V was anchored on Bottom's Bridge. The left arm
on the south side of the river ran parallel to the railroad tracks and
the Williamsburg Road to the outskirts of Richmond. The right arm
on the north side of the river ran parallel to the bank of the
Chickahominy to New Bridge. Bottom's Bridge and the railroad
bridge were the main crossing points from one flank of the army to
the other. McClellan kept his army deployed in such a position
because he planned to mass it either (1) to march over to the south
bank for a march to confront Johnston's army, or (2) to march the
soldiers on the south side back over to the north side to fight off

any attempt by Johnston to turn his right flank at New Bridge or to destroy the supply depot at White House.

McClellan feared Johnston's crossing to the north side of the Chickahominy on the bridges in his possession at Mechanicsville, above New Bridge, if he moved his entire army to the south side of the Chickahominy. McClellan's critical situation resulted from his speculation on what tactics Johnston would adopt.

McClellan's prerogative to make a decision was preempted by natural forces. During the afternoon of May 30 a heavy thunderstorm broke out of the sky. Rain poured down on the armies encamped in the environs of the Chickahominy. Torrents of rain fell until midnight; occasionally streaking lightning lighted up the sky; and the noise of thunder filled the air. The next day appeared dark and dreary. The soldiers huddled in their soggy uniforms any place they could escape the unremitting rain. Suddenly, at noon, the sun shone dimly. Battlefield sounds changed, too. Instead of thunder, the soldiers along the Chickahominy heard the booming of cannons in the direction of Richmond. Johnston, expecting the storm of the previous night to swell the river and thus prevent McClellan, with his army divided by the swollen river, from joining his forces, preempted the prerogative to make a decision. He made the decision to attack Keyes' IV Corps and Heintzelman's III Corps on the south side of the river. Keyes' corps seemed trapped. When notified of Johnston's attack, McClellan, faced with another critical situation, frantically attempted to rush reinforcements. The weather and rain-soaked terrain prohibited his soldiers from making a rapid movement. On the south side Keyes' corps could not rally in the rain and mud to repulse Johnston's attack. White Oak Swamp to the south protected Keyes' left flank but his right flank could be surrounded. A Confederate column marched to the unprotected flank. Fortunately, the muddy roads prevented Johnston's force from making the attack with a large number of soldiers.[24]

If Johnston had been able to push his soldiers between the right of Keyes' corps and Bottom's Bridge, the two corps south of the Chickahominy River would have been cut off and lost to McClellan. Late in the afternoon the dim sunshine disappeared and another storm burst with a deluge of rain, vivid lightning, and heavy thunder.

The Chickahominy had reached an almost impassable condition. At 2:30 p.m. McClellan ordered Sumner to march the two divisions in his corps over the river. As Sumner approached the Upper or Grapevine Bridge with his soldiers, he could see the bridge's flooring rising with the flowing water. It seemed only a matter of seconds before the bridge would flow away with the forceful current. The engineer soldiers had a difficult task to keep

Sumner's Bridge

the green logs of the roadway tied in place by slender long twigs used for rope; cracks appeared when logs bobbed up due to the swift current. The engineer officer at the bridge met Sumner on his approach. He urged Sumner not to cross.

"General Sumner, you cannot cross this bridge."

"Can't cross this bridge? I can, sir. I will, sir!"

"Don't you see the approaches are breaking up and the logs displaced? It is impossible."

"Impossible? Sir, I tell you I can cross. I am ordered."

Sumner had received orders to cross; he was determined to cross.

The troops in Sedgwick's division followed the troops of Major General Israel Richardson's division, led by Sumner. As the corps crossed on the bridge the tree trunks of the roadbed slipped and rolled under the soldiers' and horses' feet. Wagons and gun carriages had to be pushed over the bridge by soldiers whose feet continuously slipped out from underneath them. It was a pitch dark night made darker still by the dense woods. The approaches at each end of the bridge were a muddy morass. Tired, wet, mud-covered soldiers continued to cross late into the night. Ironically, just as the last soldier stepped off the bridge, the strength and tension binding the bridge materials together disintegrated. The bridge collapsed into the mud and water with a thunderclap. Only the weight of the soldiers, horses, wagons, and gun carriages on the bridge provided the force to keep it in place.

Sumner, with a soldier's instinct, marched through the woods to battle Johnston's soldiers heading towards Bottom's Bridge to trap the two Union corps south of the river. Leading his corps with bayonets fixed, Sumner and the first soldiers to cross met and drove Johnston's soldiers back from the bridge. Only night brought the battle to an end.

Johnston set his goal to crush Keyes' corps, but Sumner's arrival foiled his plan. Johnston also anticipated the previous day's storm to swell the river, but the capricious water reacted differently. The full force of the deluge of rain did not flow downstream until twenty-four hours later.

At that critical time of the battle McClellan did not order all the corps on the north bank of the Chickahominy to cross. He said the storms that had weakened the bridges forced him to that decision.

The critical situation continued to face McClellan and his engineer officers. The army's need for bridges accelerated. McClellan and his corps commanders looked to the engineers to construct other bridges over the river to enable the entire army to be posted on the other side. Johnston, aiming to keep the Union army divided, sent a force to each bridge site to intimidate his foe.

Second Phase of Bridge Building

On the subject of the first five bridges, McClellan wrote, "Rains demolished a great amount of our labor, and our first bridges, with their approaches, were not constructed with reference to extreme high water, were washed away or rendered impassable. To build bridges requires an immense labor force. Replacement bridges would have to be much larger, more elevated and stable. The soldiers must work in the water exposed to the enemy's fire from the opposite bank."[25]

At 7 p.m. May 31, almost twelve hours after the attack started at Fair Oaks, McClellan decided to issue orders to the engineers to build bridges. When the bridges were in place the army would march over the river to the south side.

Thus started the second phase of the engineers' bridge building. The first bridge would be for Porter's corps posted in the New Bridge area.

New Bridge Ponton Bridges. Responding to the urgency of the battle situation, the Engineer Battalion at New Bridge made an unsuccessful attempt to build a ponton bridge during the night. The darkness and the dense woods blotted out the dim light that might shine in the night sky and enable the engineers to work at their task. The river's water level rose rapidly; the rising level in turn produced more energy in the current. Captain Duane, who had been assigned the task to join the separate pontons into rafts in the river, found the darkness, the powerful current, and the rising stream too much of a force; he abandoned his task for the night.

Early in the morning Duane resumed the bridge construction. Finally, after arduous work, the battalion engineers were able to construct two ponton bridges.[26]

Because the river valley was flooded, extra guy lines were required to hold the pontons in position. At the two bridges Barnard ordered Lieutenant O. E. Babcock to make an examination of the approaches on the Richmond side. Babcock crossed over with twelve engineer soldiers. The Confederates fired upon them, inflicting wounds on some of the engineers, and those who were wounded became the Engineer Battalion's first serious battle casualties. The two bridges were close enough to Richmond for the soldiers at the bridges to hear the city's ringing church bells.

New Bridge Trestle Bridge. The engineers also started repairs on the trestle bridge at New Bridge. By working through the night they had the bridge ready for traffic at 8:15 a.m. on June 1. A crossing at New Bridge was easier than at some other bridge because the approaches were by way of an existing raised earthen causeway.

Lower Trestle Bridge. About a mile below New Bridge Captain William A. Ketchum, of the 15th New York Engineers, received orders to construct the lower trestle bridge. Every task in its construction moved along smoothly until Ketchum reached the sixth trestle. Then, due to the rapid rise of the water, he found it necessary to raise the abutments. In trying to raise the abutments, he in turn raised the shore end of the balk. When he raised the balk, the whole structure, pushed by the current, moved inshore and fell with a thud.

Undiscouraged by the failure, Ketchum immediately started to work clearing away the wreckage. He commenced rebuilding. He connected the structure with the far shore at 2 a.m. on June 2. The bridge was 350 feet in length, consisting of 7 trestles and 7 pontons to support the roadway.

Ketchum's difficult bridge-building job had its annoyances. In his report to Barnard, he stated, "I would also beg leave respectfully to report that I was very much annoyed by the constant interference of officers of higher rank than myself who came to me ordering me to hurry up the work, and representing that they had the authority of the commanding general."[27]

Upper Trestle Bridge. At the same time that Ketchum received orders to build the lower trestle bridge, Captain Ira Spaulding of the 50th New York Engineers received orders to build the upper trestle bridge about a mile above New Bridge. Due to the high water

Spaulding had to remove the timber to the high ground to prevent the current from washing it away. When he had constructed about three-quarters of the bridge, the second trestle cap from the riverbank broke, requiring Spaulding to have the engineer soldiers dismantle all the bridge except one span to put on a new cap. When he completed the construction of the bridge across the stream, he also discovered that the rapid current was fast undermining the legs of the trestles in the main channel. He was compelled to have forty feet of the bridge in the center dismantled to put in a ponton boat to hold the roadway. Because of the delay caused by the reconstruction the time spent in constructing the bridge exceeded Spaulding's estimated building time. At noon on June 1 he set the south bank abutment in place to complete the bridge.

Describing Spaulding's bridge to Barnard, Colonel Stuart spoke with the highest praise of the skill, energy, and endurance exhibited by the officers and men who built the bridge. He also mentioned their lengthy exposure in the stream which had become very deep and rapid before the trestle could be placed and secured, and of their utter indifference in regard to the enemy's shot and shell which fell in close proximity to them. The unexpected and high rise of the river made it necessary for the men engaged in the construction of the bridge to work for nearly twelve hours in the cold water. Frequently, they had to dive to place the legs of the trestles and then swim to reach the opposite shore. They had to do a large amount of the work in the darkness of the night.

Railroad Bridge. Only the railroad bridge withstood the force of the rising water on May 31. McClellan used that bridge to supply his soldiers on the south side of the river. Alexander took planks and laid them between the rails so the infantry and cavalry could also use the bridge to cross to the south side. Until the other bridges were completed, the railroad bridge was the only connection between the divided wings of the Army of the Potomac.

As light appeared on the second day of the battle the contesting armies renewed their combat with fierceness. Johnston assaulted McClellan's army with all his available soldiers. McClellan's soldiers held their ground. At noon Johnston called a halt to the gunfire of his soldiers, and ordered them to withdraw from the field. McClellan's soldiers lacked the energy to pursue their foe. Later in the day the Union soldiers learned that Johnston had been injured when he fell off his horse.

At a critical moment the Confederate soldiers were without a battlefield commander. General Robert E. Lee, well known to McClellan, later in the day assumed command of the Confederate army in the Fair Oaks' battle. During the afternoon Professor T. S. C.

Lowe, in his observation balloon, soaring over the battlefield, reported the Confederate soldiers were marching toward Richmond. At night the Union army observed campfires on the edge of the city. Both armies sought a night of rest. McClellan considered the battle of Fair Oaks a victory for his soldiers. If the battle were a victory for the Union army, it cost the Union 5,000 casualties. The cost to the Confederates totaled 8,000 casualties.[28]

Exhausted by the battle of Fair Oaks, the contending armies welcomed the opportunity to rest and reorganize. Porter's and Franklin's corps remained in position along the north bank of the Chickahominy, because McClellan did not issue orders to them to cross to the south side, and Stoneman's cavalrymen reconnoitered in the area of White House to watch the enemy's movements.

Third Phase of Bridge Building

McClellan vowed not to order his immobilized army to battle again until strong bridges spanned the Chickahominy River. Another month of intermittent rain and sunshine passed by without the armies engaging in combat. During that month McClellan's engineers occupied themselves in their third phase of bridge building. Eight of the nine bridges that crossed the river at the Fair Oaks' battle were repaired or rebuilt as required by their condition. The only bridge destroyed by the heavy current was Sumner's Lower Bridge.

McClellan and Barnard decided to build four additional bridges, raising to twelve the total number of bridges (trestle, ponton, railroad) spanning the river for the eight miles between Bottom's Bridge and New Bridge.

Spaulding's Footbridge. A short distance below the Lower Trestle Bridge, near New Bridge, Spaulding found an old beaver dam that he visualized could be converted into a narrow foot bridge. A detail of 250 engineer soldiers from his 50th New York Engineers reconstructed the beaver dam into a bridge. Where there was a break in the dam, three pontons running lengthwise across the stream were fastened to support the remainder of the roadway.

Duane's Bridge. Below Spaulding's footbridge Duane and the Engineer Battalion constructed one of the most important trestle bridges to cross the river. Construction work on the 900-foot-long bridge, with corduroy roadway, started on June 11, and work continued night and day until June 17 when the bridge reached the south bank of the Chickahominy. Throughout the days engineers worked in water over their heads because from such a position they could more easily float the heavy logs into place.

Major General Daniel P. Woodbury

Miller, *The Photographic History of the Civil War*

Woodbury Bridge. General Woodbury and work parties from the 15th and 50th New York Engineers built Woodbury Bridge a short distance below Duane's trestle bridge, which, with its approaches, stood out as one of the remarkable bridges built by the engineer soldiers. They built the bridge during six days of rain. The causeway to the bridge, a corduroy road 15 feet wide, covered with four to six inches of gravel and clay to prevent disintegration of the corduroy, zigzagged through the swamp. The causeway and the bridge covered a distance for about a mile. An earth embankment on each side protected the bridge against rising water. Countless number of soldiers who crossed the bridge admired the engineer-soldiers' bridge-building abilities. Proud of their work, the engineers fastened a homemade sign on a pole on the north end abutment that read:

"Woodbury Bridge
"On the way to Richmond
"Built by the Volunteer Engineer Corps
"From June 8 to June 14, 1862"

Woodbury and Alexander Bridge. The twelfth bridge constructed under the supervision of General Woodbury and Colonel Alexander crossed the Chickahominy between Woodbury Bridge and Sumner's Upper Bridge. Alexander selected the construction site, and Woodbury and Alexander led the work details from the 15th and 50th New York Engineers in the construction work. The bridge measured 1,080 feet long and 11 feet wide.

McClellan's Change of Base

After being immobilized and out of combat for a month, McClellan chafed to restart the Army of the Potomac marching against its foe. Lee's forces continued to build up, while McClellan's forces continued to decrease, especially from the diseases contracted in the swamplands. With the twelve bridges (ponton, trestle, railroad) ready, McClellan expressed a determination to return to battle.

Woodbury Bridge

His immediate order called for the abandonment of the supply line and depot on the Pamunkey River, and with the navy's aid, the establishment of a new base on the James River. If the change of base could be successfully accomplished, and unknown to the enemy, McClellan's army would have the benefit of fighting a battle with the aid of naval gunboats off the shore. Such a deployment could not be made easily in the face of the enemy. Besides, to McClellan's soldiers and the public, it suggested retreat.

Just as quickly as McClellan acted forcefully on a decision, his bane of precaution arose to fill him with doubts and uncertainties; he withdrew his march order. He decided not to shift operations to the James River until forced to do so by the battle situation. As a precaution, though, he had some of the supplies and ammunition at White House moved by boat to the James River.

At the same time that McClellan considered a change of base, a reconnaissance by the engineers provided evidence that Lee had erected heavy defensive works by New Bridge. Based on the new intelligence, McClellan decided he had better engage his foe in battle before the defensive works became too strong.[29]

In the interim period when McClellan debated with the idea of a change of base, he also made a change in the disposition of his soldiers. Porter's corps was posted on a line from Mechanicsville to Cold Harbor, and the two divisions in Franklin's corps were shifted— General William F. Smith's on June 5 and General Henry W. Slocum's on June 18—to the south side of the Chickahominy. Only Porter's corps and Stoneman's cavalry division remained on the north side of the river.

Ironically, it seemed each time McClellan made a bold decision on a tactical move, a disturbing situation appeared to inflict him with doubts. As he prepared to make his all-out attack against Lee, he received alarming news. Anticipating McClellan's tactics, Lee decided to resort to a bit of tested Confederate tactics. He diverted Lincoln's mind from the events on the peninsula to those in the Shenandoah Valley, and the implications of the latter events on the safety of the Union's capital city. He also turned loose General Thomas J. Jackson's cavalry in the Valley. In bold movements, Jackson cleared the Valley of Union troops. A terror gripped Washington; Jackson might capture the city! Lincoln immediately ordered McDowell to deploy his corps at Fredericksburg back to the Potomac River.[30]

The defeat in the Valley and the transfer of McDowell's corps meant that the other prongs of attack that McClellan planned to bring to bear against Lee's army, McDowell's corps and the small armies in the Valley, were ripped from his armor. Lee knew that reality, too. He ordered Jackson to join him on the Pamunkey River.

McClellan abandoned his plan to attack Lee. He harbored the fixation that Lee had more soldiers in his army than he did in the Army of the Potomac. Lee, to prove it, entered into battle against the two river-separated wings of the Army of the Potomac.

To McClellan the twelve substantial bridges meant either part of his army could maneuver back and forth over the river to meet the battle situation. The main body of the army was in position on the south side; Porter's corps with two divisions and the army's reserve force were on the north side. Lee and Jackson headed for New Bridge and Gaines Mill to strike Porter.

A critical situation faced McClellan. To extricate his army, he had a choice of dangers. He could transfer all his soldiers to the north or south side of the Chickahominy. With his eyes fixed on Lee, McClellan was determined to avoid any further humiliation of defeat. He decided to join the two wings of the army on the south side of the Chickahominy River.[31]

A Veritable Jumble

On June 25 McClellan issued an order to his quartermaster officer to evacuate White House. The task was carried out on land and on water. (1) Wagons were loaded with supplies and sent down the road to Bottom's Bridge to cross the Chickahominy. (2) Boats of all types were loaded with supplies to carry down the York and up the James River. Approximately 700 boats carried supplies away.

At night bales of hay were piled around and over supplies still at the depot to start a fire in the event of a Confederate raid. The Confederates did not interfere in the evacuation of White House. The day they did decide to attack only rubbish fell into their hands.

For days 2,000 wagons, and their teams of animals and teamsters, and 2,500 head of cattle kept up their marching to their destination twenty-five-miles away at Haxalls Landing, on the James River, south of Malvern Hill.

The long moving train, a veritable jumble, crossed safely at Bottom's bridge. The soldiers, animals, and wagons kept moving all day to White Oak Swamp Creek. For the laboring soldiers and animals the climate in the severe swamp was hot and suffocating. The engineer and pioneer soldiers labored to repair roads and hoist wagons out of the mud.

White Oak Swamp Creek Bridges

General Barnard sent General Woodbury with his engineer brigade ahead to White Oak Swamp Creek to build bridges to cross the approaching wagon trains, herd of cattle, and soldiers. The creek flowed at a right angle to the Chickahominy River on its southern bank. Woodbury rebuilt White Oak Bridge on the creek and prepared a corduroy road through the swamp. Next to the White Oak Bridge he built a second bridge. A mile upstream on the creek Major John B. Magruder, 15th New York Engineers, built a third bridge. The engineer soldiers constantly performed maintenance tasks to keep the three crossings on White Oak Swamp Creek in operating condition. Constant repair work with shovels and axes was needed as the wagons and herd of cattle kept moving without a break.

A quartermaster officer of one of the divisions who led his wagon train towards the bridges reported, "We joined the current of wagons setting toward the bridges after a hard fight for the road, no officer being present with authority to prescribe the route that trains should take or order of march. At all narrow places or crossroads, where other trains came in there was the usual conflict, cutting in and breaking up the trains, degenerating sometimes into personal contests between officers, teamsters, and wagon masters, and very often in the breaking of wagons and the killing or maiming of public animals. With infinite labor I at last got my train into the road and together and after a few hours march we reached the bridges."[32]

The soldiers marching south with the wagon trains threw away blankets and coats at the White Oak Swamp Creek Bridges in such a quantity that one muddy spot was repaired by spreading blankets over light brush, and adding earth. A heavy wagon moved over the spot as though on a rubber mat. The bridge was of crude log construction imbedded in the mud. Every wagon needed to be assisted by the soldiers at the crossing. Lined up from Savage Station to the White Oak Swamp Bridges were all the known required items of equipment of an army: wagons, horses, mules, soldiers, cannons, ponton wagons, caissons, and ambulances. At almost every step an officer urged on the teamsters and wagon masters. Twenty rows of wagons moved side by side on approach routes to the White Oak Swamp Creek Bridges. An artist's view of the scene depicts an impression of hysteria. Teamsters swore, horses and mules balked, and officers shouted to persons within earshot. Amidst the Army of the Potomac's jumble, Babel made its second appearance on earth on Virginia's terrain.[33]

Many varieties of reptiles inhabiting the Virginia White Oak Swamp Creek area made known their presence. From the stagnant water an odor filled the air. Bullfrogs kept up their din and added to the noise of the rumble from the wagons. During the night the soldiers pushed the wagon trains through the tangled forest. They made torches from pine tree branches to give some dim light to the clearing. The reflection from the light on the wagons created ghostly dancing shadows. During the last night of the

Wagon Trains Moving to White Oak Swamp Creek

mass movement rain began to fall in torrents. The darkness seemed impenetrable, and the file leaders ahead were difficult to follow on the roads. Lightning, fortunately, illuminated somewhat the pine forest every few seconds, enabling the soldiers to take a quick glance in front of them to check their direction.

On June 28 the last of the wagon trains with the supplies from White House pulled into Haxall's Landing. The change of base, a tremendous undertaking in terms of physical movement, came to a successful conclusion. McClellan missed a battlefield victory, but his change of the supply base achieved a great military feat, and the members of his army who labored and endured hardships earned accolades. The role of the engineer and pioneer soldiers in the event stands out as another one of their innovative feats on the peninsula.

Lee Returns to the Attack

Simultaneously with McClellan's issuing orders to change his base from White House, Lee gave orders to attack the Yankees at Gaines Mill. A week of fierce combat engulfed the two armies. Usually the contestants' past battles lasted one day, but the appropriately titled *Seven Days' Battle* lasted from June 26 to July 1. The bloody week's fighting put an end to the campaign to defeat Lee on the peninsula.

The finality of the battle at Gaines Mill signaled the reversal of the Army of the Potomac's mission from an offensive one to a defensive one. The soldiers of the army who were able to march made a safe withdrawal to the south side of the Chickahominy. The engineer soldiers set about on the last act of the episode to destroy the bridges they had earlier built.[34]

Late one night Company C of the Engineer Battalion dismantled the ponton bridges at New Bridge. They had to work quietly as any noise would attract the attention of the Confederate pickets. At daylight they were still dismantling the bridges. A work detail sergeant instructed the engineer soldiers to defend themselves with axes and boat oars if necessary. The pontons, balk, and chess were brought onto the shore and set afire. Some pontons were scuttled in the river with their anchors.

The Confederates, though, in time did wake up to the Yankees' activity. They captured a few of the engineer soldiers and pontons. The captured engineer soldiers were later exchanged and returned to their company. They reported that the captured pontons were taken to Richmond and paraded down the main street in back of a marching band.

Company A of the Engineer Battalion destroyed Grapevine Bridge after McClellan's soldiers had marched back over it. Another detail of twelve men with Lieutenant Cross destroyed Alexander's and Woodbury's bridges. While on the job they found themselves without infantry support. Half of the engineer soldiers formed a skirmish line; the other half worked on bridge destruction with axes. A squad of Confederate cavalry rode down on the skirmishers, but rode away when fired upon by the engineer soldiers.

Stragglers and small detachments continued to arrive at the bridge. The arrival of the wounded at Woodbury's bridge prompted the sympathy of the engineer soldiers. As a result the last span of the bridge was kept partly in place or relaid occasionally until an hour or more after sunrise for the late arrivals.

The Engineer Battalion also destroyed the Foot Bridge and Duane's Bridge after the last Union soldiers had crossed.

After Porter withdrew at the Battle of Gaines Mill, Lee became convinced McClellan was heading his army towards the James River. Lee started marching his soldiers after the Yankees to make their departure from the battlefield a rout or to cut off their retreat.

McClellan's soldiers were safely over the Chickahominy River. Lee then had to stop the movement of his army to build bridges to cross that formidable obstacle.

By June 30 McClellan's army completed a redeployment south of White Oak Swamp Creek; the three bridges over the creek were destroyed. The engineer and pioneer soldiers kept the roads opened to Malvern Hill where on a commanding plateau the army took up a defensive position. McClellan had temporarily extricated his army from danger. His soldiers desired nothing more than to restore their exhausted bodies. The artillery officers placed in firing position 300 artillery pieces that covered every approach route. The engineer soldiers were posted near a road junction as infantrymen. General Heintzelman ordered them to make their position impenetrable.

Battle of Malvern Hill

When the Confederates attacked the Union position on Malvern Hill on July 1, McClellan's soldiers fired their massed artillery; casualties among Lee's soldiers mounted, and Lee decided to withdraw from the battle. McClellan chose to let the enemy retreat.

Camping at Harrison's Landing

The next day the Army of the Potomac fell back to Harrison's Landing on the James River. The soldiers set about to fortify their positions. Infantry company commanders called upon Colonel Murphy for wheelbarrows to help them in their labor of building earthworks, but he had to refuse their request stating he had only twenty wheelbarrows in his regiment to perform the regiments' assigned tasks.[35]

While the Army of the Potomac rested and replaced its battleworn uniforms and equipment, Barnard decided to organize Company D of the Engineer Battalion. He assigned Lieutenant Babcock to command the company. Barnard expected it would take time to recruit engineer soldiers; he, therefore, decided to organize Company D by the transfer of engineer soldiers from the three other companies. That decision did not provide any soldiers because of the large numbers of men on the sick list. Few soldiers were available to work on engineer jobs. A recorded anecdote emphasizes the situation. Sergeant Major Frederick Gerber one day admonished the last and only soldier of Company A fit for duty, "Ven I calls turn out Company A, you, Private Rue, turn out!"

A Bridge for McClellan's Withdrawal

McClellan ordered Barnard on August 10 to have constructed a ponton bridge at Barrett's Ferry over the mouth of the Chickahominy River, where it joined the James River. To obtain the remnants of the ponton bridge equipment, which had been carried down to Fort Monroe upon the abandonment of the depot at White House, Lieutenant Comstock with the Engineer Battalion sailed down the James River on the steamer *Metamora* to Fort Monroe, a distance of approximately sixty miles. A day later at the fort chess and balk were loaded on barges and the pontons arranged into rafts for towing up the river.

At daylight on August 13 the barges and rafts moved from the James into the mouth of the Chickahominy headed for Barrett's Ferry, about two miles up river. After the chess and balk were unloaded and the pontons tied up, the Engineer Battalion and the 50th New York Engineers started the construction of the ponton bridge. Captain Spaulding supervised construction of the bridge's western end, Lieutenant Comstock the middle section, and Lieutenant Cross the eastern end. Construction of the bridge progressed until dark. The next morning the engineers returned to work on the bridge and during the day completed construction of the 1,980-foot-long bridge. It was made up of five spans of trestle, and 96 pontons. Unthrashed wheat stacked in a nearby field was then cut and placed upon the bridge's floor planks to prevent their splintering from the traffic of soldiers, animals, and wagons and ambulances. The gunboat *Pawnee* patrolled the river to protect the crossing from enemy attack.

The Barrett's Ferry bridge was the last and the longest bridge constructed by McClellan's engineer officers and soldiers during the Peninsular Campaign. Quartermaster General Montgomery Meigs reported 5,899 horses and 8,708 mules drawing 2,578 wagons and 415 ambulances, and 12,378 artillery and cavalry horses moved over the bridge.[36] The Army of the Potomac started to cross the long ponton bridge at Barrett's Ferry on its eight-day march to Fort Monroe. The weather was clear and cool. There was no interruption to the bridge crossing. The only accidents were when a few horses fell overboard without damaging the bridge. Four days later the extreme rear guard of the army passed over. The bridge fulfilled its purpose: the army accomplished a safe withdrawal. Within a few hours the engineer soldiers had the bridge dismantled and all the equipment in tow of a steamer bound for Fort Monroe, a stopover point on the voyage back to Alexandria. General Barnard reported "75,000 men, 300 pieces of artillery, and the immense baggage trains of the army passed over a bridge of the extraordinary length of nearly 650 yards. A feat scarcely surpassed in military history." (It was surpassed by the floating bridge built at Paducah in September 1861.) Barnard omitted from his report any mention of the thousands of animals that crossed on the bridge.

Even though the Army of the Potomac failed in the mission it undertook on the peninsula between the York and James Rivers, it

Barrett's Ferry Ponton Bridge

received many words of praise for its quality as an army and a number of distinguished tactical achievements.

The engineers also received commendations.

General Heintzelman, corps commander, said that during the change of base from the York to the James River the engineers "pioneered the way for our glorious army to its new position." Brigadier General Philip Kearny, a brigade commander, said, "They saved our army."

Newspapers also made mention of the activities of the engineer soldiers. Writing about the manual labor required by the engineers to change the base from White House to Haxall's Landing, *The New York Times* stated, "They are indeed iron men."
On the same subject, the *New York Herald* said, "All honor to the New York Engineer Corps. Nothing could withstand their untiring energy, their industry and perseverance in overcoming every obstacle that could retard the movement of our troops in their change of base to the James River."

Herman Haupt

Another *par excellence* civil engineer, Herman Haupt, joined the Federal army in the spring to make available his engineering skills on the military railroads.

Haupt attended the United States Military Academy from July 31, 1831, to July 1, 1835, and upon his graduation he received an appointment as brevet second lieutenant. He resigned from the army September 30, 1835.

He then accepted employment in Pennsylvania with the Norristown Railroad. He left the railroad in 1836 to accept a position with the Commonwealth of Pennsylvania as an assistant engineer. He continued his service to the state for three years. From 1847 to 1849 he worked for the *Pennsylvania Railroad*. He then entered the teaching profession to teach engineering. In 1851, he authored a book on the subject of bridge building. From 1856 to 1862 he was professionally engaged in northwest Massachusetts in the construction of the five-mile-long Hoosac railroad tunnel through the Hoosac range, the southern continuation of the Green Mountains, located east of the Berkshires.[37]

With the expanding importance of the inchoate railroads to the army's logistical system, and the need for engineers with the professional skill to build and maintain railroads, Secretary of War Edwin Stanton approached Haupt in the spring to accept an appointment in the United States Military Railroads Service. After discussing the terms of an appointment with Stanton, Haupt acquiesced to Stanton's request, but only after Stanton agreed to Haupt's terms. Haupt stipulated he would serve in the army as long as the public's requirements could be satisfied. In his words he said he would be useful, not ornamental. He made it clear to Stanton he would keep away from political aspirations, and in spite of his previous uniformed military service, he expressed an anathema to wearing a uniform or displaying insignia of rank. He relented on those two terms when he understood they were necessary to him to exercise the authority of his position. With the arrangement of his appointment completed, Stanton appointed Haupt a colonel with duty as chief of construction and transportation, Department of the Rappahannock in Virginia.

On April 25 Haupt reported to General McDowell, the department commander. Ironically, thirty years earlier both officers were cadets in different classes at the United States Military Academy, and the recognition of that event prompted a cordial rapport between them.

McDowell informed Haupt on April 29 of his first assignment, to reconstruct the fifteen-mile section of the Fredericksburg and Potomac Railroad between the army's depot at Aquia Creek Landing and Fredericksburg. McDowell, who had orders at the time from the president to deploy his army to the south to aid McClellan on the York-James Rivers peninsula, could not perform his mission until the railroad had been returned to operations.

McClellan's and McDowell's cooperation was dependent on the support of the railroad and the supply depot at Aquia Creek Landing on the Potomac River.

On May 17, McDowell received orders to march south adjacent to the sixty-mile route of the railroad to cooperate with McClellan and to threaten Richmond from the line of the Pamunkey-York Rivers.

Haupt's initial tasks on Fredericksburg and Potomac Railroad were (1) to rebuild bridges the Confederates had burned and restore three miles of torn-up tracks and cross ties, and (2) to rebuild the wharf building burned out at Aquia Creek Landing. The sites of bridges to be built were at Accokeek Creek, Potomac Creek, and Rappahannock River. Haupt estimated the jobs would require three to four weeks of serious work.[38]

In his approach to his tasks, Haupt decided the bridges he would build would be trestles, and built in the shortest time with timber collected in the surrounding areas of the bridges. At the outset of the initiation of the jobs, Haupt had to depend on a work force of soldiers detailed from the infantry regiments. Neither one of the parties found the arrangement to their liking. Haupt stated different details of soldiers arrived each day, who had different attitudes and skills, and he had to spend time each day instructing the soldiers on their work and making work assignments, which reduced their time spent on job tasks. The soldiers themselves found manual labor objectionable and demonstrated an unwillingness to labor for Haupt. They believed they joined the army to fight battles.

Haupt had the added tasks within the scope of his duties for the Department of the Rappahannock to reconstruct seven sabotaged or burned bridges on the Manassas Gap Railroad. On the jobs he put to work Negroes who were emigrating from the South to Washington, D.C., and passed through the army's lines.

Haupt also recognized in addition to a source of labor he needed a permanent efficient construction organization. He needed one that provided logistical support. The surrounding terrain furnished the necessary wood, but the woods also provided hiding places for the hostile force that attacked the working crews cutting timber. The hostile force also sneaked out of the woods to sabotage and destroy railroad equipment, and set bridges afire. It then returned to the woods, after some of its members made off with stolen engines.

Haupt with small untrained crews and unenthusiastic soldiers stressed his need for a civilian construction corps. General Halleck opposed his request. He believed the soldiers in the engineer units should do the construction work. Haupt agreed to Halleck's proposal if permanent engineer regiments under his command were assigned to the construction corps.

The first task Haupt started work on was reconstruction of Aquia Creek Landing with its one-acre wharf. His soldier work crews, with officers as assistant engineers, also relaid three miles of rails by working around the clock for three days.

Accokeek Creek Bridge. Haupt next turned his attention to the bridges. He commenced work on the Accokeek Creek bridge site after timber had been cut and delivered. He supervised the construction of a trestle bridge 150 feet long and 30 feet high. In the exceptional time of fifteen hours his work crew completed the construction of the bridge, and on May 14 McDowell rode across it on an engine.[39]

Potomac Creek Bridge. At the Potomac Creek bridge site Haupt's construction crew faced the obstacle of a 440-foot chasm. Previously a deck bridge, eighty feet above the water, had spanned it, but it had been burned by Rebels who were ever ready to deny bridges to the Yankees.

Haupt faced the added task of organizing a construction work force. He chose the soldiers he needed, between 100 to 120, from the 6th and 7th Wisconsin Volunteer Infantry Regiments and 19th Indiana Volunteer Infantry Regiment, and formed them into squads for particular tasks.

Potomac Creek Bridge

Haupt, *Reminiscences*

Many soldiers were deterred from working on the bridge because they had to climb about on ropes and poles eighty feet high to their workplaces. They were inexperienced in bridge building and many lacked mechanical skills as they were ordinary soldiers who mostly came from farms. The men had to work under difficult conditions for long hours, in the rain, in the heat of the sun, and with scarce food. They were Haupt's source of labor; he had to lead them to give their best. The bridge they built testifies they did their work creditably.

The round sticks of timber with the bark left on were cut in the nearby woods. They were then dragged approximately a mile and a half to the bridge site by oxen, or loaded on a wheeled frame for delivery. At the creek embankment they were rolled down and into the water where they were framed and elevated by sliding beams.

Haupt started to build the bridge on May 3. In the exceptional time of nine days his work force built a 400-foot long, 80-foot high frail-looking structure with three stories of trestle work with a supporting crib foundation. A trestle bridge of more than one story was considered impracticable. The soldiers worked all day and at night with the aid of lanterns. Approximately 34,760 linear feet of timber were used to construct the bridge. After two weeks of difficult and perilous work the soldiers cheered as railroad engines began to roll over the bridge headed for Fredericksburg. Haupt emphasized he did not seek permanence in the construction of the bridge, but the saving of time to rapidly return the railroad to operational service.

As quickly as the Yankees built a bridge, just as quickly Rebels were waiting to come out of the woods with determination to burn or destruct the product of Yankee labor.

General Cullum, author of the army's manual on floating bridges, wrote, "Haupt's *Potomac Creek* bridge one of the simplest, boldest, and most remarkable bridge structures ever built. The work of the soldiers who built it impressive."[40]

General McDowell reported he was impressed by the bridge. He added the bridge carried ten to twenty trains a day in both directions, and it withstood the force of the freshets.[41]

The author Karl A. von den Steinen remarked Herman Haupt was the "most brilliant engineer of his time."[42]

President Lincoln on a May 23 visit to the bridge site expressed his delight at Haupt's accomplishment. "I have seen most remarkable structure that human eyes ever rested upon. That man Haupt has built a bridge across Potomac Creek 400 feet long, nearly a 100 feet high and running trains over it. There is nothing in it but bean poles and cornstalks."[43] When one views the photograph of Haupt's bridge, one is quick to appreciate President Lincoln's wonderment.

Rappahannock River Bridge. While Haupt supervised the construction of the first two bridges, Daniel Stone undertook the task to build the third one, Rappahannock River Bridge. The bridge was needed to haul supplies to the army encamped south of the river. Stone collected timber from any nearby source he could find. The amount of construction in the area rapidly depleted the supply of timber. Stone built a 600-foot-long, 43-foot-high trestle bridge over the Rappahannock River.

The plans were canceled for McDowell to march out his army on May 26 to the aid of McClellan. The change in plans also called a halt to the maintenance on Haupt's three bridges. He reported to McDowell's headquarters on the upper Rappahannock River where McDowell instructed him to inspect the work crews reconstructing seven damaged or burned-out bridges on the Manassas Gap Railroad, which supplied McDowell's army.

Jackson in the Valley

In the Shenandoah Valley, General Jackson defeated the forces of Brigadier General Robert Milroy at McDowell and Major General Nathaniel Banks at Winchester. The defeats gave a scare to President Lincoln. He envisioned Jackson making a threatening march on Washington. He ordered Major General John C. Fremont and Major General James Shields to march their separate forces to converge on and trap Jackson.

Jackson, aware that the combined Union forces outnumbered his force, in an adroit tactic on June 8–9, sent one wing of his force to strike Fremont at Cross Keys where it mauled and routed him.

The other wing of the force furiously attacked Shields' advance guard at Port Republic and forced it to fall back to the main body.

The victories gave Jackson control of a ford on the South River at Port Republic. He anticipated the enemy might regroup. His cavalry force and wagon train safely crossed the river and established a defensive position. Two days earlier Lee had told Jackson, "Should an opportunity occur for striking the enemy, do not let it escape you." Jackson grasped the opportunity.[44]

Another Army in the Washington Area

As the Army of the Potomac returned to the Washington area the president, and the public as well, had the jitters Lee would march his army north to renew battle. To aid in the protection of the capital city and to reinforce McClellan in his determination to battle and defeat the Confederate army, Lincoln issued orders to the secretary of the army to organize the Army of Virginia. The units constituting the new army were McDowell's, General Franz Sigel's, and General Nathaniel P. Banks' corps. Lincoln placed the command of the army under General John Pope who had battle experience leading troops on the banks of the Mississippi River. His mission was to intercept General Jackson and to cover the Shenandoah Valley entrance leading to Maryland. Advancing on Lee's line of communications to Charlottesville and Gordonsville, Pope, by August 12, had marched to Culpeper. When McClellan turned away from further battle on the peninsula, Lee turned his army west to meet Pope's advance.

On August 18 Pope issued a general order to his army that all railroads, and especially the Orange and Alexandria Railroad, within the limits of the Army of Virginia, were placed under the exclusive charge of Colonel Haupt. He also ordered no orders regulating the running of trains, construction or repair of the roads, or transportation of supplies or troops were to be given except by authority of army headquarters through Colonel Haupt.

Upon engaging Lee's army in battle near Cedar Mountain, Pope assessed his army to be lacking in a will to engage the enemy in combat. He decided to march his soldiers back to the safety of the north side of the Rappahannock River. The corps of General James Longstreet and Jackson pursued Pope's army. Pope withdrew to the north bank of the river where he fought off his pursuers.

Jackson, in a deceptive movement around Pope's right flank on August 26, crossed the Rappahannock and skillfully masked his movement. Pope thought Jackson was heading for the Shenandoah Valley through Front Royal and Luray. A few days later Jackson appeared at Manassas where he captured and pillaged the town.

When Pope engaged Longstreet and Jackson in battle on August 30 they forced him from the battlefield south of Bull Run.

Pope reported to Halleck he needed the support of McClellan's army to protect the Army of Virginia from the onslaught of Lee.[45]

McClellan's army at the time was continuing its debarking at the port in Alexandria. General Halleck, whom Lincoln made general in chief on July 11, ordered McClellan to send Franklin's and Sumner's corps to the aid of Pope. The two corps arrived a day later, but the demoralized condition of the Army of Virginia made it impossible for the two corps' battle-hardened soldiers to rally Pope's soldiers.

As Pope's army retreated east along the Orange and Alexandria Railroad, Jackson's soldiers destroyed the bridges over Bull Run to disrupt the railroad. On August 27 Haupt's construction force rebuilt the railroad bridge over Pohick Creek. He ordered buildings in the area torn down and the material salvaged to be used to rebuild the bridge, which his workmen completed by 10 a.m. on August 28.

On August 30 Haupt organized a work crew to repair, for the seventh time, the Union Mills Bridge, over Bull Run, and the work was completed the next day. Pope depended upon the railroad to supply his troops and animals and to evacuate the wounded.

Chagrined at Pope's defeat at Bull Run and unable to satisfy the public's clamor for a victory, Lincoln dismissed Pope and at the same time brought to an end the existence of his army. The corps of Banks, McDowell, and Sigel were assigned to the Army of the Potomac.

McClellan Repeats Failure

General Lee's victory over Pope tuned the morale of his soldiers to a high pitch. Three times the Union soldiers incurred defeats with high casualties in an attempt to win a battle in Virginia; three times Confederate soldiers forced the Yankee soldiers from the battlefield.

Lee selected that martially spirited time to make his initial offensive march into Maryland and to use his victorious army's presence there to win another victory. He expected the fruits of another victory would be to encourage residents to join their fortunes with the Confederacy. He also expected to destroy the Baltimore and Ohio Railroad tracks in Maryland. He planned to follow up such a success with a march north to destroy the Pennsylvania Railroad tracks in Pennsylvania. The disruption of the railroads would cut off Union communications between East and West, except for the Great Lakes canal system farther north. Disruption of communications with the West would then require, according to

Bull Run Creek Bridge Reinforced with Haupt Trusses

Lee's analysis of the strategic situation, the Union to immobilize a large force to protect Washington.

A week after his success at Bull Run, Lee marched his army east of the Blue Ridge Mountains to Leesburg. His army crossed the Potomac River on a ponton bridge constructed by his engineer soldiers. After two days of unopposed marching, his soldiers arrived at Frederick, Maryland.

Engineer Battalion Chronicle

The Engineer Battalion, accompanying the Army of the Potomac on its march north to battle Lee's initiative, chronicled its march.

September 7. The Army of the Potomac and the Engineer Battalion left Washington in the heat. The engineer soldiers were in poor condition (the Peninsular Campaign had been strenuous for the 280 men in the battalion). The army crossed the Potomac River at fords.

September 11. The army camped at Rockville. Foraging soldiers found good food. Orders were issued soldiers could not carry unnecessary baggage.

September 12–13. The army arrived near Frederick.

September 14. The roads were choked with wagons and artillery. To make faster time the engineer soldiers took to marching in open fields. At night McClellan's soldiers reached the west side of South Mountain.

September 15. McClellan's soldiers moved out at 6:30 a.m. on a rapid, hard march to Turner's Gap. Lee retreated to Sharpsburg on Antietam Creek and decided to fight there. McClellan's soldiers took up the battle, but failed to break Lee's line.

[Concurrently, Lee sent Jackson to attack Harpers Ferry because he planned to move his supply line farther west and out of reach of the Union army. Jackson's soldiers responded, attacked, and captured the town.]

September 16. Battalion's reveille at 4:00 a.m. At daylight the engineer soldiers discovered they were lying among dead of enemy in the battle for Turner's Gap. "Silent companies" ate breakfast. At 6:00 a.m. moved out for Boonsboro; roads choked. Marched to Antietam and constructed two fords at the creek for artillery and one for infantry by cutting down banks of the creek and paving bottom in soft places with stone. Finished the construction at 10:30 p.m.

[Jackson and his soldiers returned from Harpers Ferry to rejoin Lee.]

September 17. Battalion's reveille at 4:00 a.m. Engineer soldiers built another ford for infantry at creek. McClellan opened battle with a series of uncoordinated attacks which forced the Confederates to give ground, and almost to a decisive moment where the Rebels were about to break ranks and flee the field. The Yankees needed a bold assault along the entire line to achieve their first victory against Lee. They lacked the overpowering strength to make the assault.

September 18. Battalion's reveille at 4:00 a.m. Engineer soldiers were issued forty rounds of ammunition; posted as infantry. The two contending armies spent the day peering at one another from their campsites. At night Lee slipped his army unobserved over the Potomac River on a ford at J. Miller's farm to end his first act of trampling in rebellion beyond Virginia.

September 19. The Engineer Battalion crossed Burnside bridge on way to Sharpsburg, and then on to Harpers Ferry.

September 21. With the Union's recapture of Harpers Ferry the Engineer Battalion and the 50th New York Volunteer Engineers raised the burned and sunken pontons, and built ponton bridges over the Shenandoah and Potomac Rivers with the expectation the Army of the Potomac would follow after Lee's army.

To the surprise of President Lincoln, General Halleck, and the public, General McClellan continued to encamp his immobilized army in Maryland. In response to incessant prodding to march his army, McClellan responded he had to regroup his army, await food for his soldiers and animals, and replenishment of horses and supplies to fill the wagon trains, and ammunition.

On October 24 the Engineer Battalion and 50th New York Volunteer Engineers, in anticipation of the army's movement, constructed two ponton bridges, each 1,100 feet long, across the Potomac River at Berlin, Maryland. Finally, after a month spent revitalizing his army, on October 28, McClellan redeployed the entire army over the bridges into Virginia.

The Pennsylvania Independent Engineer Company met the Army of the Potomac at Harpers Ferry and preceded it on its march through Loudoun Valley to rebuild the bridges Lee's army burned or destroyed on its retreat march. At Lovettesville the company received orders to turn around, return to Harpers Ferry, and to rebuild the suspension bridge across the Potomac River.

McClellan's march of his army into Virginia signaled he was again ready to seek out and do battle with Lee. At Warrenton he halted his army to camp. The plans he had in mind were to attack either General Longstreet's and General Jackson's corps separately, or to assault Lee's entire army at once and drive it back to Gordonsville. McClellan, though, forfeited another opportunity to engage his nemesis in battle. President Lincoln removed him as commanding general, Army of the Potomac, and assigned the command role to Major General Ambrose Burnside.

Ponton Bridge across Potomac River at Berlin

Fredericksburg: Tarnished Glory

Immediately upon assuming command of the Army of the Potomac, Burnside, aware his military and civil leaders wanted decisive battles, presented President Lincoln and General Halleck with what he considered a bold plan. He would lead the Army of the Potomac on a directional march to give General Lee the impression of an attack against his forces at Culpeper or Gordonsville. When Lee deployed his soldiers to meet the feint, Burnside would quickly order his army to change direction to march to Fredericksburg, cross the Rappahannock River, and march uncontested down the turnpike to seek out Lee's army. In its conception the plan seemed a bold and plausible maneuver possible to accomplish. The proof of it, though, depended upon all the actions that comprised its entirety being carried out at the prescribed places and times.

If Burnside fought at Culpeper or Gordonsville he would have long supply lines exposed to enemy cavalry raids. Also, the Confederates would be able to split up their army and retreat piecemeal along the routes leading to Richmond. If Burnside shifted his army to Fredericksburg he would have a shorter supply line, and be able to keep his army between the capital city and the Confederate forces. He believed the shorter route on the turnpike offered the opportunity to assault Lee's entire army.

The burden for the success of Burnside's quick-march maneuver rested upon the army's engineers. Before the army could march against Lee, it had to cross the Rappahannock. The engineers would be called upon to haul the pontons to Falmouth on the north bank of the river, and then to construct bridges on the day Burnside's army arrived at the crossing site north of Fredericksburg. Both the infantrymen and engineers had to adhere to a precise time schedule on the day appointed to cross the river. If the engineer soldiers with the pontons arrived a few days ahead of the arrival of the infantrymen, the enemy would have evidence to second-guess Burnside's plan. If the infantrymen arrived ahead of the pontons and did not have the bridges in place to enable them to cross the river immediately, they would lose the tactical advantage of taking an unprepared enemy by surprise. Any Union officer botching the timing factor would give Lee's soldiers time to march into the town and fortify it.

A week after McClellan withdrew his army from Maryland he sent an order to Captain Duane to dismantle the bridges on the Potomac River and haul the pontons to the army headquarters. While camped at Warrenton, and before his relief as army commander, McClellan mentioned to Burnside that he was considering the idea of crossing the Rappahannock near Fredericksburg; to be prepared to do so he wanted the pontons near at hand. The reception of McClellan's information might have influenced Burnside when he took command of the army.[46]

Anticipating the army's deployment, Lieutenant Comstock, Burnside's newly appointed staff engineer, ordered the Engineer Battalion on November 3 to break camp and to move to Falmouth, Virginia. The move placed the engineers in advance of the army, and in an isolated position. They adhered to military discipline; they posted pickets around the battalion on the march and in their encampments. An engineer soldier reported the environment at Falmouth was cold and stormy. The corporals of the guard details constantly made their rounds to keep awake the guards on their posts. As the temperature lowered, the engineers built huts and sod houses as a means to keep warm. The battalion activity report states a Thanksgiving Day celebration on November 27, but without any details.[47]

General Halleck, accompanied by General Meigs and Colonel Haupt, visited Burnside's headquarters on November 12 to discuss battle plans. Upon hearing of Burnside's plan, Halleck mentioned that the proposed plan differed from the one Lincoln outlined in his letter of October 13 to McClellan. Lincoln's letter, quoting a military maxim—"operate on the enemy's communications as much as possible without exposing your own"—emphasized his point by telling the field commander to take the route nearest the enemy and destroy his line of communications. In his concluding remark, atypical of a commander in chief, Lincoln said the letter was to be interpreted as a suggestion and not as an order.[48]

The proposal to march to Falmouth and cross the Rappahannock River was contrary to Lincoln's suggestion. Burnside, instead of taking the march route nearest to Lee following his line of communications, chose to break off contact and march his army away from Lee's. Burnside assessed any march to battle Lee at Gordonsville or Culpeper as dangerous to his line of communications because of the deteriorated condition of the Orange and Alexandria Railroad. Haupt emphasized that point to Burnside and President Lincoln, and added the railroad lacked the facilities to support an army the size of Burnside's. The capture of Fredericksburg, Burnside believed, made available a secure line of communications on the Richmond and Potomac Railroad, which, at the time, under Haupt's supervision appeared to be in good condition.

At the meeting Haupt reported he was prepared to undertake the speedy reconstruction and opening of railroad communications out of Aquia Creek and Fredericksburg. The buildings and wharf would be rebuilt at Aquia Creek Landing. He assured Burnside he was prepared to begin work upon receipt of orders. He also said he would need a cavalry detachment to provide security on the construction sites and to protect material at Belle Plain and Aquia Creek.

During their November 12 discussion Halleck did not offer any support to Burnside in his battle plan. He offered a counterproposal that Burnside march along the Blue Ridge Mountains, maintaining contact with Lee's army and his line of communications to the Confederate base at Staunton. Although Lincoln had said his letter was not an order, Halleck was reticent to reject it as such, and would not sanction any deviation from his interpretation. In the critical matter as to the Army of the Potomac's point of attack, Halleck withheld his decision, deciding only that there was a need for him to discuss it with the president.[49]

Burnside mentioned the critical item, the movement of the pontons to the Rappahannock. Halleck said he would order the Engineer Brigade to bring the pontons down to Falmouth. Adhering to his word, Halleck sent through the order. He telegraphed General Woodbury, who was in Washington with part of the brigade, to start moving the ponton train.

The morning after Halleck's return to Washington, November 13, Burnside received a message that the president did not approve the proposed plan of operation, but he did assent to it, with the further cryptic advice if he intended to carry it out, he was to move rapidly. The president also approved a change of base from the Orange and Alexandria Railroad to the water termination route at Aquia Creek Landing and Belle Plain. Ignoring this ambiguous response, Burnside decided to proceed according to his plan.[50]

On November 14, informed by Halleck that the president had approved the change of base, Haupt immediately called upon General Woodbury and quartermasters for necessary transportation. The next day several transports with troops were sent to Aquia Creek Landing and Belle Plain. The next morning Haupt, accompanied by Woodbury, Ingalls, and two assistant quartermasters, traveled down the Potomac to the facilities to decide upon plans of construction. Two days later a work force under William W. Wright, an engineer, began the construction work. In four days approximately 800 feet of wharf had been made ready to receive supplies and railroad equipment.

In a chain reaction all the officers involved in Burnside's battle plan with responsibility to move the pontons proceeded to violate all the military maxims of completed staff work, planning, coordination, and liaison.

The general in chief, the commanding general of the Army of the Potomac, and the commanding general of the Engineer Brigade made decisions based upon their misreading of what they thought were the facts in the proposed plan and orders. Their decisions precipitated an outcome earning the title of a blunder.

General Burnside based his decision on the knowledge he had of McClellan's orders to Duane to move the pontons. He thought that by November 12 the pontons had moved from Berlin to Washington or Alexandria, and he expected that in a few days they would be at the river. Actually, the pontons were still at Berlin. McClellan's order to Duane on November 6 to move the pontons had not been received at the bridge site by the engineer officer in charge. At the November 12 conference Halleck failed to mention that the pontons had not reached Washington. Because Burnside was not told that information, he believed that Halleck would attend to the rapid movement of the pontons. Halleck, it appears, failed to take positive action; he did not give General Woodbury specific instructions as to what day Burnside needed the pontons.[51]

Expecting the pontons for the bridges to arrive in a few days, Lieutenant Comstock telegraphed Woodbury on November 14 asking for the location of the pontons, and the readiness of the engineers to move them. Woodbury expressed surprise when he received Comstock's telegram. He did not know Burnside wanted the pontons so soon. He surmised that the army would march to Fredericksburg, but he had not heard any date mentioned. He also suspected that someone else lacked information. Halleck did not tell him when the pontons were due at their destination at the time he issued orders two days before to dismantle the bridges at Berlin. Woodbury, recognizing the need for clarification, called on Halleck to tell him that if Burnside needed the pontons on the Rappahannock the same day his army arrived there, he should delay the army's march five days. Halleck refused to grant a delay. Inexplicably he did not relay Woodbury's suggestion on a five-day delay to Burnside, and he did not give Woodbury any further instructions. As a result actions were not taken to expedite the movement of the pontons.[52]

Later in the day Comstock sent another telegram to Washington asking that a second ponton train be sent on the way. The next day Woodbury sent Comstock a telegram stating that Captain Spaulding of the 50th New York Volunteer Engineers had just arrived with thirty-six pontons, and that forty or more were expected to arrive later in the day. He advised Comstock too that a ponton train was to leave on November 16 or 17, depending on whether or not the quartermaster furnished animals to move the wagons.

According to Captain Spaulding he had "just arrived" in Washington at 10:30 p.m. on November 13. After he had arrived he had to spend a day looking for Woodbury. In his report Spaulding wrote how he walked from office to office trying to find someone who could tell him his instructions. Two days later Woodbury ordered Spaulding to start moving the ponton train of thirty-six pontons he had brought down from Berlin, and the twelve then in the engineer depot in Washington, to Falmouth. Woodbury did not think it important to impress Spaulding with the need to hurry because a battle waited upon the ponton train.[53]

Spaulding moved the ponton train by road to the Occoquan River, twenty miles below Washington. Upon arrival there he decided, to make the movement easier, to fasten the pontons together forming rafts, and in that form float them to the Potomac River, and then on down to Aquia Creek. The chess and balk were left at the river's bank. They were to continue by the animal-drawn wagons overland on the muddy roads. The rafts of pontons arrived at Belle Plain on Potomac Creek, fifteen miles from Falmouth, on November 18. As the wagons were still moving overland on the muddy roads, there were no wagons to carry the pontons to their destination. No one took the time to notify Comstock that the pontons were destined for Belle Plain, and wagons should be sent there to move the pontons to Falmouth.

Woodbury, in his reply to Comstock, said the second train of forty pontons would leave on November 16 or 17, depending on receipt of additional animals from the quartermaster. Actually that ponton train did not leave until four days later because of the wait for 270 new animals and the necessary teamsters. After crossing the Occoquan River, it too became bogged down in the mud. The entire train was then sent by rafts from the Occoquan to the Potomac River, and then down to Aquia Creek, where the officer in charge received orders to proceed to Belle Plain.

Burnside, unaware of the mixup and delay on the movement of the pontons, started his army marching from Warrenton to Falmouth. The head of the column of soldiers began to arrive near Falmouth on November 19. The main body of the army started to reach camp the next day. To Burnside's surprise the pontons for the bridges were not there. His surprise turned to anger. He looked for Woodbury. When he found Woodbury he told him that for his failure to be ready to build the bridges across the Rappahannock he was placed under arrest, and would remain in that status until he made a satisfactory explanation for his failure.[54]

Watching the movement of the enemy army, Lee moved his army east along the south side of the Rappahannock. He was not yet in Fredericksburg the day Burnside's soldiers began their arrival on the north side of the river opposite the town. The turn in the tactical situation prompted General Edwin V. Sumner to ask Burnside for permission to ford the river and have his Right Grand Division attempt to occupy Fredericksburg. "No, Sumner," said Burnside, "wait for the pontons." Burnside wanted his line of communications by bridges in place between the two banks of the river before engaging in battle. The bridges would assure him a route to bring over reinforcements and supplies, or to withdraw, if necessary.[55]

Finally on November 25 the two ponton trains arrived from Belle Plain. Burnside's army had been camping for five days, waiting for orders to cross the Rappahannock. The Confederate forces were not sitting idly in their camp; they marched into Fredericksburg and massed in battle formation on the hills on the south side of the town out of range of Union guns. Burnside's crossing site was on a line in front of an alert and safely posted enemy.

Alarmed about the delay in crossing the Rappahannock, Lincoln visited Burnside the next day at Aquia Creek to discuss what changes Burnside contemplated in his initial battle plan. Burnside's obstinacy for his plan seemingly was persuasive enough to forestall the president from issuing a countermand of Burnside's plan.[56]

Burnside set in motion his operation on December 10 to cross the river for the attack on Lee's army. Comstock issued a terse order to the Engineer Brigade for two ponton bridges to be thrown across the Rappahannock River at the upper or western end of the town of Fredericksburg; one ponton bridge to be thrown at the center of the town; and two ponton bridges to be thrown at the lower or eastern end of the town. The distance between the extreme bridges extended two miles. The Engineer Battalion was ordered to construct one bridge, the easternmost, and the 15th and 50th New York Volunteer Engineer regiments were to throw the other four.

To protect the engineers while at work, each bridge was to be covered by an artillery battery and an infantry regiment. The ponton trains were to arrive at the bank of the river at three o'clock in the morning. The wagons with the pontons, chess, and balk were to be unloaded and the pontons placed in the water by daylight. If the engineers were not interrupted by the enemy, they were to have all the bridges built within three hours after daylight.

At 3:00 a.m., December 11, amidst cold and foggy weather, the engineer soldiers started to move the bridge trains from headquarters' area of the army to the riverbank. The engineer soldiers were required to put their weight against the wagons to guide them cautiously down a plateau that rose thirty feet above the riverbank.

Upon reaching the assigned bridge site at the easternmost site, the Engineer Battalion immediately encountered difficulty. Because of the steepness of the riverbank the engineer soldiers

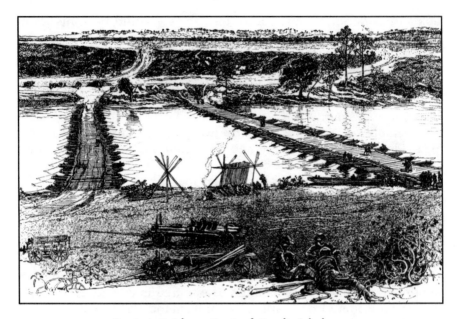

Ponton Bridges East of Fredericksburg

Library of Congress

were unable to bring the wagons close to the water's edge. Thus they had to unload the pontons, chess, and balk 200 yards from the bridge site, drag the bridge components across a plowed field to the edge of a bluff, and then carry them down the steep embankment. At the river's edge they only had a narrow strip of level ground to walk on. It was a muscle-straining job for the engineers to carry pontons 31 feet long, 1,600 pounds in weight. The unforeseen delay in bringing the equipment to the river's edge delayed the starting of construction for two hours.

At 7:00 a.m. the Engineer Battalion's soldiers began work with the enemy unaware of the construction of a bridge. They could not work rapidly because they had to chop through ice, almost a half-inch thick, that closed the river. When they broke through the ice they had to work standing in the freezing water. The enemy remained in the dark about the building of the bridge until 9:00 a.m. Engineers were just starting to put the approaches down to the south shore when a Confederate picket on the plateau above the south bank of the river became aware of the bridge. He seized a brand from his fire and waved it over his head. Signal guns in the town responded with fire, which aroused hostile pickets. The engineer soldiers pushed construction of the bridge; infantrymen formed for their protection; artillery on the bluffs fired at the enemy. The enemy fire wounded Private James Savage of Company C. Privates Allen McDonald and J. A. Curtis were captured. The gunfire of the Union soldiers protecting the engineer work party forced the enemy riflemen back, clearing the way for the engineers to complete a 400-foot floating bridge by 11:00 a.m.

A guard of twenty engineer soldiers was posted at the bridge. The other engineers were released to return to camp. An engineer soldier reported they were wet, tired, and hungry. They watched columns of infantrymen waiting to cross the Rappahannock and engage in the "deadly and destined to be fruitless onslaught on Confederate forces."

The 15th New York Volunteer Engineers worked on a bridge on the west side of the one built by the Engineer Battalion. To start work on the bridge Lieutenant H. V. Slosson left the staging area with the ponton train at 1:00 a.m. After a difficult trip, "a most tedious and toilsome march, in a dark night, with rain in torrents, most time rendering roads almost impassable from the depth of the mud," the ponton train arrived six hours later at the riverbank where the engineers unloaded the pontons.

The engineer soldiers started construction of the bridge, "and the volunteer engineers made the timber fly," but they were interrupted in their work by a picket force concealed behind houses and barns on the south side of the river. The Confederates kept their positions without molesting Slosson's engineer soldiers until the last balks were about ready to be put in place. Then they rapidly ran forward 200 paces, peered over the riverbank, ascertained the position of the bridge abutment, and hastily retired behind houses. Confederate infantry companies then appeared on the brow of the hill, deployed as skirmishers, and sent a volley of fire on the engineer soldiers, wounding six of them. Bullets pierced the pontons in many places.

Engineer soldiers who had finished their tasks on the bridge hastened to return the fire with great spirit. Their conduct under fire for the first time pleased Slosson. The artillery immediately opened fire and dispersed Lee's skirmishers in confusion. Twice afterwards the skirmishers tried to rally, but each time the artillery fire scattered them in confusion. The delay caused by the arrival of the enemy skirmishers held up the completion of the 420-foot bridge until 9:00 a.m.

Later in the day Comstock ordered Slosson to build a second bridge adjoining the one already in place. A 440-foot ponton bridge was constructed without Confederate opposition.

The Engineer Battalion and Lieutenant Slosson's engineer soldiers had in readiness three ponton bridges for General Franklin to cross his Left Grand Division over the Rappahannock east of the town.

Near the center of Burnside's army's position on the river the 50th New York Volunteer Engineers were forced to work in the face of enemy fire. The Confederates were determined to stop the engineer soldiers in their work to bridge the river. The engineers, led by Captain James H. McDonald, started building the bridge at 3:00 a.m. About three hours later when the bridge spanned two-thirds of the river, the Confederates fired upon the engineers working on the bridge from the house near the shore and from behind walls and fences. During the shooting Captain Augustus S. Perkins and two engineer soldiers were killed, and several incurred wounds. The infantry protecting the engineer work party from the northern shore were too far away and could do little harm to the Confederates by return fire. The unarmed engineers, unable to return the hostile fire, were driven off the bridge.

In an attempt to drive away the attackers, Union soldiers opened artillery fire on the town. The indiscriminate firing failed to silence the Confederates. A haze hanging over the river made it impossible to pick out targets. The engineers returned to work and attempted to finish the bridge, but without success.

With construction still stymied at ten o'clock Woodbury led eighty volunteers from the 8th Connecticut Infantry under Captain Wolcott P. Marsh, Lieutenant Roger M. Ford, and Lieutenant Andrew M. Morgan to the unfinished bridge. One-half of the force was placed in a safe position on the shore as a protective force. The other half started marching to the bridge. Before the soldiers in the force could start across on the unfinished structure several of them were shot down by Confederate riflemen. The others ran for cover; they refused to move out on the bridge. Woodbury's heroic efforts came to naught.

By noon the fog cleared up. The artillerymen again opened fire on the Confederate position and were able to zero in on and silence their targets. The engineers returned to work led by Captain McDonald, but as soon as the work party reached the work site the enemy poured a heavy fire on them, wounding McDonald, a sergeant, and three privates. The firing range was so short and the fire so heavy it became impossible for the engineers to work. They again deserted the bridge for protective cover.

Because the 50th New York Volunteer Engineers could not muster a force to complete the bridge they were taken off the job.

Building Ponton Bridge West of Fredericksburg

Rossiter Johnson, *Campfire and Battleground*

Their failure marked one of the few times during the war that an engineer unit failed to do its assigned job. The failure, though, because they quit under fire, brought them the most disgrace. To finish the bridge the 15th New York Volunteer Engineers, led by Major John B. Magruder, were brought up from the bridge at the eastern end of the army's line. They arrived at three in the afternoon. Magruder divided Company E into crews to row four pontons. The crews then embarked twenty-five soldiers of the 89th New York Volunteer Infantry in each ponton and landed the infantrymen on the other side of the river under cover of well-directed rifle and artillery fire. After the one hundred 89th Regiment's infantrymen landed, the Confederate riflemen, who were able to stop the work of the engineers during the early part of the day, seeing resistance hopeless, surrendered to the infantrymen. The 15th New York Engineers then rapidly pushed completion of the 400-foot bridge by dusk.

The fifth and sixth bridges at the upper end, or western, of the army's line also were constructed under enemy harassment, and their delayed construction held up the crossing of Sumner's Right Grand Division. The two ponton bridges were started at three o'clock in the morning. They were almost finished, in three hours, when the Confederates, taking advantage of every possible means of concealment, commenced heavy fire of musketry upon the 50th New York Volunteers work party and the supporting infantry. Captain Wesley Brainerd and many engineer privates were wounded

Building Ponton Bridge at Fredericksburg

and disabled in the attempt. Twice during the day the engineers made attempts to finish the two bridges; each time the Confederates drove them back from the work site with considerable losses in killed and wounded.

In desperation a force of about 120 infantrymen from the 7th Michigan and 19th and 20th Massachusetts Infantry Regiments crossed over through the icy water in six pontons rowed by engineer soldiers. After the infantrymen landed they rushed to the buildings held by the enemy, and the enemy soldiers surrendered without offering resistance. The engineers finished the bridges without further opposition.[57]

The engineers' failure to complete the bridges across the Rappahannock by the scheduled time delayed Burnside's army's attack for twelve hours. The staff engineer officers and grand division commanders were critical of the regimental engineer officers and soldiers. General Woodbury reported he was greatly mortified to find in the morning that the engineers would not continue their work until "actually shot down." Some of the officers and men, he said, showed a willingness to work, but the majority seemed to think their task a helpless one. "Perhaps," he added, "I was unreasonable."

"It is generally considered a brave feat to cross a bridge of any length under fire," Woodbury concluded, "although the time of danger may not last more than a minute or two. How much more difficult to build a bridge exposed for hours to the murderous fire, the danger increasing as the bridge is extended. I found a loop-holed block house uninjured by our artillery directly opposite the upper bridges and only a few yards from their southern abutment. I also found in the neighborhood a rifle pit behind a stone wall some two-hundred feet long and cellars enclosed by heavy walls where the Confederates could load and fire in perfect safety. There were many other secure shelters."[58]

Captain Spaulding endured chagrin from the actions of the engineer soldiers under his command; especially in the regiment's four attempts to finish the center bridge.

"Some of the non-commissioned officers and privates showed the effects which are usually produced upon unarmed men placed for the first time under heavy fire and without means of repelling the attack. They were panic stricken and it was difficult to make them join in the repeated attempts to complete the bridge. They were worse than useless. The conduct and bearing of many of them," Spaulding concluded, "was deserving of special praise. Some of the privates deserve to occupy the places now held by unworthy men as non-commissioned officers and when I receive the official reports of commanders I shall be happy to bring the names of these men to General Woodbury's favorable attention."[59]

General Sumner who waited all day to cross his Right Grand Division over the river on the fifth and sixth bridges spoke harsh words about the engineer soldiers. "The engineers were annoyed during the day by fire of sharpshooters secreted in houses near landing of the bridges. The engineers failed to accomplish their assigned mission. Only under the care of the gallant men of the 7th Michigan, 89th New York, and 19th and 20th Massachusetts Regiments who crossed the river at two points in pontons and carried handsomely the houses and shelters occupied by the Confederates, did the engineers finally complete the bridges."[60]

By nightfall Union forces had crossed the Rappahannock River and taken up guardposts at the six bridge sites. All the next day soldiers of the Army of the Potomac marched over the bridges. Fog concealed their movements.

The river crossings were made without a mishap, except for an incident on the second bridge. For hours on that bridge a steady stream of soldiers and wagons had crossed. Then all of a sudden a spirited colonel who thought he could inspire his regiment more by martial music than by monotonous, dull tones of wagon wheels and soldiers' shoes on the bridge's roadway ordered his regimental band to strike up music to parade the regiment over the bridge. As the marching soldiers picked up the rhythm the second and third bridges began to sway to the cadence, and were about ready to topple over and spill the soldiers, animals, and wagons into the icy water. The engineer officer present, sensing the danger, jumped on his horse and started galloping against the traffic across the bridge, forcing some soldiers into the water as his horse cleared a path, shouting, "stop that music, stop that music." The music and swaying of the bridges stopped, which prevented a disaster.[61]

On December 13 a bright sun lighted up the Rappahannock valley. The Union flags fluttered in the breeze. The colorful scene of massed soldiers dispelled the dreary picture of the previous day. Below Fredericksburg, Franklin's Left Grand Division fought Jackson in a series of engagements. Franklin completely misunderstood Burnside's orders. Unable to fight his way to Fredericksburg against Jackson's forces, he had to fall back to his bridgehead on the Rappahannock.

The soldiers in Sumner's Right Grand Division met with a slaughter as they attacked Confederate soldiers stationed behind a stone wall on Marye's Heights in the rear of the town, deployed for a defensive battle. At the stone wall Sumner's soldiers made six charges against Lee's well-entrenched soldiers. Each time Lee's soldiers repulsed Sumner's soldiers.

For two days the Confederate soldiers repelled the Union soldiers. General Joseph Hooker's Center Grand Division had received orders to pounce upon the Confederates when Franklin's and Sumner's divisions routed them at Fredericksburg. General Hooker's soldiers crossed the river in desperation to take Marye's Heights. Lee's soldiers also cut down Hooker's soldiers. On the third day of the bloody battle which produced many casualties, a violent storm occurred at Fredericksburg. Employing the weather as a shield, the Army of the Potomac, under orders of General Burnside, withdrew over its ponton bridges to the north bank of the Rappahannock River. The Union artillery on Stafford heights protected Burnside's army from a Confederate pursuit, and enabled it to withdraw unmolested.

On February 15 the Engineer Battalion received orders to dismantle its bridge. At the north end of the bridge engineer soldiers met surviving infantrymen and artillerymen who were returning from battle. When it appeared as though all the soldiers had crossed, the engineers started taking apart the roadway. The anchors for the pontons were not raised; instead the engineers cut the hawsers. A ponton was kept in the water to ferry stragglers. Infantrymen and artillerymen provided protective fire at the bridge. The ponton wagons arrived at the riverbank, and the engineer soldiers loaded the pontons, chess, and balk onto them. With the departure of the ponton train the Rappahannock River closed the book on a gallant effort.

The Engineer Battalion returned to its camp at Aquia Creek Landing where its soldiers spent the ensuing time building a 600-foot shed, covered with pine boughs, for the animals. The battalion chronicler's last inscription for the Fredericksburg campaign reads: "Due 6 months pay."[62]

The 15th New York Volunteer Engineers received orders at midnight February 15 to take up its two bridges. Until the early hours of the morning Franklin's soldiers continued to recross to the safety of the north bank of the river. The engineer soldiers started to break up the first bridge at three o'clock the next morning; they completed the dismantling job in an hour. At daylight the second bridge was dismantled and the pontons hidden in the woods above the riverbank. The 50th New York Volunteer Engineers took up its three bridges on the western flank six hours later.

With its return over the Rappahannock River from the battle of Fredericksburg, the Army of the Potomac inscribed another disastrous defeat on its records. Its human cost added up to 12,653 casualties. The Engineer Brigade's casualties were: killed, eight engineer soldiers and one officer; wounded, forty-nine engineer soldiers and one officer; and missing, two engineer soldiers.

After the Fredericksburg fiasco attempts were made to place responsibility for its outcome. The Congressional Committee on the Conduct of the War held hearings from December 1862 to February 1863, and elicited testimony on Burnside's initial plan and his orders for the movement of the pontons. At the conclusion of the hearings the committee published the testimony and refrained from any criticism of the president or military officers. It left it to the readers of the report to decide for themselves who was responsible for the battlefield failure.

In the aftermath of the battle the usual relief of some officers from their commands occurred.

Burnside lost his command of the Army of the Potomac, but he was permitted to resume his position as a corps commander. He received harsh criticism, but he deserved respect for forthrightly assuming responsibility for his failures. He declared, "I am responsible." He could say nothing else. Few commanders were willing to speak out as frankly as Burnside.

Dismissal befell Woodbury as commander of the Engineer Brigade. The Chief of Engineers banished him to Fort Tortugas in the Florida Keys to tend to the fort's defenses. He contacted yellow fever within the following year and died.

The Western Theater
Missouri Engineer Regiment

Early in the new year General Halleck issued orders to John Pope to move his force down the Mississippi River, in conjunction with gunboats, and seize the town of New Madrid. He was then to capture the strong river fort at Island Number 10 that blocked the river to traffic. A successful operation meant restoring Union control of the Mississippi River.

Colonel Bissell's engineer regiment began its participation in the operation on March 4 with a three-and-a-half days' march in severe weather from Commerce to New Madrid. There it constructed siege works before the town. The Confederates withdrew from the town. Bissell's regiment then started constructing siege works to attack Island Number 10.

To find a means of opening river traffic, Colonel Bissell reconnoitered the area and determined that a road across the swamp was impracticable, but that a canal could be dug through the marshland for small steamers. It was not found practicable to make the canal deep enough for the gunboats within a reasonable time. Even so, the work was a prodigiously laborious job. The canal was twelve miles long, six miles of it through heavy timber. A passage fifty feet wide was made through the swamp by sawing off large trees four and a half feet under water. The construction work progressed for nineteen days, with untiring energy on the part of the engineer soldiers, and was completed on April 4. General Pope said in his report that Colonel Bissell was "full of resource, untiring, and determined. He labored night and day, and his engineer regiment completed work which will be a monument of enterprise and skill." Assistant Secretary of War Thomas A. Scott inspected the canal and reported to Secretary of War Stanton that it was a herculean job.[63]

Colonel Bissell's regiment looked upon their work achievement as "memorable work" that earned for the regiment status and an enviable reputation.[64]

An Adjectival Bridge

Captain William F. Patterson's Kentucky Company of Mechanics and Engineers received orders from General Thomas' headquarters at the end of March to report to General George W. Morgan's division at Cumberland Gap Ford. The division's mission was to prevent Confederate troops from marching through the gap from Virginia into Southeast Kentucky.

After its arrival at the division's camp, Patterson's company worked with a large detail from the infantry regiments to construct 40 miles of roads and bridges to aid in the planned Union flank movement upon Cumberland Gap through the Cumberland Mountains.

Patterson chronicled how on the march through the mountains he was called upon to solve a critical problem that brought a halt to the column.

He titled his report "Incidents," a story of how a bridge he designed and whose building he supervised restored the column's march. He believed it one of his major engineer feats, which explained his creating a record of it.

"Incidents" is included in this story of Civil War bridges for two reasons: (1) because of the unique, innovative qualities of his expedient; and (2) because his expedient exemplifies the creative skill of the Civil War engineers who stood in the face of situations similar to Patterson's, but after analysis and assessment of the situations requiring bridges they conceptualized in their minds bridge designs, and then set the engineer soldiers to work to build them.

The "Incidents" Patterson wrote about in the spring of 1862 follow:

Incidents

"Leaving the almost dry side of the North Fork of the Kentucky river we at once began the ascent of a steep hill and an old worn out road was our guide (if indeed the road had ever had been such an article of civilization).

* * * * *

"There was relief, beyond the trouble of making the road. The main part of our command on the ridge to our left was arriving. General George Morgan marched on to Hazlegreen and so far as our peace was concerned there was no one to molest or cause apprehension. The first day since we left the pass that party could march a foot without constant insults from Morgan's sharp shooters concealed here and there on our flanks. As we moved along in the road on and out of it, it was all the same, for the ground was dry and hard and level enough to go anywhere and we began to feel not unlike old times in the woods at home, when the roads were free, and to meet any one would be to have good refreshing chat about the latest news of the war.

* * * * *

"Following the trail we began to descend rapidly along the side of a ravine, a small stream apparently on our left. Soon the train was halted, word came along the line for Patterson to the front. I made my way with no little difficulty for there was no more space than was required for the trains so narrow was the way. I found our quartermaster, Major M. C. Garber, our brigade commander, Brigadier General Absalom Baird, and others at what seemed to be the end of our journey, at least with wagons.

"Major Garber said, 'we see no way for our train beyond this place. You see this precipice? No wagon can go over this place and unless you can devise some plan for a road all we can do is to burn our train and make our way as best we can. You know we must somehow join our command. The time is against us now. If anything can be done it must be done in a very short time.'

"General Baird turned to me and said, 'What do you think of it, Captain?' I said it is a bad place but we can cross it before night. 'Then call for what help you need.' All the troops save the teamsters came down and while some prepared a hasty meal by the clear water, other workers sat around. This was about noon.

"In times past a mill had been in use here, the mill and dam had washed out and against our shore leaving a precipice about thirty feet high, just the end of our road. This must be filled up or bridged over. Green brush was abundant which we crossed and recrossed interlacing with earth from the hill side above.

"In less than three hours the first wagon was crossed safely. Short lines were attached to the rear of the wagons to which men held on holding back, the earth was kept loose by constant packing. Very large quantities of loose earth was carried over with each wagon, shoveled onto brush, which was again covered with brush and then another wagon of dirt. Six or eight wagons thus passed over and made our road compact requiring no further attention than the corn of the season.

"This work was all complete in about three hours. When our train was again in steady motion ascending a steep hill on the opposite shore Major Garber came to me and said, 'You have done a good work and shall have your choice of all the horses in this army. Take your time, take any horse you fancy, no difference who may see and hold back.' I did accordingly but afterward thought that man did not lose a winner when I took his horse. I soon gave him away."[65]

* * * * *

In the sense of a definition of a bridge—a structure spanning a chasm, road, river and affording a passage—Patterson's expedient he described in his foregoing "Incidents" fits the definition.

Wire Rope Bridge

Mottelay and Copeland, *The Soldier in Our Civil War*

Patterson, as he progressed through the Civil War, continued to achieve self-satisfying and prideful engineering feats. In the Vicksburg campaign he became a *par excellence* engineer by his original bridge designs.

General Meigs' Wire-Rope Bridge

Throughout the war there were other without bounds examples emulating Captain Patterson's imaginative bridge building feat.

Quartermaster General Meigs, a Corps of Engineers officer, reported on his success to provide a bridge in a critical situation.

During the army's operations in the mountains of Virginia, he received a requisition for light and portable bridge equipage suitable to bridge mountain streams and chasms.

Meigs quickly took steps to initiate the fabrication of equipage to be used for the construction of a wire-rope suspension bridge. The equipage Meigs provided was suitable for bridging streams and chasms with steep and high banks on mountain roads in Virginia. The wire-rope suspension bridges were also constructed over the Shenandoah and Rappahannock Rivers during the year's campaigns.[66]

Colonel Innes: The Daily Business of War: Bridge Building

General Don Carlos Buell's Army of the Ohio occupied Nashville in February. The planned movements of his army south presaged a busy time for Colonel William P. Innes' Michigan engineer regiment on railroad construction.

General Halleck, who had been appointed commander of the army forces in the West, ordered Buell to march his army south in support of Grant's march against the Confederate army at Shiloh. On March 16 Buell's cavalry marched out to provide security to Innes' regiment at the bridge sites between Nashville and Columbia. The infantrymen began to march a day later. The Michigan engineers provided construction parties at stream and river crossings, guarded by the cavalry, to provide Buell's soldiers rapid crossings.

On arrival at Columbia, Innes confronted the burning bridge over the Duck River. It had been set afire by Rebel partisans or soldiers aware Buell's army was on the march and would need the bridge. The Duck River was also at flood stage. Innes started his engineer soldiers at work to build a timber trestle bridge, but the work proceeded slowly, and with difficulty, because of the flood stage of the river.

Buell, on his arrival at the bridgehead on March 30, observing the progress on the bridge construction and aware of his orders to be at Savannah on the Tennessee River within a week, ordered Innes to complete the bridge with pontons.

Under severe working conditions Innes' engineer soldiers completed the bridge for Buell's force to cross the Duck River and complete its 90-mile march to join Grant.[67]

As the spring and summer progressed, other bridge building tasks were assigned to Innes' regiment. In June eight companies of the regiment were busily at work rebuilding the Memphis-Charleston Railroad from Memphis to Stevenson, Alabama. At the same time two companies were assigned to work on the line from Huntsville east to Stevenson, building and rebuilding bridges.

Innes reported, "I had two companies at the same time engaged on what is called the heavy trestle near the tunnel (seven miles from Gallatin), rebuilding about 1,050 feet of it, about 64 feet high."

Another work detail constructed at Richland Creek #2 a bridge 300 feet long and 30 feet high.

The regiment then moved to Columbia with two companies and repaired the bridge across Duck River that had been washed away by high water. Buell had crossed his army over the earlier bridge on his march to Savannah.

Innes' engineer soldiers also rebuilt Crow Creek Bridge #3 and built a bridge at Cowan.

By August 28 work had been completed so that the railroad operated to Stevenson. The railroad was essential for support of Buell's army.

Innes wrote in the record, "More work done by his regiment's engineer soldiers in a short time than had been done by any other work crew."[68]

In September General Braxton Bragg conducted a daring march north into Kentucky (emulating Lee's march into Maryland). Buell ordered Innes to march his regiment to Kentucky. Bragg's march was another demonstration of the Confederates marching behind the line of communications of the Union army to the consternation of its generals. As a result of Bragg's invasion pressure was placed on Innes' engineers to keep the railroads supporting Buell in operational order. They were connected to the depots in Nashville, which had to support Buell's army as he engaged the front line of Bragg's army. As Bragg began to retreat from Kentucky he made every effort to destroy the bridges on the railroads and over the creeks and rivers. When Buell, marching against Bragg, arrived at Bowling Green, and on the bank of the Big Barren River, he found the bridge destroyed and the river flooding its banks. Innes' regiment was ordered to rebuild the bridge, and it did so in the same form built earlier in the year. Timber trestle bridges were built out from the banks, and joined in the middle by a ponton bridge.[69] Innes summed up his summer activities with the expression, "his war business was building bridges, and fighting the enemy an occasional exception."

War on the Railroad Tracks

After the capture of the railroad center at Corinth in May, Grant gave immediate attention to operating conditions of the railroads. They were vital to the logistical support in the conduct of battles. They delivered the necessities of battle—food, forage, equipment, supplies, and ammunition. The importance of the railroads was just as vital to the Confederates, but their importance was to tear up and destroy and immobilize the railroads in the Union's hands to deny its army its sustenance and ability to continue combat. Control of the iron rails became a war in itself; both combatants allocated much of their resources to achieve their purposes.

The exertion to rebuild and repair railroads consumed the labor and construction skill of the 1st Michigan Volunteer Engineer Regiment. In pursuit of the railroad mission Colonel Innes received orders to repair and open the Memphis-Charleston Railroad from

Corinth east to Decatur, Alabama, a stretch of approximately 75
miles, south of the Tennessee River. Innes' records chronicle the
following work to rebuild railroad bridges:

Five miles east of Corinth	One trestle
Knowles Mill	Two trestles
Bear Creek	Rebuilt Bridge 300' long
East Bear Creek	Built-repaired two bridges 150' long
Buzzard Roost	Rebuilt 70' span
Spring Creek-Tuscumbia	Rebuilt bridge 216'
Farm Creek	Rebuilt bridge 330'
Courtland	Two bridges, one 240' and another 70' long 2/3 rebuilt
Mall's Creek	Rebuilt bridge 100' long
Richmond Creek	Rebuilt one bridge 375' long and 28' high and another 300' long and 30' high.

Material for repair work, he reported, amounted to 23,000 board
feet of lumber. The necessary iron was salvaged from wrecked
bridges.

Innes wrote, in summary, the railroad work covered rebuilding 110 miles of destroyed track and bridges. "The regiment," he
boasted, "was figuratively in advance of all other troops so we had
to do picket duty as well as labor." Yet, a few weeks later, he wrote
to the army commander protesting the detail of his engineers to
picket duty to protect railroads. "It was," he declared, "an
infantryman's task."[70]

Rebuilding a Trestle Bridge

Mottelay and Copeland, *The Soldier in Our Civil War*

Chapter 3

1863
Innovative Bridges for the Armies' Victories

The Cruel Mud March

In the aftermath of the Fredericksburg blunder, Burnside chafed with a determination to defeat the Confederate soldiers dug in behind fortified earthworks atop the south bank of the Rappahannock. A victory would reverse the stigma of his defeat and elevate him to the stature of a bold, popular battlefield leader. Instead, he precipitated another failure and his relief from the army's command. He also subjected his soldiers and animals to a cruel foot march.

Burnside ordered his army on January 20 to march approximately 15 miles west of Fredericksburg along the northern bank of the Rappahannock to Banks' Ford and United States Ford. There they were to cross the fords on ponton bridges to be built by the engineer soldiers, and once across envelop the left flank of Lee's army.

At 10 a.m. the Engineer Battalion, with an infantry division as an escort, started marching astride the animal-drawn ponton train. The day turned out dark, dreary, and with a freezing temperature. Alternately rain and snow fell upon the soldiers, animals, ponton train, and terrain. A high wind swept continuously down the river valley. To ward off the cold wind, soldiers changed position one after another to lee of their comrades. If a soldier stumbled out of the ground path he was attempting to follow he lost his way. The frozen ground thawed from the grinding of the heavy traffic. The wagon wheels and animals' and soldiers' feet ground the thawed earth into mud, which led them to become mired in it. The engineer and infantry soldiers labored strenuously to lift the wagon wheels out of the mire and to give help to the animals to move the 30 pontons, the wagons with the balk and chess, and tools. The brawn of the horses and mules could barely budge their own bodies much less the train of wagons.

In the dark air the interval lengthened between the wagons of the ponton train. The severe weather and crumbled terrain thwarted the march. Fatigued teamsters and soldiers despaired of reaching the fords.

To the horror of the commanding officers, sabotage occurred. Linchpins on the wagon wheels were "treacherously pulled out," and ponton wagons dropped to the ground. At the additional catastrophe orders were immediately sent down from higher echelons to engineer officers to put guards on each wagon "to bayonet the first soldier found meddling with the wheels." Lieutenant Cross of the Engineer Battalion made his way forward of the ponton train to examine its condition. He found disruption of the movement of the train occurred along the line. Some teamsters, overwhelmed with helplessness, and considerate of their animals, unhitched them and rode them away.

Lieutenant Cross toiled to keep the teamsters on their wagons, but many fled. A wagon overturned in a stream. Soldiers held up the heads of the mules to prevent their drowning. Other soldiers waded into the stream, unloaded the balk and chess from the wagon, pulled out the wagon, reloaded it, and hitched the mules, and attempted to continue the march.

The ordeal for the engineer soldiers and the wagon animals lasted for 24 hours. They were able to move about a half mile in an hour of march. They had been without food and rest for the day. They endured severe hardships, and were in a state of bodily exhaustion.

Finally, those engineer soldiers able to reach United States Ford with some of the ponton wagons, unloaded pontons and dragged them over the poor muddy paths to the water's edge. They waded into the ford to float the pontons into position to form a bridge, but the fierce wind would not permit them to stand up to do the work, even when they anchored their weary limbs in mud to their knees.

The soldiers set about to build pine bough shelters and to collect kindling to start fires. A Regular Army battery nearby gave the engineer soldiers hardtack to eat. They welcomed the nourishment. They also attempted to dry themselves out and sleep through the rain.

While Burnside's soldiers and animals struggled against the weather and mud, with little headway, reports on the severe conditions impeding the march reached Burnside's headquarters. He quickly realized the futility of his battle plan and march orders. He called a halt to the march to outflank Lee's army.

On January 23 the engineer soldiers abandoned the ponton train and started to plod their way back to Falmouth. Along the far side of the riverbank enemy soldiers taunted them with banners they held up imprinted with the words "Burnside's Mud Scrape." The next day the engineer battalion's soldiers available for duty marched back to United States Ford to recover and return to Falmouth the abandoned animals and ponton train.[1]

A later report stated two engineer soldiers died from disease incurred on the "mud march."

One of the participants in the march wrote in his diary:

> Thousands of the boys in blue, after horses and mules could do no more in pulling the pontoon [sic] wagons that must be gotten through to the Rappahannock, to build the bridge on which the Army was to cross were put on the ropes to tug and pull, and pull and tug hour after hour and way into the night; but they were Virginia roads, and it was no use; so after days and days of mud and rain the campaign was abandoned, and worn and weary we marched back to our camps at Falmouth and beyond, and in passing saw the greetings of Johnnies over the river in Fredericksburg, on a banner bearing the cheerful legend, "Burnside stuck in the mud."[2]

President Lincoln decided on the need of a new commander for the Army of the Potomac. He replaced Burnside with Major General "Fighting Joe" Hooker, who had been a division commander in McClellan's campaign against Richmond. Hooker stated he was determined to abandon the military doctrine of attacking an enemy posted behind a fortified position. His tactics would be to maneuver around Lee's flanks to force him into an open battlefield.

Hooker selected his senior staff officers and commenced the preparation of his plans for the spring campaign.

He assigned Brigadier General Gouverneur K. Warren as chief engineer officer of the army. Warren had earned an outstanding reputation in the prewar corps of topographical engineers. His cohorts said his "intellect fitted for high command; a courage that knew no fear."[3] Brigadier General Henry W. Benham replaced General Woodbury as commander of the army's engineer brigade.

Hooker also discussed with General Haupt the rebuilding of the railroad bridge over the Rappahannock River. The two generals were in complete accord on the plans to employ the railroad to haul supplies as the army marched toward Richmond.

In Hooker's spring campaign Haupt's task would be to rebuild the 400-foot railroad bridge the Confederates had destroyed on the Rappahannock River. His work waited upon General Sedgwick's crossing the river and attacking and capturing Marye's Heights. (Sedgwick's attack succeeded, but in the sequence of Hooker's battle other corps failed in their attacks. General Ingalls then advised General Haupt to cancel the rebuilding of the Rappahannock River bridge.)[4]

Chancellorsville

To carry out his battle plans, Hooker ordered a maneuver around Lee's left flank. The battle was to start with the cavalry, Stoneman's Sabers crossing the Rappahannock at Kelly's Ford, 22 miles above Fredericksburg, and, after maneuvering around Lee's left flank, destroying the Fredericksburg and Richmond Railway and the Virginia Central Railroad, which provided Lee's route of railroad communication with Richmond. Stoneman was then to roam behind Lee's battle lines, destroying supply depots. General Sedgwick, leading the I and VI Corps, was to cross the Rappahannock east of Fredericksburg to make a diversionary movement.

Hooker was to lead the V, XI, and XII Corps and to march to United States Ford west of Fredericksburg, cross the river, and march to Chancellorsville. The III Corps was to remain at Stafford Heights to reinforce, if necessary, the forces under the leadership of Hooker or Sedgwick; the II Corps was to remain in reserve at Banks' Ford.

The engineer soldiers received orders to march ahead on April 27 to construct the necessary ponton bridges across the river. General Henry W. Benham's plan called for the construction of the ponton bridges to be completed by 3:30 a.m. on April 27.

The infantry soldiers looked upon the engineers as a source of information on battle events. Whenever they met the engineers passing by with the ponton trains they speculated on their engagement in a battle. Their question to the engineers expressed their anxiety, "Is the news good or bad?"

East of Fredericksburg. The battle plan called for five bridges across the Rappahannock east of Fredericksburg:

At Franklin's Crossing during the night of April 28 the engineer soldiers of the Engineer Battalion and the 15th New York Volunteer Engineers lay still and quiet along the road; the fog concealed them. On the scheduled time the infantrymen arrived at the riverbank. Quietly the engineers and infantrymen dragged and carried on poles 100 pontons down the riverbank. They were quiet enough at the river so that the Confederate pickets were unaware of their presence. The engineers placed the pontons in the water, and after boarding 60 infantrymen in each one, ferried them to the far shore. When the pontons grounded on the shore the infantrymen disembarked and deployed on the riverbank to be a protective force for the engineers engaged in building the three bridges.

The engineer soldiers completed the first ponton bridge at Franklin's Crossing at 7 a.m., the second at 7:15 a.m., and the third one at 10 a.m. Upon completion of the three bridges the engineer soldiers who were tired, hungry, and wet set up a camp at the bridge sites.

At Pollock's Mill tactical events unfolded in a different course. To insure silence when moving the pontons to the bridge site, infantrymen were assigned to carry the pontons, for the other two bridges, the last mile to the river's edge. A carrying party of 72 soldiers was assigned to carry each one of the 1,600-pound pontons. Infantrymen objected to such manual-labor tasks. They joined the army to fight the Rebels. A lieutenant reported his soldiers took such work in the "familiar way, with internecine conflict." The infantrymen hauled the pontons out of the 50th New York Volunteer Engineers' camp at 11:30 p.m. Hand carrying the pontons turned out to be too heavy a task for them. They collapsed with exhaustion from the weight of the pontons, and, at the same time, could not remain quiet on a dark, unknown path. To complete the movement of the pontons, the engineers had to send for the ponton wagons, reload the pontons onto the wagons, and then, accompanied by the noises of the wagons, clattering of timber, shrieking mules, and swearing teamsters, move the pontons in a laborious task to the river's edge.

A further delay occurred when an argument broke out between Benham and the commander of the infantrymen assigned to carry the pontons to the river, and who were then to cross over in them to form a protecting force for the engineers while they built the bridge. When daylight broke engineers were ready with the pontons, but the infantrymen were not ready or were unwilling to be rowed across the river. Benham pleaded with the soldiers to rally around the engineer soldiers, board the pontons, and cross to the far shore. While sitting on his horse haranguing the soldiers, Benham attracted the attention of the Confederate soldiers on the far side of the river. They began to fire at him. Their rifle fire hit Benham's horse. Benham moved to the water's edge, and as he leaned over to talk to an officer, his horse fell to the ground. Benham slid off the dead horse. Eventually the infantrymen were persuaded to be ferried over the river. The engineers then started construction of the two bridges.

While working on the bridges the engineers were under cannon fire. One shell bored through the strake of a ponton. The engineers also worked in a fog, and as they worked, the Confederate soldiers who could hear them, but not see them, taunted them with words, saying how they would fill them full of lead as soon as they could see them. Three Union soldiers were wounded. One engineer soldier who participated in the battle wrote years later in his reminiscences that "the engineers were never the same after it."[5] Finally, at 11 a.m., eight hours late, the 50th New York Volunteer Engineers completed the two bridges. On the five ponton bridges built across the Rappahannock at Franklin's Crossing and Pollock's Mill Creek, 25,000 soldiers and their supporting guns and supplies, under command of General Sedgwick, crossed the river.

West of Fredericksburg. In a struggling march with the elements on the night of April 28 the engineer soldiers of the 15th and 50th New York Volunteer Engineers headed west of Fredericksburg through the wilderness to build the four bridges across the Rappahannock. Rain fell upon the soldiers and animals. A thick fog settled into the river valley. The terrain lacked roads or paths. The engineers corduroyed with logs the muddy paths made by the ponton wagons, animals, and soldiers to be able to bring the pontons up to the bridge sites.

The 15th New York engineers hauled a bridge train to Banks' Ford where the II Corps was camped as the reserve force. Because the corps would cross the river on the demands of the battle, the ponton train was parked amidst the trees.

The two most difficult bridges to build were the two at United States Ford, 13 miles above Fredericksburg, under the supervision of Major Ira Spaulding of the 50th New York engineers. It rained all during the preceding night while the engineers were hauling the pontons the 13 miles to the bridge sites. The engineers had to lead the ponton train through a crooked, muddy trail in the dark forest. They did not reach their destination until 8 a.m., five hours after the designated time. Extra horses were needed to pull the ponton train through the mud and forest. The engineers had to build a primitive road to the river. By three o'clock in the afternoon they finished construction of the two bridges. On the Confederate side of the river the engineers had to build a road up the riverbank for the use of the supply wagons. Hooker, with the V, XI, and XII Corps, crossed the Rappahannock the next morning.

At Kelly's Ford, 22 miles above Fredericksburg, under the supervision of Lieutenant Comstock, Captain Timothy Lubey with a company from the 15th New York Volunteer Engineers built a canvas ponton bridge. Stoneman's 9,000 cavalrymen crossed the river on Lubey's bridge, and then forded the Rapidan River.

General Lee assessed quickly Hooker's attempt to turn his left flank. His intelligence officers also informed him that Hooker had divided his army into two forces, with a force above and below Fredericksburg. Lee decided to make separate attacks on the flanks of his enemy. The first would be against Hooker's corps at Chancellorsville.

Lee sent a portion of his cavalry force against Stoneman's Union cavalry, and kept the balance of the force stationed at Chancellorsville to watch Hooker. He also assaulted the Union right flank in the wilderness. A small force remained on the Union left flank to hold Sedgwick east of Fredericksburg.

Hooker established a defensive position on May 1 at Chancellorsville, and only sporadic fighting occurred during the day.

Hooker's right flank interfaced with a defenseless position where it joined the open country. Lee decided to outflank Hooker's unprotected flank by sending Jackson's Confederate cavalry there on May 2. As evening approached, Jackson maneuvered his troopers around Hooker's right flank. The attack brought tragedy to Lee's army; one of Jackson's troopers mistakenly shot him.

At daybreak the next day Major General J.E.B. Stuart, who replaced Jackson, renewed the attack. The Confederates forced the Union soldiers to give up ground; by ten o'clock in the morning Lee's soldiers had retaken Chancellorsville. On the Union's left flank, Lee's soldiers surrounded Sedgwick's I and VI Corps but Sedgwick held the road to Banks' Ford. He fought off Lee's soldiers and retreated to the safety of the river.

Alert to the perilous Union tactical situation, the engineer soldiers accomplished one of their most successful bridge building projects. Lieutenant Colonel W. H. Pettes of the 50th New York Engineers and Company H rushed a ponton train from the ponton bridge he had dismantled at Pollock's Mill Creek at midnight on April 30 the sixteen-mile distance to Banks' Ford, where on May 3 between three and four o'clock in the afternoon he rebuilt a mixed bridge of pontons and trestle over the river under heavy fire of shot and shells from an enemy battery. "To the firm resolution with which this company proceeded with the work," Colonel Pettes reported, "may be attributed the safety of General Sedgwick's corps when it was so disastrously repulsed and surrounded by the enemy. The company lost a sergeant killed by a shell. The bridge was also dismantled under heavy fire of artillery from the enemy's earthworks and finally brought off in safety."[6]

The following afternoon Lieutenant Colonel John B. Magruder of the 15th New York Engineers used the ponton bridge train brought to Banks' Ford on the day the campaign started for the II

Corps reserve force to construct another bridge at the same site. Sedgwick's soldiers who reached Banks' Ford retreated on the two rapidly constructed bridges to the safety of the north bank of the Rappahannock.

Also on the afternoon of May 4 the three ponton bridges built at Franklin's Crossing at the start of the campaign were dismantled by the engineers and brought in rafts, with enemy soldiers following them along the riverbank and firing at them, to the town of Fredericksburg where they were used to rebuild a bridge across the river. That night the engineer soldiers camped at the bridge. Between 2 and 3 a.m. on the morning of May 5 a force of 17,000 soldiers from Sedgwick's II Corps marched over the bridge in 45 minutes to the north bank of the Rappahannock. The bridge was then quickly dismantled.

As Sedgwick's soldiers safely retreated over the Rappahannock, Lee withdrew his attacking forces and decided to make a final attack to destroy Hooker's force. He found to his surprise that the Army of the Potomac had deserted the battlefield and recrossed the Rappahannock to safety.

To help Hooker escape, the engineers kept open the two ponton bridges at United States Ford which they had constructed on April 30. Lieutenant Colonel Clinton B. Colgate of the 15th New York Engineers moved a ponton bridge train on May 4 from Franklin's Crossing to United States Ford and built another bridge across the river. At intervals, wagons with a ponton had to be taken down the bank separately, held by a cable. The bridge was started at 12:26 p.m. and finished by 2:30 p.m. The major part of Hooker's army crossed back over the river on the three bridges.

After Hooker's retreat had started, a violent storm broke out; the river rose nine feet. The ponton bridges started swaying. Twice pontons broke loose from one of the bridges, but the engineers immediately reported to work by wading into the river to do arduous repair work. The bridges were taken up at sunset on May 5 and moved a safe distance from the riverbank.[7]

Later that night the weary engineer soldiers with only muddy ground to sleep on collected piles of brush to use as mattresses. The next day they were on the march again headed for Falmouth. They plodded through mud for ten hours without a minute's rest. Five of their ponton wagons were abandoned because they became mired beyond retrieval.

The return to Falmouth brought to an end another unsuccessful attempt of the Army of the Potomac to defeat the Confederates in battle. An Engineer Battalion soldier inscribed with frankness in the records, "Union Army again beat."[8]

Gettysburg

After Chancellorsville, the defensive positions the contending antagonists withdrew to, on opposite banks of the Rappahannock River, fenced them into limited terrain to maneuver to attack in force. Lee sought a maneuver to force his enemy to a battle on open ground. To accomplish his objective, he deployed his army away from its defensive position. He expected his tactics to open up an opportunity, if the enemy marched after him, to select the terrain where it would be beneficial to attack the enemy head on.

Lee on June 3 marched his army away from its encampment on the Rappahannock River. His long line of soldiers headed westward searching for fighting ground. The 76,000 soldiers of the Army of Northern Virginia deployed over the Blue Ridge Mountains and down into the Shenandoah Valley. The army was divided into three corps under Generals James Longstreet, Ambrose P. Hill, and Richard S. Ewell. There was also a cavalry division under General J.E.B. Stuart. The army's soldiers were concealed by the Blue Ridge Mountains as they marched down the Shenandoah and Cumberland Valleys.

On the march, Stuart's cavalry, Lee's eyes and ears, received orders from Lee to march on the army's right flank, but he was not to march to the right flank of the Union army, unless he could return quickly to join Lee. The Union army, though, marched faster than Stuart had expected. His cavalrymen were forced to an isolated position on the Union flank, which prevented them from cutting through the Union column to return to Lee to report intelligence. They had to march north beyond the enemy, and then circle west.

The engineer soldiers performed their tasks to insure the army's mobility. Their main tasks were to build the fords and bridges on the Potomac River for the armies to cross, the major obstacle on their march routes.[9]

Lee Crosses the Potomac. At the Potomac River from June 15 to June 25 Lee's soldiers, with the water level at a seasonal low, forded the Potomac at Williamsport, southeast of Hagerstown, and at Falling Waters, six miles south of Williamsport. The record notes there was a ponton bridge for the wagon trains and artillery at Falling Waters, probably built by pioneer companies from the infantry divisions. The absence of engineer officer reports in the records prevents searching further details on Lee's army's river crossing.

Lee's larger plan seemingly did not include any specific Northern location, but rather a march on open terrain in the North until somewhere, according to his expectations, he would make contact with and defeat the Union army. In anticipation of a victory he also hoped to pillage needed supplies from the area, either factories, warehouses, or farms. He expected another bonus. The presence of his army in Maryland and Pennsylvania might bring about a willingness of the Federal government to negotiate an end to the rebellion. Reading Northern newspapers, Lee, and perhaps his Confederate soldiers, detected what they assessed to be low Yankee morale and a distaste for the continuance of the bloodshed. The Confederate soldiers never doubted they would continue to whip the Yankee soldiers just as they had done at Bull Run, the environs of Richmond, Fredericksburg, Antietam, and Chancellorsville. They believed they would achieve victory until the Yankees decided they had enough and quit the battlefield. Victory in Pennsylvania would be a big lift too for the morale of the people in the South.

Hooker's Response. Lee's departure from the Rappahannock, and his march west over the mountains and into the valley, alerted Hooker to a new tactical situation. The Army of the Potomac, an estimated 115,000 soldiers strong, hastily packed its equipment, guns, and supplies, and started marching after Lee, who had a two-day head start. Hooker's army marched on the east side of the mountains.

To bolster his army to meet Lee's challenge, on June 27 at Frederick, Maryland, Hooker asked General Halleck for the soldiers stationed at Harpers Ferry to be placed under his command. His request precipitated an argument with Halleck and President Lincoln; President Lincoln said "no." Disgruntled, Hooker asked to be relieved of command of the Army of the Potomac. Lincoln assented to the request and appointed Major General George Gordon Meade to command the Army of the Potomac. Meade had served successively as a division commander in McClellan's ill-fated campaign, and as V Corps commander at Chancellorsville under Hooker.[10]

Union Engineers Bridge the Potomac. On June 4 at 3:30 a.m. the Engineer Brigade was awakened at its camp at Falmouth and given its marching orders. General Warren, Hooker's chief engineer officer, issued instructions to General Benham to remove the ponton bridges from the Rappahannock River, assemble the bridge trains, and transport them to Alexandria.

The brigade's bridge trains arrived at Alexandria on June 16. There Benham received further orders to place a ponton bridge train in the Chesapeake and Ohio Canal at Georgetown by daylight the next day. Benham set to work the engineer battalion and a detail of 250 engineer soldiers from the 50th New York Volunteer Engineers rearranging the pontons and balk and chess, and animal teams, to be transported to the canal. At 2 a.m. further orders arrived for the

ponton train to proceed up the canal to the area of Edwards Ferry—
Noland's Ford—Hauling Ferry (north of Barnesville where the
Monocacy River joined the Potomac). Captain Charles N. Turnbull,
whom Benham placed in charge of the movement up the canal,
reported the pontons were in the canal and under way by 6 a.m.
On June 20 Captain Turnbull completed the movement of the
ponton train to Edwards Ferry.

At 8:30 p.m. that night Captain Turnbull received orders
from army staff officers to construct a ponton bridge over nearby
Goose Creek, south of Leesburg, which flowed into the Potomac
on the Virginia side. Soldiers had to cross the creek to approach
Edwards Ferry.

Turnbull also received orders to bridge the Potomac River. At
the Potomac bridge site construction parties worked from each
shore, Virginia-Maryland, and according to the Engineer Battalion's
report, a fire was built on the Virginia shore to aid the engineer
soldiers on the Maryland shore to align the bridge pontons with
the pontons being placed in the water on the Virginia shore. By
daylight on the twenty-first the engineers completed the bridge, a
1,340-foot ponton bridge of 64 boats, and 3 crib trestles. Later in
the day Turnbull received orders to build a second ponton bridge
nearby at Edwards Ferry.[11]

The Army of the Potomac's officers and soldiers, plus 2,000
mules, 31,000 horses, and 4,500 artillery-caissons, and wagons
and ambulances, had been massing in northern Virginia in the
area of the bridges for a number of days, waiting either to ford the
river or to cross over the bridges.

On June 24 the XI Corps crossed over the Potomac on the
Edwards Ferry bridges.

On June 25 the I and III Corps crossed over the Potomac on
the Edwards Ferry bridges. Major General Julius Stahel's cavalry
division crossed over the Potomac at Young's Island Ford.

On June 26 Headquarters, Army of the Potomac, the II Corps,
V Corps, VI Corps, and XII Corps crossed over the Potomac on the
Edwards Ferry bridges.

On June 27 Brigadier General John Buford's cavalry division
and Brigadier General David McM. Gregg's cavalry division crossed
over the Potomac on the Edwards Ferry bridges.[12]

"Soldiers continuously crossed," reports stated, "and the engineers constantly worked to keep the fords and bridges in shape."[13]

After completing its crossing of the Potomac, the Army of the
Potomac marched north parallel to and east of Lee's army. Meade's
intelligence sources kept him informed of the progress of Lee's soldiers' march north. Meade's soldiers too were on a parallel march,

seeking out the enemy, ready to do battle, and tactically deployed between Lee's army and the city of Washington.

On June 27–28 the Engineer Battalion, and the detail of the 50th New York Engineers, dismantled the three ponton bridges. To prevent the pontons' falling into the enemy's hands, or being vandalized, or torched, the Engineer Battalion's pontons were formed into a bridge train on wagons to accompany the battalion on its march north with the army, and the pontons of the 50th New York Engineers were rafted and placed in the Chesapeake and Ohio canal to be returned to the engineer depot in Washington.

At the completion of its work to form up the bridge train, the Engineer Battalion received orders to march north approximately 12 miles to Buckeystown, where it arrived at midnight. A remark in the records described the march "a hard one after a hard day's work."[14]

The next day the battalion was ordered to march six miles to Frederick. On arrival there, Company B was assigned the duty to patrol and keep order in the town. At 1 a.m. on the thirtieth the battalion was awakened and turned out, and at 2 a.m. started on a "hard forced march of approximately six miles to Liberty. On arrival four engineer soldiers fainted at the muster formation."[15]

On July 1 the Engineer Battalion marched 12 miles to Taneytown with infantrymen of the army.

At 2 a.m. the next morning, Captain George H. Mendell, commanding officer of the battalion, received orders from General Meade to march the battalion to the vicinity of the railheads at Westminster and Union Bridge. Their assignment was to guard against any enemy cavalry raids on the railroad trains that arrived with supplies from Baltimore, and the wagon trains which transported the supplies to the battlefield. "You may find some infantry there from other corps," Meade's orders stated. "If in your judgment they are an insufficient force to guard the large number of wagons assembled there, you will report the fact, and hold your command in readiness to move elsewhere. If you find the force small and insufficient, the major general commanding desires that you take charge of the whole and dispose and instruct the troops on duty in such a manner that they will be able to make a vigorous and determined resistance against any raid."[16] The battalion's engineer soldiers performed the duty assigned to them by General Meade, with the additional duty to guard the prisoners of war marched there to the collection point, during the ensuing battle at Gettysburg. All they knew of the battle was the gunfire they heard in the distance.

General Haupt's Attention to the Railroad

On the withdrawal of the Army of the Potomac from Falmouth on June 13 to march after Lee's army, Haupt abandoned the Aquia Creek Railroad, depot, and wharf facilities. After Haupt's action, it would only be a matter of time before the Confederates would move into Aquia Creek either to put the Union's abandoned facilities to their use, or to vandalize and burn them.

Haupt had planned when Meade assumed command of the army to discuss with him the feasibility of operations of the railroads to supply his army, but he had to forego his intentions inasmuch as communications by rail and telegraph had been cut by the enemy in Maryland and Pennsylvania. Haupt had anticipated Meade's army would operate in that area.

Thus Haupt concluded his first task called for him to conduct a reconnaissance to Harrisburg to determine the effects on the railroads of Lee's soldiers marching about in southeast Pennsylvania. He had gathered information the Baltimore & Ohio line to Frederick had been cut by the Confederates, and the North Central Railroad, an important connection with the North on its route from Baltimore, through Hanover Junction, into Harrisburg, had also been torn up by Stuart's cavalry.[17]

Faced with many decisions in the immediacy of taking over command, Meade made the decision to use the Western Maryland Railroad from Baltimore to Westminster as his main supply line for his army. The railroad lacked some equipment, track, and cars, but with the Baltimore & Ohio and North Central closed, it was the only available railroad for his army's needs, and he would have to do his best with it. The town and the railroad would provide a safe and direct supply line. The line would have wagon-train roads fanning out to the main points of the Union's troop locations at Taneytown, Uniontown, Union Mills, Littlestown, and Manchester.[18]

On June 28 Haupt decided it was imperative for him to journey to Harrisburg to survey the railroad situation firsthand. He arrived there by the roundabout trip to Philadelphia. At the city, after surveying the situation and piecing together information, Haupt concluded he could not replace the Columbia-Wrightsville railroad bridge over the Susquehanna River, which had been destroyed by the Confederate cavalry, in time to be of use in the current campaign. He also sent a message to General Halleck to forward to General Meade, that General Lee was withdrawing his forces from the line of Carlisle-York, with the apparent intention of not attacking but of falling back and concentrating his army near Chambersburg or Gettysburg to crush in detail the Army of the Potomac before it could fully concentrate or its new commander take full charge.[19]

On July 2 Haupt journeyed to Hanover, east of Gettysburg, transferred to the Gettysburg branch and proceeded to Oxford where a large bridge across the Conewago Creek had been burned. He decided on the mode of repairs for it, and set crews to work to do the repairs. On the next day, the third, after finishing the bridge repairs, he issued instructions to the foremen to proceed on the line to make repairs as necessary, and work on to Gettysburg. Haupt then took a carriage to Gettysburg where he met for three hours with General Meade. He then returned to Oxford to complete the railroad to Gettysburg.[20]

Haupt reported his assistant, Adna Anderson, rebuilt with two divisions of his work force 19 bridges on the North Central Railroad. Many contrabands, skilled in the use of an axe, were employed on the jobs. The rebuilding work was speeded up by the use of expedients bypassing an attempt for a permanent structure, and all 19 were returned to traffic within a few days. The branch lines Littlestown and Gettysburg, destroyed by Stuart's cavalry, were also returned to operations.[21]

On July 4 Haupt reported the rebuilding of the 120-foot railroad bridge at Hanover, east of Gettysburg, enabling trains to move closer to the army.[22]

Later reports of the Army of the Potomac's surgeon general stated that 3,500 wounded were evacuated by train from Gettysburg, and 4,000 who had been brought to Littlestown and Westminster were evacuated by train to Baltimore and Washington.[23]

At Gettysburg's Battlefield

Lee's and Meade's armies fought a gruesome battle for three days.

Casualties for the Army of Northern Virginia reached 3,903 killed; 18,735 wounded; and 5,425 prisoners of war or missing.

Casualties for the Army of the Potomac reached 3,155 killed; 14,529 wounded; and 5,365 prisoners of war or missing.

Lee's long-harbored goal had been to bring to battle the Union army on an open battlefield with the expectation his generalship would destroy his foe. Gettysburg presented that opportunity to Lee, but denied him the achievement of his goal.

When Meade assumed command of the Army of the Potomac his immediate objective was to engage Lee in a defensive battle. His generalship on the battlefield achieved a credible outcome of his objective.

In the focus of Confederate and Union strategy, both generals failed to achieve their government's stated strategic goal.

Lee failed to defeat the Union soldiers on the battlefield and force their surrender. Also, the strategy to march into Maryland to cause a popular uprising of the citizens against the war, and to raid for food, forage, clothing, animals, and materiel of war for the army, fell short of accomplishment.

General Meade for his part demonstrated a complete lack of familiarity with the strategy conceptualized early in the war, which was to engage the rebellious force in combat and destroy it. President Lincoln found it necessary to castigate Meade for his perception of his achievement in the battle of Gettysburg, which failed to be an achievement in accord with the national strategy.[24]

Post-Battle Deployments

Anticipating Lee's retreat to the Potomac River after the cessation of hostilities on July 3, Meade ordered General William H. French's III Corps to garrison Maryland Heights from the Monocacy River to Williamsport, where reoccupation was completed by July 7.

General French sent a cavalry detachment to Williamsport to reconnoiter for the presence of a ponton bridge, and to destroy it. Major Shadrack Foley, 14th Pennsylvania Cavalry, reported on July 4 his detachment destroyed a ponton bridge at Williamsport with axes, but because the pontons were waterlogged he could not burn them. He reported the depth of the water at the Potomac River at ten feet. Also, he captured a detachment of the 12th Virginia Cavalry, consisting of 1 officer and 16 enlisted men, guarding the bridge. The Confederate prisoners reported the pontons were those captured in General McClellan's peninsular campaign. French's cavalry also skirmished with the enemy at Williamsport on July 8.

On July 5 General French sent another cavalry detachment to Harpers Ferry where Confederate soldiers were in the process of placing floorboards on the railroad bridge. The detachment captured the Confederate soldiers and ripped up the floorboards.[25]

General Lee reported his wagon trains, guarded by Stuart's cavalry, started out for Williamsport on July 7 in the rain, and only stragglers were captured on the march. On the subject of the rain, Lee wrote, "It was one of the most inclement nights I have ever known at this season of the year. It rained without cessation, rendering the roads by which we marched to the river very difficult to pass and causing much delay."[26]

General Lee also wrote in the record on his June crossing of the Potomac at the start of the campaign, "I had calculated upon the river remaining fordable during the summer so as to enable me to recross at my pleasure, but a series of storms commencing the day after our entrance into Maryland has placed the river beyond fording, and the present storm will keep it so for at least a week. I will have to accept battle if the enemy offers it. It is all in the hands of the Sovereign Ruler of the Universe."[27]

General Meade, prompted by a message from President Lincoln to pursue the Confederates, issued orders to his army on July 6 to march and follow Lee's army back to Virginia.

The Engineer Battalion reported it accompanied the army "on a hard march." A remark in the battalion's records states while on the march, "We passed the 7th New York Infantry 'which looked trim and clean' in comparison to 'rough and covered' battalion." After a 22-mile march to Frederick in the rain and through mud the "cross and tired officers and men camped."[28]

At 6 a.m. the next morning [seventh] the Engineer Battalion resumed the march with Meade's headquarters' reserve train. The army's trains crowded the roads. After four days' marching, the battalion's soldiers reached Antietam Creek on July 11, and camped for three days.

On July 10 General Lee wrote in a message to President Davis, "The Potomac continues to be past fording owing to the rapidity of the stream and limited facilities we have for crossing. There is no intelligence on the movement of the enemy."[29]

On July 12 General Lee reported to President Davis, "All goes well. The army occupies a strong position covering the Potomac from Williamsport to Falling Waters. Subsistence supplies though are precarious. The river has now fallen to four feet, and Major J. A. Harman is building a bridge with crude boats put together from the wood taken from barns. The river will be passable tomorrow [thirteenth]. Should the rain continue to subside our communications with the south bank will be open by tomorrow. Had the late unexpected rise not occurred there would have been no cause for anxiety as it would have been in my power to cross the Potomac on my first reaching it without molestation."[30]

General Lee reported on the night of July 13, the Potomac River being in a fordable condition, his army started crossing over the river. The soldiers were able to ford the river, but the wagon trains, ambulances, and artillery crossed on the bridge. Because of the condition of the road leading to the river, the long, strung-out line of wagon trains, with their escorts, did not complete the march to the bridge until July 14 at daylight. The crossing of the rear guard completed its crossing at 1 p.m.[31]

Generals Buford and Hugh J. Kilpatrick were to make a cavalry attack against Lee at the Williamsport bridge on the day Lee completed his crossing, but they arrived too late to engage Lee's soldiers.[32]

While camped at Antietam Creek for three days the Engineer Battalion's engineer soldiers built a four-crib trestle bridge across the creek. They tore down a nearby barn and used its timber for the bridge's construction.

Early on the morning of July 15 a message arrived at the Engineer Battalion's headquarters reporting the enemy had crossed over the Potomac River. A late afternoon order by General Warren sent the battalion on a forced march to Harpers Ferry. On arrival at the town's bridge the engineer soldiers were immediately given work assignments. One work party spent a day replacing one of the bridge's suspension wires. Another party replaced the flooring that had been taken up to deny the enemy the use of the bridge. Another party raised the pontons that had been sunk in the canal. The sick and wounded in the town were then placed in the pontons and transported to the east to Berlin.

On July 16 General Lee reported to President Davis his army was encamped at Bunker Hill, Virginia, and would rest a day. He also reported he learned the enemy crossed at Harpers Ferry, and "if he follows us I will lead him up the Valley." Lee's demonstration of skillful and inspiring leadership of his soldiers brought to an end the chronicle of the battle of Gettysburg.[33]

The Engineer Battalion marched from Harpers Ferry east to Berlin on July 17 where the engineer soldiers received a new issue of clothing. At two o'clock the next morning they were roused and set to work building a 60-ponton bridge over the Potomac River. They completed the bridge by 10 a.m., at which time the Army of the Potomac started the crossing over of its soldiers, animals, wagons, ambulances, and artillery. Units of the army also crossed the Potomac at Harpers Ferry, and some crossed over the Shenandoah River. The army spent two days crossing the river, and began a march to Lovettsville.

With traffic on the bridge ending after two days, the engineer soldiers dismantled the bridge at Berlin and collected the pontons and equipage and regrouped. After a two-day march the Engineer Battalion arrived at Goose Creek where they built a five-crib 75-foot trestle bridge from boards taken from nearby barns. Upon a report the enemy was in the area the engineer soldiers were placed on guard duty on the army's wagon trains.

The battalion then set out on a march to Warrenton, where it arrived on the twenty-fourth at one o'clock in the morning. For the Engineer Battalion its arrival marked the close of the Gettysburg campaign. The battalion's chronicler wrote for the record, after all their marching on their feet, performing strenuous manual work on arrival at rivers and battle sites, "Sunday church bells were ringing and everything seemed home like."[34]

Bridge-Building Feats in the West
Vicksburg

Grant's generalship, determination, and ingenuity achieved a superb battlefield victory on July 4 at Vicksburg.

Earlier attempts in the closing days of 1862 and opening days of 1863 to march against Vicksburg to achieve the Union's strategy to possess and control the Mississippi River met with failure.

Grant, chagrined with the destructive attack of the Confederates against his depot at Holly Springs, the defeat of Sherman's and Flag Officer David D. Porter's joint expedition on the Yazoo, and the receipt of news Major General John A. McClernand was organizing a river expedition against Vicksburg, decided to transfer all of his forces to Milliken's Bend, Louisiana, and to take personal command of the expedition against Vicksburg.[35]

Brigadier General John B. Sanborn wrote at the time Grant moved down river it was not the best of time. A low morale pervaded the Union armies. They had failed to advance in the East. There had been some victories in the West, but the failure of Grant's overland march to Vicksburg, in the fall of 1862, especially the destruction of the depot at Holly Springs, and General William T. Sherman's defeat at Chickasaw Bayou struck a blow to the Union's morale. A cold, stormy winter, with snow in Memphis, added to the soldiers' woes.

There were doubts, he added, about the plan Grant had adopted to move his army to Milliken's Bend to attack Vicksburg, and a fear he would not remain throughout the campaign. "Sadness, gloom, determination and vigor seemed to be strangely mingled."[36]

Operations on the West Side of the Mississippi

General Grant arrived January 29 at Milliken's Bend to take personal command of operations against Vicksburg. He acted firstly to organize the Army of the Tennessee into XIII, XV, XVI (to remain in Memphis), and XVII Corps. He acted secondly to find a feasible route for his army to march to Vicksburg.

An engineer staff officer stated the campaign Grant organized for Vicksburg was the "most distinctively one" because of its dependency on engineer-pioneer soldiers to surmount the obstacles interposed by nature, and by powerful, vigilant, and skillful foe, through means and methods not mentioned in any textbooks; and the requirement to be eyes and ears of everything topographic to find the best and most expeditious methods of moving the soldiers of Grant's army to the desired point.[37]

Corduroy Road

Photographic File, U.S. Army Engineer School

Grant spent the ensuing months of the new year detailing his officers and soldiers to work on proposed military expedients to restore mobility to his army, he called "experiments," to find the nearest practicable route where his army could set foot on dry soil, set up a supply base, and march to Vicksburg.[38]

(1) He assigned his staff engineer officer, Captain Frederick Prime, the task to provide staff supervision in the recommencing of work on the canal which Brigadier General Thomas Williams had started to dig on June 27, 1862, on Flag Officer David G. Farragut's expedition up the Mississippi River, across the De Soto Peninsula to enable transports and naval vessels to bypass Vicksburg. Captain William F. Patterson's Kentucky Company of Mechanics and Engineers provided technical assistance to the working parties on the canal and performed such other work to build two miles of corduroy road, and a half-mile long and seven-foot high levy.

Captain William L. B. Jenney, General Sherman's staff engineer officer, reported when Sherman received orders to furnish soldier working parties to do pick and shovel work on the canal, soldiers who thought they were in the vanguard of a successful campaign, remarked: "It was no bigger than a plantation ditch, and ends in slack water within enfilading fire of enemy. How could it be thought of such importance?"[39]

(2) Lieutenant James H. Wilson, Corps of Topographical Engineers, and a naval force reconnoitered the opening of a route up the Yazoo River to attack the Confederates' flank.

(3) Flag Officer Porter with a fleet of ironclads and army transports, with soldier-working parties aboard, reconnoitered a route through Steele's Bayou on the east side of the Mississippi River.

(4) General James B. McPherson reconnoitered the opening of a roundabout route south of Vicksburg through Lake Providence

to the Red River, and into the Mississippi River to land a force on the Confederates' left flank. In pursuit of the project, Companies D and G of the Missouri Engineer Regiment, commanded by Captain Eben M. Hill, constructed a passage for the river fleet from Baxter's Bayou to Macon Bayou by cutting passages through levies. From Macon Bayou the engineers successfully cut a passage through streams and bayous to the Mississippi River. Because of the distance to travel on enemy terrain and the hazards to navigation in bayous and small rivers McPherson abandoned the project.[40]

Colonel Manning F. Force, 20th Ohio Volunteer Infantry Regiment, reported his regiment arrived on February 23 to work at Lake Providence. The lake was bordered by live oaks, moss, and glistening magnolias. He camped his soldiers in a cotton field, on wet ground, but he built for his tent a board floor and porch. The regiment, he added, lived royally on stray cattle, sheep, hogs, and pond fish, and worked with the 30th Illinois Volunteer Infantry Regiment in building a corduroy road across a swamp.[41]

After expending a prodigious amount of manual labor, which took a physical toll by disease on the soldiers and contraband workforce, the "experiments" proved to be futile in finding a route for the army to march out of its west bank mudhole. Grant, though, concluded he had not expected much from the labor, except it kept his army occupied.[42]

On March 29, resorting to what he expected to be his final and successful expedient, Grant assigned General McClernand the task of making a reconnaissance for a road south along the west bank of the Mississippi River and an embarkation point for his army to cross the river, which would provide an approach to Vicksburg from the south end of Pemberton's army's camp.

McClernand assigned the reconnaissance task to Brigadier General Peter Osterhaus, Ninth Division, with Captain Patterson and his Kentucky Company of Mechanics and Engineers to supervise the engineer tasks. On April 2 the expedition reached Richmond, Louisiana, after fighting off a Confederate cavalry force. Osterhaus decided the next mission would be a reconnaissance in force along the road to New Carthage.[43]

In his first task on the expedition Captain Patterson's company supervised in the next two days the construction of a timber trestle bridge 390 feet long across the rapid stream of Roundaway Bayou. Logs and boards for the bridge were salvaged from nearby plantation houses and outbuildings. At 5 p.m., April 4, Osterhaus' expedition crossed the bridge on the way to New Carthage. A Confederate cavalry force took up a position far enough ahead of

Osterhaus' force on the flooded bayou terrain to make its presence known and to gather intelligence on the enemy.

Osterhaus' reconnaissance from Smith's Plantation confirmed New Carthage in its flooded condition could only be reached by boat. He further learned all the boats and flats in the area had been commandeered by the Rebels. To be able to convey a force to establish a foothold at New Carthage, Osterhaus ordered Captain Patterson to use the nearby sawmills to construct 20 pontons and flats. Patterson initiated the task with the assistance of infantrymen.

Osterhaus reported to General McClernand on April 10 the practicability of the route he established. McClernand gave his concurrence and ordered other divisions to march on the route in preparation for their transfer to the Mississippi River.

Two events intervened to change the course of events on the watery battlefield occupied by Osterhaus' expedition.

(1) On April 16, according to Grant's and Porter's plan, naval gunboats and transports successfully sailed by Vicksburg and anticipated joining Grant's army somewhere down river to accomplish the movement of the army across the river.

(2) The next day Grant arrived at McClernand's and Osterhaus' command post, and after making an estimate of the situation, he calculated it would be a tedious and long, drawn-out operation, with a dearth of barges and boats, to transport his army to New Carthage. Thus, he ordered Lieutenant Wilson to examine the land to the south to locate a suitable line of march to the Mississippi River nearer to Vicksburg.

After completing his terrain survey Wilson reported to Grant that to cross a large force and to build a practicable line of communications to New Carthage it would be timesaving to march the soldiers down the primitive roads, building bridges as needed over the bayous.[44]

On Wilson's recommendation Grant ordered roads to be repaired and corduroyed and bridges built from Smith's Plantation to Perkins' Plantation, twelve miles farther south. Captain Patterson's company and division pioneer soldiers worked day and night reconstructing drainage culverts on the bayous, corduroying the roads, and building bridges. The tasks also laid difficult burdens on the infantrymen who, in addition to the physical strain of the march in the environment, were assigned duty to cut, strip, and haul timber for corduroying roads and building four bridges. The route increased the march from Milliken's Bend to the new ferrying point to forty miles.

Timber Trestle

Photographic File, U.S. Army Engineer School

Patterson's company constructed a bridge where Gilbert Bayou joined Bayou Vidal from a large flatboat 200 feet long, anchored across the main channel of the bayou by a cable and chain on the south end and braced with wood against a tree on the north end. Spans were built from each end of the flatboat towards the bayou's bank. The roadway was fixed in place by heavy beams pinned to the floor planks. Using only their axes and other handtools, the engineers-pioneers and infantrymen finished the 730-foot part floating and part fixed bridge after 14 hours' work, on April 17.

Patterson's company marched south and next built a 250-foot bridge on 16 flatboats, with piers and trestles on each end, between the mouth of Negro and Mound Bayous, where they emptied into Brushy Bayou.

On April 22 Brigadier General William E. Strong, a staff officer on General McPherson's staff, witnessed what he believed a brilliant, exciting, and interesting incident that escaped the deserved special attention of the public. "To illustrate," he declared, "the most perilous and gallant performance of the war was the running of the Vicksburg batteries by the wooden transport fleet, manned by volunteer soldiers."[45]

The fate of Grant's army depended upon the transports' success; they were essential to transport soldiers and supplies across the river.

On April 25 Brigadier General Alvin P. Hovey reported his Twelfth Division completed a four-days' march from Gilbert's Bayou to Perkins' Plantation. To enable the division to complete its march, Patterson's company built four bridges over about one thousand feet of water and cut two miles of road through the woods, which opened up "a great military route" through overflowed lands from Milliken's Bend to the Mississippi River. During this severe bridge-building task, Hovey reported, "Many of my men worked for hours up to their necks in water, and I take occasion to thank them for their devotion and energy there displayed."[46]

Reaching Perkins' Plantation after their strenuous march, Hovey's soldiers expected to embark on transports, barges, and ferries. When McClernand arrived on the scene he learned that transports available to ferry the soldiers over the river to the Mississippi shore were insufficient. He ordered the soldiers to march farther down to a point where boats might be available and would have a short turnaround time on a trip shore to shore.

The leading soldiers of McClernand's XIII Corps, after a 22-mile march from Perkins' Plantation, arrived on April 29 at Dishroon's Plantation, thirty days after starting their march. The men had marched a total road distance of approximately seventy miles while struggling against the rain, mud, bayous, and insects, and fighting off Confederate cavalry attacks. They had crossed 2,000 feet of bridging built by Captain Patterson's company and pioneer and infantry soldiers. They had spent an inordinate amount of time dragging their own feet and yanking animals out of the mud, and putting their shoulders to wagons and gun carriages whose vessels were stuck in the mud. They completed a dreary and rigorous march on terrain where they were lacking conveniences to accommodate their appetites, health, sanitation, and security. There was, also, scarcely any dry ground to accommodate all the soldiers and provide them a place to camp, bathe, cook, and sleep comfortably, and to be buried in if they met with death. Likewise, there were few accommodations for the horses and mules who supported the march. The only compensation to the soldiers was the stimulation of their sensitivity to the natural world with the arrival of spring with its beautiful scenery and invigorating climate, the hope of something new accompanying the spring, and the stimulation of their morale with the realization they were now about to go over the river and confront the long sought enemy in battle.

On the Battleground

A different situation pervaded on the east side of the river. General John C. Pemberton, commander of Confederate forces at Vicksburg, found it difficult to assess Grant's intentions. He had reports of many Union troop movements. He misread Sherman's ruse marching north on April 29 as a march of Grant's army north up the river to attempt a landing on the Yazoo River. The cavalry raid Grant ordered Colonel Benjamin H. Grierson to conduct through northern Mississippi, which had been in progress since April 17 harassing the countryside and tearing up railroad tracks and destroying depots, turned the Confederates' attention away from Grant's march to Dishroon's Plantation.

Bayou Pierre

At the break of dawn on April 30 Grant's soldiers awaiting their turns to board all types of boats to be ferried over the Mississippi were face to face with the "Father of Waters"—one of the tough obstacles that stood in their path to reach Vicksburg.

The first wave of boats headed for the far shore at Bruinsburg, 30 miles south of Vicksburg. After the boats dropped their anchors as near the shore and as permitted by the water's depth, the soldiers debarked and waded ashore. To their surprise they were free of Confederate gunfire as they trudged through the heavy brush on the river's bank.

Colonel Force, 20th Ohio Volunteer Infantry, wrote soldiers landed at a narrow strip of bottom land which intervened between the river and the lofty, precipitous bluff. A roadway, walled in with high vertical banks, cut through the bluff and led from the river bottom up to the tableland above. A small force could have held the pass against an army, but it was left unguarded by the Confederates, and Grant's soldiers marched through it.[47]

The regiments of McClernand's corps continued to move inland. It was the first dry ground Grant's soldiers had placed their feet on in four months. All day long navy vessels and army transports and barges ferried Grant's soldiers over the river.

By nightfall 18,000 soldiers of McClernand's and McPherson's corps were safely across and camped in the enemy's presence.

With the success of the amphibious operation to restore his army's mobility, Grant declared he was overcome by a "degree of relief scarcely equaled since his army stood on dry ground on the same side of the river with the enemy."[48]

Grant's success, General Sanborn wrote, with the transports running by the batteries of Vicksburg, the march down the west side of the Mississippi, the crossing of the river, and the marching inland, endowed him with superhuman effort and power. From that time on his genius and his energies seemed to burst forth with new life. He rose to the ultimate pitch of determination and energy, and the whole army partook of his spirit.[49]

The next morning Grant's army broke camp early, and he ordered the XIII and XVII Corps to continue the battle for Port Gibson.

At 1 a.m. when McClernand's soldiers approached Magnolia Church, four miles from Port Gibson, the soldiers in General E. A.

Carr's Fourteenth Division came under light enemy rifle fire, followed by artillery fire. Carr ordered a return of the fire which silenced the enemy's. The soldiers of his division became the first to achieve the long sought goal to engage the enemy on the battlefield. In the remaining nighttime McClernand ordered his soldiers to rest on their arms.

McClernand at dawn ordered Osterhaus' Ninth Division to attack the enemy's right flank. Soon after marching out of their bivouac, Osterhaus' soldiers met the enemy who demonstrated considerable force and determination to engage in battle, but Osterhaus' soldiers showed they were also caught up in the long sought battle. Osterhaus pressed his soldiers forward until formidable obstacles, terrain and enemy fire, halted their progress and demonstrated the impracticability of a successful frontal attack.

In the afternoon, Osterhaus, leading a bold charge of his soldiers, routed the enemy. Joined by General A. J. Smith's Tenth Division, the soldiers of the two divisions pursued the enemy to within a half mile of Port Gibson.

Early in the morning McClernand also ordered General Carr's Fourteenth Division to attack the enemy's left flank. Carr pressed his soldiers forward to a range of hills where he found the enemy drawn up on the crests. The hostile lines immediately opened fire on each other and brought on an earnest, ensuing struggle. McClernand then sent General Hovey's Twelfth Division to support Carr's division. All four of McClernand's XIII Corps' divisions and General J. A. Logan's Third Division of the XVII Corps were in place on the battlefield. Fierce engagements followed throughout the day, but after an obstinate struggle the Confederates were beaten back from the field.

"The shades of night soon after closed upon the stricken field," McClernand wrote in his report, "which the valor of our men had won and held, and upon which they found their first repose since they had left Dishroon's Landing 24 hours before."[50]

General John S. Bowen, commander of Confederate forces at Grand Gulf, decided initially to meet McClernand's and McPherson's soldiers on the south side of Bayou Pierre, but he soon recognized there were too many vulnerable points on his extended line of battle for the strength of his soldiers. He reported to Pemberton he had fought "20,000" of Grant's soldiers since dawn, and was outnumbered. "Under cover of dark," he told Pemberton, "will cross to other side of Bayou Pierre."[51]

Separate bridges spanned both the North and South Forks of Bayou Pierre. The fleeing Confederates destroyed them. On the bank of the South Fork a rear guard was left to prevent the rebuilding of

Suspension and Floating Bridges, South Fork, Bayou Pierre

Harper's Pictorial History

the bridge. While McClernand's infantrymen battled the Rebels to drive them over the river, on orders of Colonel Wilson, of Grant's engineer staff, Captain Patterson's company in a joint task with Captain Stewart R. Tresilian, commander of the Pioneer Corps, XVII Corps, started the building of a 160-foot long, 12-foot wide floating bridge, which they completed in four and one-half hours. Plenty of buoyant materials were found by tearing down the barns and cotton gins in the neighborhood. All the approaches over quicksand were covered with layers of logs.[52]

Grant's soldiers marched over the bridge in the direction of Grindstone Ford on the North Fork of Bayou Pierre, eight miles east of Port Gibson. The burning suspension bridge across the bayou, which the retreating Rebels set afire, stopped their march. With the help of local Negroes the Yankees put out the fire.

Captain Patterson, quick to devise ways to overcome an obstacle, each way a unique one, requiring a structure conforming to the terrain, at midnight on May 2 set the soldiers to work salvaging timber planks in the area. He then had them lashed with telegraph wires to the suspended rods hanging from the chains spanning the bayou. Cross-tie timbers were fastened to the vertical planks tied to the suspension rods. Over the cross ties a road covering of boards, ripped from buildings, were put in place by spikes and lashings. Ramps were built at each end for the traffic to move over. The bridge opened for traffic at 5:30 a.m., May 3. After the soldiers and animals had crossed, curious as to how well the bridge held up under the weight of traffic, Patterson examined it from end to end and found it free of any weak spots.

Captain Andrew Hickenlooper, General McPherson's staff engineer officer, wrote, "The bridging of the South Fork of Bayou Pierre in four hours and the complete reconstruction of the suspension bridge, nearly 300 feet in length and 40 feet above the bed of the North Fork, in a single dark and stormy night by engineer and pioneer soldiers, assisted by troops worn out by two days and nights of continuous marching and fighting, will ever remain as examples of what may be accomplished by the intelligent direction of American soldiers."[53]

When General Grant landed on the east side of the river he received a message from Major General Nathaniel P. Banks, Army of the Gulf, which stated he could not arrive near Port Hudson until a week later and would only have 12,000 soldiers. The president desired the two generals first to make a joint attack to seize Port Hudson below Vicksburg. Grant had other alarming news. Confederate reinforcements were marching from the east to Jackson; they would attempt to join the forces at Vicksburg.

Grant's review of his army's tactical situation revealed there were opportunities present to achieve the desired battle victory. The army was on firm terrain in a favorable position to capture Vicksburg. The soldiers were in a position to conduct a quick strike. There was a pause in the action because Grant faced a decision on whether to wait for the arrival of General Banks' 12,000 soldiers. If Grant waited, he could lose the advantage of his position. A bold act to employ the soldiers present, could stop the arrival of the Confederates' reinforcements. Grant followed his innate bold spirit. Orders were issued to the army to march and attack the enemy. The orders called for the army to march between General Joseph E. Johnston who was marching from the east to Jackson and General Pemberton who was marching from Vicksburg. Because Grant's army was south of the two antagonists, the army could march to the north and deploy between the two bodies of troops. Then by turning first to Johnston on the right flank and then to Pemberton on the left flank, Grant's army could attack each one separately for victories.

By May 6 Sherman's XV Corps had completely reversed its march north, turned south on the west bank, followed the march route of the other two corps, crossed the river and joined Grant. His corps also brought with it 200 wagons filled with rations and the India rubber ponton bridge train.[54]

On the same day Sherman reversed his march, Grant ordered all supply wagons to be completely filled. In a startling move, he cut his army loose from its camp. All supplies and equipment were piled into wagons. Grant's orders to his soldiers were to live off the wagons and the countryside farms. The Union soldiers started marching northeast.

Grant's actions puzzled Pemberton. He sought out Grant's line of communications in the belief its destruction would bring about the defeat of the enemy. His efforts were to no avail; intelligence officers informed him Grant's wagons were carrying his supplies and the land fed the soldiers.

On May 6 Captain Patterson wrote to his wife from Willow Springs, "Through another terrible battle, Grand Gulf. First to enter Port Gibson, within 30 miles of Vicksburg. Rebels burned splendid bridge but to no avail. We built a floating bridge in one to two hours to go across. Grant and McClernand in thick of battle."[55]

Grant marched boldly east and won a battle against Johnston at Raymond on May 12. Colonel Force wrote in his report of the battle, "I remember noticing the forest leaves, cut by rifle balls, falling in thick eddies, still as snowflakes. At one time the enemy in our front advanced to the border of the creek, and rifles of opposing lines crossed while firing. Men who were not shot were burned by the powder of the rifles that sped the balls."[56]

Two days later Grant's army won another battle at Jackson, the capital city. Under supervision of engineer officers the soldiers destroyed every item that could be put to use for military purposes.

Battle of Champion's Hill

Pemberton's army from Vicksburg as well as Grant's from Jackson were marching on May 16 to an area where there were difficult natural-terrain obstacles: (1) Edward's Station, approximately 22 miles from Vicksburg, and on the march route of Pemberton's soldiers; (2) Baker's Creek, east of Pemberton's march route, which coursed north and south; and (3) Champion's Hill which loomed up on Grant's soldiers' westward-bound march routes.

Early in the morning Grant rode horseback out to Bolton and surveyed the situation of the impending battle at the Vicksburg-Jackson and Bolton-Raymond railroads' crossings. To the troop commanders he gave on the spot orders for tactical dispositions. He recorded he then passed on to the front. He arrived at Hovey's division, on the north road, at the halt with his soldiers and the enemies facing each other. The enemy troops in front of Hovey's division were in a strong position on a narrow, high ridge on the Confederates' left flank. The top of the ridge was a precipitous hillside. On the left side of the road were Hovey's soldiers positioned amidst dense forest and undergrowth, and on the right of the road was a valley and a ravine.

At 9:30 a.m. Hovey reported to Grant a strong enemy on his front. McPherson posted two divisions, Logan's and Brigadier General Marcellus B. Crocker's Seventh Division, on Hovey's right.

On the center of the Union line Smith's and Hovey's divisions of McClernand's corps were posted, and two of the corps' divisions, Carr's and Osterhaus', were on an approach march to post on the left flank.

At 11 a.m. Hovey ordered his soldiers into battle. In a fierce encounter with the enemy Hovey's soldiers bore the brunt of the determined combat. Grant ordered McPherson to reinforce Hovey. Brigade's of Logan's division struck the enemy's left flank, and because the north road the division's troops were on took a westerly course Logan's soldiers were in a position to strike the left and rear of the Confederate line. After three hours of continuous and severe combat Hovey's soldiers were reaching the point of exhaustion. Logan asked Grant to order Hovey to make an attack and simultaneously he would surround the enemy on his left flank. Grant passed the order to Hovey who implored his soldiers to rally to the attack; they responded and at 2:30 p.m. drove the enemy from the field.

On Hovey's left flank Smith's division's soldiers forced the enemy, who offered little resistance, to withdraw.

Grant on the Raymond Road on the left observed the enemy's retreating. He also noticed on the ridge on his left flank a column of soldiers. He discovered the column to be Carr's division, with McClernand, and then on Carr's left flank Osterhaus' division. He ordered Osterhaus to pursue the enemy. He ordered Carr to march hastily to the Big Black River and to cross it, if he could, and Osterhaus to follow.

In the aftermath of the battle, Grant stated at the time of Hovey's attack he had expected McClernand to have Carr's and Osterhaus' divisions on the field when the battle commenced; they were two and a half miles away. McClernand reported his divisions were delayed due to the hilly terrain, and in dense forest his soldiers could not see the enemy's infantry and artillery formations. McClernand described Osterhaus' division's march route as through "broad field, thick wood, chaos of abrupt hills and yawning ravines."[57]

Grant's conclusion that Hovey's division bore the brunt of the battle is supported by the casualties incurred:

Division	Killed	Wounded	Missing
Hovey's	211	872	119
Smith's	51	239	27
Logan's	128	528	15
Totals	390	1,639	161 [58]

If Grant implied criticism of McClernand for his divisions' failure to be on the battlefield when expected, there is another plausible conclusion. If Smith's division, which met the enemy on the corps' center, and Logan's division, which reached the rear of the enemy on the army's right flank, had been promptly reinforced, the enemy's army might have been entrapped. Instead a crafty and determined enemy army escaped the battlefield to fight again. From the Union's viewpoint Grant's skillful deployment of his troops confined Pemberton to Vicksburg and prevented him from joining Johnston.[59]

Grant sent a communication to Sherman with notice of the outcome of the day's battle, and ordered him to march his corps to Bridgeport, north of Grant's right flank. He sent orders to Major General Frank P. Blair to join Sherman's corps.

Battle at Big Black River Bridge

General Carr's division as ordered by General Grant pursued and attacked the fleeing Confederates at the Big Black River bridgehead. After a few hours of skirmishing, and passing over ground without cover and overcoming obstacles, Carr's soldiers were gallantly successful assaulting and capturing the enemy's position. The entire garrison of 1,751 soldiers and 17 pieces of artillery were the Union's trophies. Other enemy soldiers fled to a steamer, forming a bridge across the river near the railroad bridge, permitting many of them to escape to the commanding bluffs on the west side. The enemy on the west bank of the river immediately set afire the steamer and the railroad bridge with cotton balls soaked in turpentine.

Sherman's corps reached Bridgeport on the Big Black River.

Captain Christian Lochbihler, Company I, 35th Missouri Infantry, who hauled the India rubber ponton bridge train all the way from Milliken's Bend, received his opportunity to build a ponton bridge on the army's right flank. During the night his company built a bridge at Bridgeport for Sherman to cross his soldiers in the morning.[60]

On the left flank of the line Captain Patterson and his company of engineer soldiers demonstrated again their ingenuity to build a bridge. He and his soldiers felled tall pine trees on the riverbank into the river. Patterson's soldiers then stripped the trees of their limbs and floated them into position at right angles to the flow of the river to reach shore to shore and anchored them. Soldiers collected timber for balk and chess from the burned-out railroad bridge and nearby houses and warehouses to place on the felled tree stems reaching across the river for a roadway.[61]

At the center of the army's front occurred, perhaps, the unique achievement of bridge building, which Captain Hickenlooper of

Vicksburg, India Rubber Ponton Bridge

Rossiter Johnson, *Campfire and Battleground*

General McPherson's engineer staff, described: "The army was indebted for the celerity of its movements to the quickness of perception and inventive genius which enabled a volunteer engineer officer to construct in one night a bridge capable of safely passing an army corps with its immense trains across Big Black river, 30 feet in depth, without having at his command a single pioneer corps because they were left behind in the rapid pursuit of a fleeing foe, or a stick of framed timber, or a tool of any kind except ordinary woodsman axes. By the lurid light of brush fires, tired soldiers, at work raised a structure."[62]

To Captain Tresilian, the subject of Captain Hickenlooper's above remarks, the task to build a bridge in such a short time weighed heavily on his thoughts. Alas! An idea emerged from studying his surroundings and the application of his mind to the problem. While looking at the buildings along the river's bank, an inspiration alerted him when he noticed a warehouse filled with bales of cotton. Instantly, he remembered that a bale of cotton would float.

With a mental image of a bridge quickly forming in his mind, Tresilian hastened to the bridge-building job. He had brush fires lighted for light. He put the tired soldiers from the 48th Indiana, 59th Indiana, 4th Minnesota, and 18th Wisconsin Volunteer Infantry

Regiments to work to build the bridge. They tore down wooden warehouses for timber and hauled it and the bales of cotton to the river's bank. They recovered nails from the wood.

A squad of soldiers first measured the width of the river. They anchored a guy line, woven from rope used to tether the horses, to the picket and prolonges to drag artillery carriages, on their side of the river and then by use of a two-man raft carried it quietly to the enemy side where they anchored it. The needed bridge span was accurately measured from the guy line's length.

The soldiers selected two beams 12 inches by 16 inches and 35-feet long from the timber moved to the river's bank and laid them parallel on the ground 10 feet apart. The beams were joined together by one-inch strips nailed two and one-half feet apart. The structure the soldiers fabricated looked like a wide ladder. Uprights were nailed to each end. Two cotton bales, one on top of the other, were then placed on the cross pieces and pressed against the end uprights. The bales were kept tightly in place by nailing strips criss-cross in front of them. Additional bales of cotton were placed and fastened in the same way until they filled the length of the ladderlike frame, which took on the form of crated bales of cotton.

In the light from the brush fires, Tresilian and his soldiers built three 35-foot sections of crated cotton bales and timber, and dragged them into the river where they were floated into place. All three sections were fastened together end-to-end to form the bridge. Each section of the bridge was tied to the guy line soldiers had strung across the river to prevent the bridge from breaking up and floating down the river. Planks were fastened on top of the sections for the roadway, and logs and brush were used to make a fill upon which to construct the abutments and approach roads.[63]

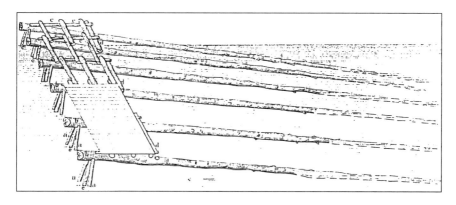

Vicksburg, Timber Trestle Bridge

Haupt, *Military Bridges*

Vicksburg, Cotton Bales Bridge

Harper's Weekly

On the morning of May 18, General William E. Strong described the terrain the soldiers in Grant's army observed upon their crossing of the Big Black River: "There lay spread out before the Army of the Tennessee a long line of high rugged irregular bluffs, clearly cut against the sky, crowned with cannon which peered ominously from embrasures to the right and left as far as they could see. Lines of heavy rifle pits surmounted with head logs ran along the bluffs connecting fort with fort and filled with veteran infantrymen.

"Fortifications covered city and both flanks rested on a great river. Approaches were over and across a succession of bluffs lying parallel to each other or nearly so. Summits were quite free from timber or underbrush, but the sides were abrupt and difficult to scale. Between the bluffs and at their base were streams along the banks on which grew dense thickets of willow and quaking aspen. Down the steep sides of these bluffs was a perfect labyrinth of fallen timber and limbs entwined and interlaced. Guns from the intrenched line were trained with deadly accuracy for a space of at least two thousand yards in their direct front.

"The position of the enemy was stronger than that of the Russians at Sebastopol, approaches were frightful. Enough to appall the stoutest heart.

"Line upon line of gallant men, moving over such a country, opposed the while to the deadly fire of cannon at short range, supported by a magnificent corps of sharpshooters and a solid line of infantry concealed in deep rifle pits and protected by head logs.

"A widely swiftly flowing river was at our backs. We were face to face of fortified crests of Vicksburg's hills. At last enemy at bay! The country 50 miles every direction had been thoroughly exhausted of forage and supplies. We could not go back. We had to go forward."[64]

In the face of what they observed on the battlefront, Grant's soldiers made a spirited attack on the enemy's entrenchments, but owing principally to encountering rough, unknown ground covered by fallen trees and entanglements, the assault became too disorganized and dispirited to succeed. Grant's soldiers expected to find the enemy soldiers too discouraged and demoralized to put up an effective defense or too spread out to cover their entire line. Such a condition might have occurred the night before on the enemy's side. A night free of battle made a difference. On the morning attack the Yankees spent too much time on strange terrain finding and taking up their positions. In addition they had been marching and fighting for three weeks. They were tired and deserving of rest, while the roads were prepared, and supplies of rations, ammunition, and clothing were brought forward.[65]

To develop the new supply base on the Yazoo River to receive the supplies brought down from Memphis, Sherman sent Captain Jenney to survey a road from the army's position to reach Johnston's Place Landing. Within a day the road along Thompson's Lake was so far completed as to admit passage of wagons. At the landing the four companies of the 1st Missouri Volunteer Engineer Regiment, which had been transferred from duty keeping the roads and bridges opened on the west bank of the river, built a ponton bridge 350-feet long over the head of Chickasaw Bayou to complete the road. Later the engineers built a permanent timber trestle bridge to replace the ponton bridge because all the supplies and ammunition were brought to Vicksburg over it and the heavy traffic wore out the ponton bridge's roadway.[66]

On May 19 Grant looked to the investment of Vicksburg. Continuous skirmishing took place during the early part of the day and Grant expressed hopefulness of carrying the enemy's works. Believing the enemy demoralized by the repeated defeats on the march to Vicksburg and being cooped up in his works, Grant ordered a general assault on the enemy's line at 2 p.m. The XV Corps, posted in a good position, carried out a vigorous assault. The XIII and XVII Corps succeeded in gaining advanced positions covered from the fire of the enemy.

McClernand reported later: "By 2 o'clock with great difficulty, my line had gained a half mile, and was within 800 yards of the enemy's works. The ground in front was unexplored and commanded

Johnston's Place Landing Ponton Bridge

by the enemy's works, yet, at the appointed signal, my infantry went forward under such cover as my artillery could afford, and bravely continued a wasting conflict until they had approached within 500 yards of the enemy's lines, when exhaustion and the lateness of the evening interrupted it." Captain Peter C. Hains, the corps' staff engineer officer, reported while there were casualties in the corps there was no loss of confidence in the soldiers on their being able to take the enemy's works.

On May 21 Grant made the decision to order another assault to carry Vicksburg.

"There were many reasons to determine me to adopt this course," he wrote in the record. "I believed an assault from the position gained by this time could be made successfully. It was known that Johnston was at Canton with the force taken by him from Jackson, reinforced by other troops from the east, and that more were daily reaching him. With the force I then had, a short time must have enabled him to attack me in the rear, and possibly succeed in raising the siege.

"Possession of Vicksburg at the time would have enabled me to have turned upon Johnston and driven him from the state, and possessed myself of all the railroads and practical military highways, thus effectually securing to ourselves all territory west of the Tombigbee, and this before the season was too far advanced for campaigning in this latitude. I would have saved the government sending large reinforcements, much needed elsewhere; and finally, the troops themselves were impatient to possess Vicksburg and would not have worked in the trenches with the same zeal, believing it unnecessary, that they did after their failure to carry the works."

Grant issued orders for a general assault on the whole line to commence 10 a.m., May 22. Time pieces were to be synchronized to avoid any difference in movement of the assault.[67]

At 10 a.m. on the appointed day the three army corps in front of the enemy's works commenced an assault. Grant posted himself in a commanding position near McPherson's front where he could see all the advancing columns from McPherson's corps, and a portion of the commands of McClernand and Sherman. A portion of the command of each corps succeeded in planting their flags on the outer slopes of the enemy's bastions, and in maintaining them there until night.

"The assault was gallant in the extreme on the part of all the troops," Grant wrote, "but the enemy's position was too strong, both naturally and artificially, to be taken that way. At every point assaulted, and at all of them at the same time, the enemy was able to show all the force his works would cover."

The assault failed, Grant regretfully reported, with much loss in killed and wounded, but without weakening of the confidence of the soldiers in their ultimate ability to succeed.[68]

General Grant informed General Halleck, "Vicksburg is now completely invested. I have possession of Haynes' Bluff and the Yazoo; consequently have supplies. Today an attempt was made to carry the city by assault, but was not entirely successful. We hold possession, however, of two of the enemy's forts, and have skirmishers under all of them. Our loss was not severe. The nature of the ground about Vicksburg is such that it can only be taken by siege. It is entirely safe to us in time. I would say one week, if the enemy do not send a large army upon my rear."[69]

The Siege

On May 23 Grant announced his decision to conduct a siege by regular approaches against Vicksburg.

From Grant's decision arose the demand for engineers capable of directing the operations of a stupendous siege works covering a line of investment ten miles in length. The requisition was filled, Hickenlooper reported, and well filled.[70]

An approximate mile of open land area existed between the defensive lines of the contending armies.

The siege, in a way, obviated the futility of the open assault across an open battlefield against an enemy entrenched in a well-fortified position.

After a month of laborious work on the ten siege approaches, General Grant reported to General Halleck, "The enemy are now undoubtedly in our grasp. The fall of Vicksburg and capture of most of the garrison can only be a question of time. I heard a great deal of the enemy bringing a large force from the east to effect a raising of the siege. They may attempt something of the kind, but I do not see how they can do it."[71]

Surrender

On July 3, Captain Jenney concluded General Pemberton saw all the preparations of the siege, ditches, rifle pits, sand bag embrasures, and so decided to surrender.

General Strong reported white flags were raised all along the lines of both armies. Silence pervaded for the first time in 46 days (since the first assault on May 19), and the guns were silent.

Colonel Force observed the day's strange silence was oppressive—it seemed a boding silence.

General Grant during the afternoon received from General Pemberton a letter proposing an armistice and the appointment of a commission to arrange terms for the capitulation of Vicksburg. Grant sent his answer by recently promoted Lieutenant Colonel James Wilson to General Pemberton. Later in the day Grant and Pemberton met between the lines in a personal conference on the subject of the capitulation. Pemberton asked for a commission to discuss terms, but Grant refused his request, declaring there were no terms other than unconditional surrender.[72]

July 4—Saturday—10:30 a.m. General Grant to General Henry Halleck: "The enemy surrendered this morning. The only terms allowed are their paroles as prisoners of war. This I regard of great advantage. It saves probably several days in the captured town; leaves troops and transports ready for immediate service. General Sherman with a large force will immediately face on Johnston and drive him from the state. I will send troops to the relief of General Banks, and return the IX Corps to General Burnside."[73]

With the surrender of the Confederate army at Vicksburg the Army of the Tennessee achieved for the Union in the larger picture of strategy the return of control of the entire Mississippi River to the Union.

General Sanborn conceptualized the ideals of the victory in eloquent poetic words:

"When ages shall have passed away and the proudest monuments erected by human hands shall have crumbled to dust, and heights of Vicksburg worn away by mighty river that rolls at the base, the fame and glory of the campaign that compelled Vicksburg's surrender will survive, exempt from mutability and decay, a beacon to qualities of liberty, justice, and humanity as law of life."[74]

Bridge Anecdote

At the end of the Vicksburg battle, Grant ordered Sherman's corps to pursue General Johnston. While camped at the Tallahatchee River, near Wyatt, General Sherman and his engineer officer, Captain Jenney, surveyed the houses and outbuildings for material to build a bridge across the river. While looking at beams in a citizen's house an insightful conversation occurred that reflected the beliefs of persons of both sections of the country.

Sherman told the owner he would take the beams in the house.

The owner replied, "You would not tear down the house you sleep in and sleep out on the lawn in the rain."

Sherman replied, "The bridge must be built if it takes the last house in town."

The owner replied, "The people want vouchers for the value of their destroyed houses."

Sherman said to the owner, "Call on the government of the southern confederacy. You let them burn the old bridge. I have to build a new one. I have to use your house. I give you the bridge in exchange. Take care of it."[75]

Chattanooga
Chickamauga, September 18–20, 1863

After the successful conclusion of the battle at Stones River in the opening days of the new year, General William Rosecrans camped his Union army for the winter at Murfreesboro. Bragg camped his Confederate army at Tullahoma.

President Lincoln urged Rosecrans to force the war in the West into a double-pronged attack by marching his Army of the Cumberland against the river town, Chattanooga. At the time Grant's Vicksburg campaign was in its early stage, and Lincoln and Halleck believed an attack on Chickamauga would lead the Confederate high command to transfer soldiers from Vicksburg.

Chattanooga was the gateway for the Confederates to attack up to the Ohio River. It also anchored a fortress in the path of the Union army to march to the southeastern states of the Confederacy. Other resources were the railroad center in the town, and the grain crops in eastern Tennessee.

Finally, responding a season later to the proddings of President Lincoln and General Halleck, Rosecrans on June 23 marched out of his camp at Murfreesboro and headed south to engage Bragg's army at Tullahoma. His army consisted of Major General George H. Thomas' XIV Corps, Major General Alexander McCook's XX Corps, and Major General Thomas L. Crittenden's XXI Corps. Brigadier General Robert Mitchell commanded his cavalry corps, and Major General Gordon Granger commanded the reserve corps.

Rosecrans' soldiers marched under difficult conditions, obstacle-filled terrain, and enemy cavalry attacks on the railroad transporting the supplies. Rosecrans employed tactics of feinting to Bragg's left flank and then changing tactics feinting a march on his right flank. After days of hard marching Rosecrans' soldiers succeeded in maneuvering Bragg's soldiers out of a naturally strong defensive position.

The contending armies marched in the rain. The soldiers' and animals' feet and the wagon wheels ground the terrain into a quagmire. In spite of the rough terrain and weather, Rosecrans' soldiers kept up their attack, and by a series of adept flanking maneuvers forced Bragg's soldiers to give ground and deploy southward towards the Tennessee River.

There were strong natural obstacles for Rosecrans' army to overcome as it pursued Bragg. To cross the mountains and the rivers required a maximum of time and the accumulation of a large amount of supplies. The Nashville and Chattanooga Railroad which hauled the supplies had to be kept in repair. The railroad bridges which Bragg's cavalry burned or tore up taxed the skills of the army's engineers.

Elk River Bridge

The supply trains were delayed while Colonel Innes' Michigan Engineer Regiment's engineers again reconstructed their most difficult and skillful railroad bridge over the Elk River between Allison's and Estill's Springs, south of Pulaski, Tennessee. When the Union army's soldiers marched south from Nashville they needed enormous tons of supplies delivered by the railroad, but the Rebels' constant cavalry raids on the railroad bridges disrupted the supply lines. They destroyed the Nashville and Decatur Railroad bridge. The army desperately needed supplies, but the trains could not transport supplies to the battlefield without the Elk River bridge. Innes' engineers were issued orders to rebuild it, with, according to Innes, the assistance of "citizen bridge builders." Quickly, once the work crews were on the site, they were at work cutting timber in the nearby forest. They worked during July and August in incessant rains and sunshine. The destroyed bridge delayed the shipment of food and ammunition. The work crews were constantly spurred on with the admonition the soldiers on the battlefield needed supplies. The supplies could not be hauled readily over the wagon roads because of the muddy conditions on the ground and the constant rains that made them impassable. There were also the constant cavalry raids.

The record length bridge built by Innes' engineers and the citizen artisans spanned a chasm of 700 feet in length and 58 feet in height. The work crews worked in twenty feet of water to build the trestles. Innes reported the reconstruction of the bridge an enormous task. He also assessed the bridge as the heaviest one his regiment labored on. Its unique features were an upper deck for the railroad and a lower one for the soldiers, wagon trains, and artillery.[76]

Another problem facing the Army of the Cumberland on the march was the depleted supply of forage for the animals, who were starving to death. The army could not expect to find ripe corn in eastern Tennessee until August. Rosecrans proposed to delay the progress of his army until it was supplied with ripe corn. Also, the return of his cavalry to action depended upon restoring his horses to a healthy condition.

Reconstructed Elk River Bridge

On August 4 Halleck sent Rosecrans a message to hasten the movement of his army. The message provoked Rosecrans, who replied he would march at the appropriate time. The two generals engaged in a heated brouhaha over the time spent waiting for the animals' forage.

Bragg's Confederate army withdrew from the battle, left middle Tennessee, crossed the Tennessee River at Battle Creek and Kelly's Ferry, and on July 3 entered Chattanooga. Bragg ordered the destruction of the Tennessee River railroad bridge to impede Rosecrans' pursuit. He also set to work his engineer and pioneer soldiers to build defense works at the river's crossings. With Bragg's deployment below the Tennessee River, Rosecrans' target became the battle for Chattanooga.

Rosecrans reviewed his options, and what action he decided on would be to cross the Tennessee River below Chattanooga, turn the Confederates' left flank and interrupt Bragg's communications and supply line from Atlanta. If successful, Rosecrans' deployment would cut the railroad lines to Chattanooga, and Bragg would find himself shut in between Burnside (whom Halleck ordered to move against him) on the north and east and Rosecrans on the west and south. To deceive and to annoy Bragg, Rosecrans sent an expedition to make a feint at the river north of the town. Bragg was led to believe Rosecrans' attack would be made up river on the north side. As a result he left the crossing sites below Chattanooga without guards.

By August 8 General Philip Sheridan's division had pushed forward to Stevenson-Bridgeport where facilities could be built for commissary and quartermaster stores. On August 16 Rosecrans' army began its movement over the Cumberland Mountains. His soldiers began to arrive at the Tennessee River four days later.

The engineers were called upon to perform their important role in the army's mobility. Their task was to pick the best point to cross Rosecrans' army over the river. They would also have to collect and build the means to make the crossing. Colonel Innes brought forth on the march the ponton train, which, to deny information to the enemy, he had concealed near Stevenson (inland of the river but on the railroad), southwest of Bridgeport.

The engineers made a reconnaissance along the river and selected four sites for the bridges.

(1) *Bridgeport.* Colonel Innes' regiment built a ponton bridge across the Tennessee River. The pioneers from General Sheridan's division assisted with the construction of timber trestles for the roadways to connect from the pontons to the shorelines.

Union army units that crossed the bridge to the south side of the river were: all the wagon trains, one brigade of Thomas' XIV Corps, Sheridan's Third Division, XX Corps.

(2) *Shellmound* (east of Bridgeport). Major General Joseph J. Reynolds' Fourth Division pioneers captured boats and bridge-building materials, and used them to construct a floating bridge.

Union army unit that crossed the bridge to the south side of the river was: General Reynolds' Fourth Division, XIV Corps.

(3) *Battle Creek* (north of Bridgeport). Brigadier General John M. Brannan's Third Division, XIV Corps, pioneers built rafts to ferry the division over the river.

Union army units that were ferried to the south side of the river were: General Brannan's Third Division, XIV Corps, and First Brigade (Mounted Infantry), detached from Fourth Division.

(4) *Caperton's Ferry* (south of Bridgeport). Major General Alexander McD. McCook, XX Corps, to protect the bridge site ferried infantrymen in pontons over the river to drive away the enemy cavalry present there. Pioneers in Brigadier General Jefferson C. Davis' First Division then built a ponton bridge.

Union army units that crossed the bridge to the south side of the river were: First and Second Divisions of McCook's XX Corps, and cavalry units.

At *Island Creek Ford* cavalry units forded the river.

On August 29 with bridges, ferries, and fords in place, Rosecrans' army began to cross the Tennessee River (except for General Crittenden's corps which remained on the north side of the river and marched down the Sequatchie Valley).

Rosecrans' army safely completed its crossing the river barrier on September 2, and regrouped itself in a position to threaten Bragg's army. Rosecrans learned, with his army on the south side of the river, the enemy firmly held Lookout Mountain, and was concentrating at Chattanooga. To dislodge the enemy, he recognized, it would be necessary to capture Lookout Mountain, or deploy his army to compel Bragg to quit his position because of the Union's endangerment of his line of communications.

Rosecrans adopted the option to threaten Bragg's line of communications. He began his army's movement the night of September 8–9. When his army was safely beyond the first mountain barrier, he decided to threaten the enemy's line of communications with his right flank, while the center and left of his battlefront seized the gaps and commanding points of the mountains in front.

General Thomas marched his corps on Trenton, seizing Frick's and Steven's Gaps on Lookout Mountain. General McCook's corps marched to Valley Head and seized Winston's Gap. General

Crittenden's corps crossed the Tennessee River to Wauhatchie, and made contact on his right with General Thomas, and together threatened Chattanooga by the pass over the point of Lookout Mountain.

Bragg, upon learning that Rosecrans' army had crossed the Tennessee River below Chattanooga, intending to threaten his lines of supply, made the decision to abandon Chattanooga and deploy southeastward.

On September 9 Crittenden reported to Rosecrans his reconnaissance alerted him to the information the Rebels were evacuating Chattanooga, marching southeastward, and his corps would take possession of the army's objective (Chattanooga).

Upon receipt of the news Rosecrans ordered his other corps commanders to press on through the difficult passes of Lookout and Missionary Mountains, and on to Bragg's retreating army.

General Halleck remarked it was a surprise to him Bragg abandoned the important position of Chattanooga, and because he was uncertain of Confederate intentions, he instructed Rosecrans after holding mountain passes on the west, and Dalton, or a point on the railroad, to prevent the return of Bragg. Halleck at the same time ordered Burnside's Army of the Ohio to march down to connect with Rosecrans, and other commanders of adjoining areas were ordered to secure Rosecrans' line of communications.[77]

Rosecrans received intelligence from commanders on the battlefield reporting Bragg's army was concentrating near La Fayette to dispute Rosecrans' army's advance in passage of Pigeon Mountain. Rosecrans, though, erred in concluding Bragg had retreated farther southeastward when he reviewed the intelligence given to him. Bragg remained close by to conduct cavalry raids on Rosecrans' right and left flanks and to disrupt railroads and line of communications to Burnside's army.

By word of mouth other ominous information reached Rosecrans that the Confederate high command was moving soldiers from other battlefronts to reinforce Bragg. The information proved to be true. Rosecrans assumed Bragg's army was disorganized and retreating, whereas in reality Bragg was employing a stratagem against his enemy. Reinforcements for his army were moving to La Fayette from Tennessee and Mississippi.

Reinforcements were also moving from a third source. In an outstanding deployment of troops and employment of railroads in national strategy, Lieutenant General James L. Longstreet's corps was transported approximately 900 miles through the southeastern United States from Virginia to Georgia. His corps started boarding trains on September 9, and nine days later his frontline troops arrived in Georgia; succeeding bodies of troops arrived days afterwards. The entire operation, the officers' management of it, and the skillful use of 16 deteriorated short-line railroads of different gauges to move approximately 15,000 troops, elicited admiration for the Confederate government.

Chickamauga Battle. The battle began on the morning of September 19 with General McCook's corps posted on the right flank, General Crittenden's corps on the center of the line, and General Thomas' corps on the left flank. The enemy began the battle with an attack on the Union's left flank to capture the road to Chattanooga, but failed in its attempt. Bragg then ordered an assault on the center of the line. McCook's soldiers steadfastly held their ground.

On September 20 the Confederates renewed the attack on the Union's left and center of the line. By errors of subordinate generalship in the misreading of Rosecrans' orders, a gap opened in the Union line, and Bragg's soldiers broke through. The Union's center and right of the line fell back from the battle, and the continuance of the battle was left to General Thomas' corps on the left. The top generals on the battlefield fled to Chattanooga, but the chief of staff of the Army of the Cumberland, General James Garfield, remained and joined General Thomas in the battle.

General Thomas' soldiers fought stubbornly to hold their position; they repulsed the assaults of the enemy, and through his leadership Thomas earned renown. At night the enemy withdrew. On the next day Thomas, in view of the withdrawal of the army commander and the two other corps' commanders, withdrew his corps to Chattanooga.

Rosecrans also committed a critical error when after withdrawing to Chattanooga, he also withdrew his soldiers from the passes of Lookout Mountain which guarded the line of supplies to Bridgeport. Bragg, aware of the opportunity handed to him, immediately occupied the passes and sent his cavalry across the Tennessee River north of Chattanooga to attack the wagon trains in Sequatchie Valley. Bragg's cavalry also captured points on the railroad to cut off the trains carrying supplies to Chattanooga.

Afterwards, Rosecrans wrote for the record about the battle:

> Swift was the charge and terrible the conflict, but the enemy was broken. A thousand of our brave men, killed and wounded, paid for its possession, but we held the gap. Two divisions of Longstreet's corps confronted the position. Determined to take it, they successively came to the assault. A battery of six guns placed in the gorge poured death and slaughter into them. They charged to within a few yards of the pieces, but our grape and canister, and the leaden hail of our musketry, delivered in sparing but

terrible volleys from cartridges taken, in many instances, from the boxes of their fallen companions, were too much even for Longstreet's men. About sunset they made their last charge, when our men, being out of ammunition, rushed on them with bayonet, and they gave way to return no more.[78]

Railroads Provide Mobility

The Confederate decision to reinforce Bragg forced Halleck on September 23 to face a decision on the Union's necessity to reinforce Rosecrans. Leaders of each government became well aware of the strategic importance to win the battle at Chattanooga. Both sides recognized the need for quick action, and looked to the railroads to provide the army with the mobility to ship reinforcements in a short period of time.

Halleck ordered field commanders in the West (Major General Stephen A. Hurlbut, Grant, and Sherman) to reinforce Rosecrans. He also ordered the XI and XII Corps of the Army of the Potomac to move west by railroad to join Rosecrans' army, and assigned General Hooker to command the expedition.

Halleck advised Rosecrans on September 24 that 15,000 troops would be in Nashville in a week, and added, "It is important Chattanooga be held till reinforcements arrive."[79]

On the same day President Lincoln issued an executive order to Secretary of War Stanton and General Hooker, "to take possession of all railroads to carry out the assigned military operations."

Stanton coordinated the movement with W. P. Smith of the Baltimore and Ohio Railroad who gave assurance the railroad would furnish 30 passenger cars, 200 box and rack cars, and 125 flat cars to move 3,000 troops a day.

The generals anticipated a number of human incidents on the movement, so provided for them with the issuance of instructions.

General Halleck sent a message to Brigadier General B. F. Kelley, commander of the Mountain Department, at Clarksburg, West Virginia, that troops would cross the Ohio River at Benwood, West Virginia, and continue the journey at Bellaire, Ohio. He also ordered that guards be posted at the two towns to keep troops in formation, and to order closed all nearby saloons.

General Hooker, fearful of soldiers' desertions, also issued orders to his unit commanders that their soldiers were not to leave railroad cars for any reason except to transfer from one railroad to another.

General Carl Schurz issued an order to his division officers when their Ohio regiments, present on the trains, reached the Ohio

River they were to remain with their troops to prohibit them from straggling to familiar Ohio places.

Train Movements

On September 25 J. W. Garrett of the Baltimore and Ohio reported that of the troops that moved on the Orange and Alexandria Railroad from Manassas Junction, Virginia, to the Baltimore and Ohio station at Washington, and on to Camden Yards, Baltimore, had departed for Benwood in two trains of 51 cars each.

The route laid out for the trains called for the Baltimore and Ohio to transport troops to Benwood, West Virginia; the Central Ohio Railroad from Bellaire to Columbus; the Xenia Railroad to Dayton; Dayton Western Railroad to the state line; Indiana Central Railroad to Indianapolis; and Jeffersonville Railroad to Jeffersonville, Indiana. The Louisville & Nashville completed the route's final segment to Bridgeport.

The complete journey approximated 1,200 miles.

Of interest to this story are any reports on bridges.

W. P. Smith reported at Benwood, "A substantial and superior bridge of scows and barges, strongly connected, is in full readiness to make the transfer across the Ohio River, where adequate cars are waiting at Bellaire, for the soldiers to reboard."

The building of the Benwood floating bridge for the soldiers to cross the river to change railroads attests to the native ability of artisans to anticipate, coordinate, plan, and construct expedients to conduct military operations.

At Jeffersonville, Indiana, Thomas Scott, assistant secretary of war, assigned by Secretary Stanton to monitor the troop movements, reported arrangements were completed to have ferryboats there on hand to ferry troops across the river from Jeffersonville to Louisville.

On September 28, at 3 p.m., W. P. Smith sent a message to Secretary Stanton, "Troops have been promptly and successfully transferred from Benwood to Bellaire with baggage, artillery, and all effects which were reloaded at once on Ohio side, and dispatched to Indianapolis. Not one of 30 trains, nearly 600 cars, has been delayed improperly. The actual movement of men and horses has exceeded the number asked to be provided for, 20 per cent in men, and 50 per cent in horses."

On September 29 General Hooker sent a message to Rosecrans, "head of column passed through Louisville." He reported an incident to travel, "losses of a few men. They were men who fell asleep on flat cars and rolled off trains in motion."

After an exceptionally well organized and conducted railroad operation by the railroads and the army, on September 30, at 10:30 p.m., the first train of Hooker's troops arrived at Bridgeport.

Two weeks later the rear echelon of Hooker's force arrived at Bridgeport, after transferring from Virginia a reported 5,834 soldiers in the XI Corps and 9,245 in the XII Corps. The journey achieved a record movement of soldiers by railroad.[80]

Rosecrans' Last Words on Chickamauga

On October 2, Rosecrans issued a complimentary order to the Army of the Cumberland:

> You have made a grand and successful campaign. You have driven the rebels from Middle Tennessee. You crossed a great mountain range, placed yourselves on the banks of a broad river, crossed in the face of a powerful opposing army, and crossed two other great mountain ranges at the only practicable passes some 40 miles between extremes. When day closed you held the field from which you withdrew in face of overpowering numbers to occupy the point for which you set out—Chattanooga.
>
> The general commanding earnestly begs every officer and soldier of this army to unite with him in thanking Almighty God for his favors to us. No battle furnishes a loftier example of obstinate bravery and enduring resistance to superior numbers.[81]

Halleck Revamps the Field Command

As his final action in strengthening the army at Chattanooga, Halleck wrote, "By the manner in which three armies operated in the field, it was apparent to him they needed a single commander to obtain better cooperation than had existed with the separate commanders." He concluded, "Grant by his distinguished service and higher rank earned the higher command." On October 16, the War Department issued an order that created the Military Division of the Mississippi, with General Grant its commander. His subordinate armies were: Army of the Cumberland, General Thomas; Army of the Ohio, General Burnside; and Army of the Tennessee, General Sherman. On October 18, General Grant assumed command of the division.[82]

Siege
September 24–November 25

Imprisoned and under siege the Yankees faced a problem to bring food and forage into the town. The solution to the problem would test the engineers.

Two obstacles on the northern side of the important river town placed the Army of the Cumberland in a perilous position,

Tennessee River Trestle Bridge

Battles and Leaders of the Civil War, People's Pictorial Edition

the Tennessee River and the Cumberland Mountains. South of the river Missionary Ridge to the east and Lookout Mountain to the west, separated by Chattanooga Valley, jutted out like a bipod from the town. Bragg had quickly sent his soldiers to the tops of the two strategic high points. Beyond the town, on the south side of the river, Bragg's soldiers had seized the wagon road and railroad tracks the Union needed to haul supplies to Chattanooga from its supply base at Bridgeport.

Bragg thought he had closed every transportation line into the town: wagon road, railroad, and river. He could not completely cut his enemy's supply route. The animals, horses, mules, and oxen, filled the critical role to move the wagon trains which crossed the Tennessee River at Bridgeport and made their way on a triangular course over sixty miles of winding and narrow mountain trails. They pushed northeast up the Sequatchie Valley to Anderson's crossroad through Jasper, then on poor mountain trails southeast over Walden's ridge to the two ferries and ponton bridge on the outskirts of Chattanooga, and crossed the Tennessee River into the town. Travel on the circuitous route of poor roads and trails was a back-breaking job and required exertion from the soldiers and animals. The animals bore a brunt in the raising of the siege. They were as vulnerable to battlefield injuries and diseases as the soldiers.

The ponton and trestle bridges, which the wagon trains used to cross the river to enter the town, were built by Companies D and K of the Michigan Engineers Regiment and the Pioneer Brigade of the Army of the Cumberland. Rosecrans had ordered Colonel Innes' engineer soldiers and the Pioneer Brigade's pioneers, who remained in the town in September when the army left to pursue Bragg at Chickamauga, to build the bridges so supplies could move into the town. Chattanooga then became the supply base backing up the

Tennessee River Trestle Bridge Draw-in-Place

Battles and Leaders of the Civil War, People's Pictorial Edition

army, but the base without supporting lines of communication lost the ability to build up sufficient supplies for the army upon its September 22 return.[83]

The frequent rains turned the wagon roads into muddy obstacles. Wagon wheels could not turn and animals could not pull their feet out of the mud. The flimsy supply line, dependent upon the animals' mobility and strength, came to a halt. A shortage developed on food for the soldiers and forage for the animals. Without food the Union's soldiers could not muster the strength or will to fight. On the route from Bridgeport through the mountains it was reported 10,000 horses and mules starved to death because of lack of forage and the low priority given to their feeding. Their smelly carcasses lined the wagon roads.[84]

Wagon Train Raid

The most deadly and barbaric damage to the wagon trains and animals was inspired by Bragg's orders to General Joseph W. Wheeler and his troopers to raid and to destroy railroad cars and railroad bridges, to disrupt efforts to reinforce the Union army, and to harass and destroy wagon trains and animals as they moved over Walden's Ridge on their trips to and from Bridgeport. A number of reports in the records chronicle the poignant story how Wheeler conducted his raids with violence, destructiveness, and cruelty. The following is a report by a Confederate cavalryman who participated in one of the raids:

> General Wheeler was in charge of the cavalry with General Bragg in front of Chattanooga where Rosecrans' army was behind fortifications.
>
> Bragg spoke to Wheeler for an expedition north of the Tennessee River to break Rosecrans' line of communications. Wheeler said few of his cavalry horses were able to stand the strain of such an expedition. Bragg, who expected his orders to be obeyed, said, "Make your best effort."
>
> Wheeler with his cavalry reached the Tennessee river near Cottonport, 40 miles east of Chattanooga on September 30. There the 4th Ohio Cavalry was lined up on the north bank of the river. Opposed by the Union Cavalry, Wheeler moved his cavalry farther on up the river to a ford and then crossed the river. Wheeler made his way across Walden's ridge and descended into Sequatchie Valley at Anderson's Cross Roads early on morning of October 2. There Wheeler's cavalrymen encountered the advance guard of a Union infantry escort to an enormous wagon train filled with supplies on the way to the army in Chattanooga. Wheeler ordered a detachment from two regiments to charge the escort. The Union

cavalrymen repulsed the Confederate cavalry detachment and it fled in disorder. Wheeler arrived on the scene and hearing a report of what occurred ordered a regiment to be formed. He led the regiment in an attack, which after creating a scene of panic and confusion, captured the Union escort.

Wheeler was well aware he was in the rear of Rosecrans' army. A Federal cavalry regiment posted near Bridgeport had received orders to proceed up Sequatchie Valley to support the wagon train but failed at the critical moment to carry out their assignment.

At the outset of Wheeler's attack Union teamsters turned about in hope of making an escape toward Bridgeport. Unsuccessful, they became panic stricken and took to their heels for safety, leaving their uncontrolled teams to run wild. Some of the wagons overturned blocking the road in places with anywhere from 10 to 50 teams, some mules still standing, some fallen and tangled in the harness, and all in inextricable confusion. Wheeler's cavalry for 6 or 8 miles followed along this line of wagons and at every half mile or so they instigated a repetition of panic and confusion.

As we proceeded men were detailed to set fire to the wagons and to kill the mules since it was impossible to escape with animals. The smoke of the wagons was visible for many miles and the explosion of the ammunition sounded along the valley road. Rosecrans, hearing the sound in the distance, thought the Rebels were bombarding his depot at Bridgeport.

While the wagons were burning, and before those of us who went to the end of the train could return to the columns, the Federals arrived. They formed between us and the column.

The loss was acute to Federals. They were in a precarious position in Chattanooga and on reduced rations to a cracker a day.

Wheeler reported the quartermaster in charge of the wagon train said there were 800 6-mule wagons, plus a great number of sutlers' wagons.

Rosecrans admitted to the destruction of 500 wagons and from 1,000 to 2,000 mules destroyed.

Missed by Wheeler in the raid were 30 wagons that had turned off in a narrow roadway little used and were already partly towards Walden's Ridge.[85]

Bragg estimated the casualties his army would incur from either a frontal assault or a flanking movement against Thomas' soldiers. He also observed his pincers' hold onto the town and the destructive raids on the wagon trains. He concluded it would be easier to starve Thomas' army into surrender than to spill blood in an attempt to conquer it.

President Davis journeyed down from the Confederate capital city to share with his soldiers the great feat of whipping the new commander of the Army of the Cumberland. Bold in his confidence, he told Bragg's soldiers, "We hold the enemy at our mercy and his destruction is only a question of time."

Grant's Turnabout of the Siege

A starving army, huddled behind breastworks, built for its protection with the assistance of the engineer soldiers, greeted Grant on his arrival in Chattanooga on October 23. As the first step to break out of the army's imprisonment, Grant set about to open up a supply road. He studied the dejected soldiers and declared he would not stay a prisoner in the town. He had starved out a Confederate army at Vicksburg; he was determined not to have the tables turned on his army.

Grant knew it would take the energetic engineer and pioneer soldiers to chop free the soldiers and the town. Major General William F. Smith, Thomas' newly appointed staff engineer officer, was ready with a plan on how to open the river and wagon road from Brown's Ferry. He outlined his plan to Grant that by seizing the hills, nine miles west of Chattanooga on the south bank of the river, the Union soldiers could occupy Locust Valley and control the supply road to Bridgeport.

Smith planned for supply wagons to move up to Brown's Ferry opposite Moccasin Point peninsula. The peninsula, shaped like an Indian's moccasin, was formed by a U-turn of the Tennessee River. The Confederate batteries and sharpshooters on Lookout Mountain could not reach the location with their gunfire. If the engineers built a ponton bridge across the ferry site, the wagon trains would be able to cross the river. Once across the river the wagon trains were to follow the road on the peninsula leading to the bridges crossing the Tennessee River at Chattanooga.

Grant believed Smith's plan a workable one. He approved it and placed Smith in command of the project with orders to carry it out at once.

General Smith in turn called upon Colonel Innes and his engineer soldiers to do the construction work. They started to work at once and transported the pontons they had already built to the riverbank. During the late hours on October 26–27 they loaded 52 pontons and 2 flatboats with 1,600 soldiers of Brigadier General William B. Hazen's brigade. Each ponton carried 28 soldiers and each flatboat about 80 soldiers. At 3 a.m. the contingent of pontons

General Hazen's Landing at Brown's Ferry

Battles and Leaders of the Civil War

and flatboats started floating down the river. Fog covered the valley. The fog-hidden craft moved noiselessly in the river. They passed undiscovered the point of Lookout Mountain in front of a line of Rebel pickets. An alert Confederate picket, hearing a sound, asked, "Is that a Yankee ponton?" One of his companions said, "No, it's a log." They knew it was either a log or ponton because the Confederates east of the town threw logs into the swift current above the ponton bridge at Chattanooga. When the logs floated down the river they smashed into the ponton bridge, and some with enough force broke loose the bridge pontons. If a ponton or a log came floating down the river, the Confederates guessed they had temporarily broken apart the bridge.[86]

After a nine-mile journey the soldier-filled pontons and flatboats arrived at Brown's Ferry. Daylight was just breaking through the atmosphere. The engineer soldiers turned the pontons and flatboats to the shore on Moccasin Point. When the pontons and flatboats scraped the river bottom, Hazen's infantrymen jumped out and quickly waded ashore and ran up the west river bank.

Alerted to the Yankees' presence, the Rebel pickets along the shore scattered, shouting, "Yanks, Yanks, Yanks." The Yankee soldiers hastened the running of the pickets farther inland by the fire of their musket balls at them. Unopposed, Hazen's attackers moved inland and seized a low range of hills and threw up breastworks.

General Smith sent down river Captain Perrin V. Fox of Colonel Innes' regiment, and Captain George W. Dresser, an engineer officer on his staff, and the engineer soldiers with the pontons, and balk and chess, to a point opposite Brown's Ferry, which they reached before full daylight. There they unloaded the bridge

materials and constructed a bridge 900-feet long across the river.
The bridge wobbled in a six-mile-an-hour current. Sometimes
the engineer soldiers were doubtful the bridge would hold, but
to allay their fears it held fast. At ten o'clock in the morning the
bridge opened for traffic. A *Harper's Weekly* writer wrote, "The
bridge is the best work of the kind that has been constructed by
the army at this point."[87]

The Union soldiers in Chattanooga, and the Confederate soldiers defending the river bank, too, were surprised to discover Cap-
tains Fox and Dresser and their engineer soldiers had built the
bridge. They did not think the task could be done in the face of the
enemy and in the swift current of the river.

At the same time General Hazen's brigade moved down to
Brown's Ferry, General Hooker marched his soldiers up to the two-
mile wide Valley of Lookout between Raccoon and Lookout Mountains. General Longstreet, on Lookout Mountain, watched Hooker's
soldiers. He anticipated sweeping down on them in the dark.
Hooker's soldiers knew Confederate soldiers were lurking in the
mountains; they were watchful. The Confederates were determined
to disrupt the supply road from Bridgeport to Chattanooga. At one
o'clock in the morning on October 29, Longstreet's soldiers assaulted
Hooker's soldiers. The adversaries engaged in a touch and go battle
for three hours. Hooker's soldiers held their ground. When the battle
ended, the Rebels were scrambling up the mountainside.

The Union's victorious battle to control the southwest bank of
the Tennessee River won a safe supply route to feed and equip the
hungry army. The wagon route from Brown's Ferry, across Moccasin Point peninsula, to the bridges at Chattanooga, reduced the
distance of the supply line to twenty-eight miles. Bragg's plan failed
to starve out his enemy. Yankee ingenuity lifted the siege. Thomas'
army had an uninterrupted line of communications to the depots
at Stevenson and Bridgeport.

The skill of the engineer soldiers in their role to reopen the
supply line received widespread notice. A Confederate newspaper
in Richmond stated, "This daring surprise in Lookout Valley on the
night of 26–27 October has deprived us of the fruits of
Chickamauga." Assistant Secretary of War Charles A. Dana, who
was visiting Grant at Chattanooga, reported, "Its brilliancy cannot
be exaggerated."[88]

The Nashville and Northwestern Railroad

Based on the day-to-day experience of moving supplies by
wagon trains and railroads, Grant and his staff officers concluded
there was a need for a backup railroad to transport supplies from

the Tennessee River to the Nashville depots. Before the rebellion initial steps were taken to extend the Nashville and Northwestern Railroad to Johnsonville.

Colonel Innes with a large force of his Michigan Engineer Regiment and civilian craftsmen had begun earlier the construction work. General Grant, aware of the size of the construction job, assigned the Missouri Engineer Regiment to assist on the work.

In December 1863, the Missouri Engineer Regiment, transferred from Corinth, arrived in Nashville, a new military strategic point. Troops were amassed around the city for an anticipated march south into enemy territory. The army, though, was dependent on the railroad between Louisville and Nashville for its supply line. Enemy guerrilla raids persistently cut and damaged the line. A situation developed that called for a large force to be provided to guard the railroad. Another problem was the fact the Cumberland River was not navigable to Nashville for steamers and gunboats. Grant decided, as a solution, to connect the Tennessee River to Nashville by building the Nashville and Northwestern Railroad to Johnsonville where there would be offloading of transports and supply boats, with transportation to Nashville provided by the railroad.

At the same time Colonel Bissell resigned from command of the Missouri Engineer Regiment. Lieutenant Colonel Henry Flad was promoted to colonel and assigned command of the regiment. Major William Tweeddale was promoted to lieutenant colonel, and Captain Eben M. Hill was promoted to major and command of the 3rd Battalion. To increase the engineer regiment's manpower, there also occurred the consolidation of the Missouri Engineer Regiment and the 25th Missouri Volunteer Infantry Regiment.

The regiment was detailed to continue the construction on the Nashville and Northwestern Railroad. The regiment was organized into three battalions, each with 400 engineer soldiers. To prepare to build the railroad in the spring the regiment pursued a training program conducted by Colonel Flad and Lieutenant Colonel Tweeddale.

Major Hill's battalion established its camp at Waverly, fourteen miles from the Tennessee River. The battalion's task was to build a bridge on the track route over a ravine 1,200 feet long and at a height of 800 feet at the ravine's deepest point. Hill faced a target date of two months to build the trestle bridge. The 400 workmen, employed on the bridge, worked six days a week from dawn until darkness.

Oak, hickory, and pine trees in the nearby forest were cut down and hewed into beams and poles. Spikes and bolts to fasten the trestle together were manufactured in the camp's blacksmith shop.

The track-laying was pushed rapidly toward the Tennessee River.

The engineer soldiers were proud of their work with primitive materials, hand tools, and engineering skills. They were given orders to build a bridge, and they built it.

"Little by little that great gap was filled," reported an observer. "Timber hewn down one day was dragged and put in its place in the bridge the next day. Every man in his own place doing the work required of him. When time was up, a train rolled over the completed trestle. It was the most important piece of work on the road, and so well built and solid was the structure, it remained in use for 20 years after the war till it was replaced with a steel and iron bridge."[89]

In early summer the railroad opened for traffic. The event received the *nom de guerre* "the wedding of the Cumberland and Tennessee rivers."

The battalion also constructed on the railroad several other bridges and trestlework, laid track, constructed platforms, switches, and turnouts. The engineers also built small forts and blockhouses, to be occupied by soldiers, for the protection of trestlework and bridges.

In August, the regiment transferred to General Sherman's Military Division of the Mississippi, arriving at the Chattahootchee River on August 25. From there it marched to the front, hauling siege guns, and arrived on September 1 at Jonesboro where it met the fire of enemy batteries. A month later the regiment entered Atlanta where it built and strengthened fortifications. While General Sherman pursued Hood's army, the regiment remained in Atlanta.[90]

Nashville and Chattanooga Railroad

Colonel Innes' regiment worked incessantly on the railroad during the year to keep in operation the 151-mile railroad from Nashville to Chattanooga. The line only operated between Nashville and Bridgeport on the north bank of the Tennessee. Innes' regiment continued the reconstruction work, for the fourth time, on the Bridgeport railroad bridge, but his work force was insufficient to achieve an expeditious completion. While Innes' work continued, supplies moved to Chattanooga from Bridgeport by the burdensome use of boats and wagon trains. Finally, Innes' work force completed the reconstruction of the bridge to enable trains to cross over on December 22.[91]

Running Water Ravine Bridge

There was also a critical need to complete the bridge at Running Water Ravine, Whiteside, Tennessee, to complete the fourteen miles of railroad tracks into Chattanooga.

Railroad Bridge at Bridgeport, Alabama

A pioneer officer, First Lieutenant Chesley A. Mosman, Pioneer Company, 59th Illinois Infantry, described the environment of Whiteside and the construction of the bridge. The target date for its completion was forty days.

Whiteside, where the pioneer company camped, was a half mile west of the bridge being built over the stream called Running Water. The pioneers were camped in the bottom of a canyon, as they called it. On the level ground Running Water was a noisy, broiling mountain stream which flowed with a swift current as the bed fell rapidly. A mile and a half away timber was cut in the woods for the bridge.

Lieutenant Mosman reported on December 9, "I have a hundred men at work on the bridge, mostly soldiers from Colonel William Grose's brigade who get one dollar a day extra pay. Two more bents (poles) were erected today. The pioneers have rigged up a windlass, a device for raising or hauling objects. With a windlass and tackle they raise bents in place. They completed one abutment for the bridge today."

He reported soldiers were always present from Colonel Grose's brigade to protect the bridge, and rifle pits were built to protect them.

By December 16 four bents were in place west of pier number one. The bents or trestles were built one above another in tiers, with each bent 16 feet high, and rose 112 feet from bed of stream to top of rail. Mosman reported he climbed to top of number two tier.

On December 22, Mosman wrote that at the bridge all the bents were in place to second pier on the west side of the stream and are making fair progress. He also reported the news (on the concurrently being built bridge) the train ran over the bridge at Bridgeport "this a.m. for the first time."

On December 27, Mosman reported Kendall, construction superintendent, said the bridge would be finished in ten days, with good weather. "What a godsend that will be for the poor fellows in Chattanooga who have to live on one quarter and one half rations."

Mosman wrote that January 10 was the coldest day of the year and the winter. "The teams are hauling timber for the bridge. They have the trestle work of the bridge nearly done. Only three yet to be put in on the super structure."

On January 13, Kendall said he would have the bridge finished tomorrow, the fourteenth.

Mosman reported on January 14, he witnessed the first train to go across the four-tiered trestle bridge, 780 feet in length, and 116 feet in height at center of ravine. The train consisted of an engine and five cars. "Nearly the whole brigade was there and all

Trestle Bridge Running Water Ravine

anxious to witness the sight." He reported a small train moved over at 2 p.m., and, as he observed, the bridge did not give a particle. After the train crossed, soldiers made a rush for it, and as many as could climbed aboard. Another train came over about dusk.

The first train went over to Chattanooga and returned, and both went over en route for Bridgeport. "This, of course," Mosman reported, "was of greatest importance to the army. Then the trains would pull right through to Chattanooga without stopping at Stevenson and Bridgeport. There would be no loading and un-loading at the Bridgeport bridge, and rations would be abundant in the army once more. It was also of great importance to the overworked teamsters and teams of animals who worked nearly day and night for three months in their vain endeavors to keep bread and meat in the mouths and clothes on the backs of 75,000 men." Proudly, Mosman declared, the bridge was built within four days of the estimated time.[92]

Arrival of Sherman on the Battlefield

On November 14, Sherman's soldiers began to arrive. Grant's first move was to deceive Bragg that the main Union attack would assault the Confederates' left flank. Sherman's soldiers at Bridge-port marched up to Lookout Valley. Then his army, less a division, marched quickly and unnoticed to Brown's Ferry and crossed the river on the ponton bridge. After assembling his soldiers on the east side of the river, Sherman marched them behind Chattanooga along the riverbank to Grant's left flank. The Confederates, hearing of the movement, thought Sherman was moving to the relief of Burnside at Knoxville. They failed to perceive the real purpose of the march, an attack on Bragg's right flank.

The engineer soldiers, who had concealed pontons on the river east of the town, at one o'clock in the morning on November 24 ferried 3,000 soldiers from the shelter of Friar's Island, northeast of the town, down the Tennessee River to Chickamauga River, and put the soldiers ashore at landing sites. On repeat trips other soldiers were put ashore. By dawn 8,000 soldiers had been ferried to the landing site. General Smith then supervised the construction of a 1,350-foot-long ponton bridge over the Tennessee River at the landing site. He also set the engineer soldiers to work building a ponton bridge across Chickamauga Creek. Both bridges were opened for traffic by noon for Sherman to cross the remainder of his army and march his soldiers to the northern end of Missionary Ridge. Dana, witnessing the operation, said, "I have never beheld any work done so well. I doubt if the history of war can show bridges of such extent laid so noiselessly and well in so short a time. I attribute it to the genius and intelligence of General William Farrar Smith."[93]

Decisive battles were then fought in front of Chattanooga on November 24–25. Hooker's soldiers defeated the Confederates in the battle of Lookout Mountain. Moving down the eastern slope of the mountain, Hooker's soldiers pushed Bragg's soldiers out of the valley and up onto Missionary Ridge where they encountered Sherman's soldiers. Together Sherman and Hooker drove the Rebels off Missionary Ridge southward to Ringgold, Georgia. Thus the Union fastened its grip on a victory.[94]

Newspaper Accounts

There were some soldiers in the western armies who believed editors of eastern newspapers failed to show any excitement about printing stories of the successes of the Union armies in the West.

Frank Leslie's Illustrated Weekly noticed the absence of such stories and wrote about the armies fighting in the West. By the close of 1863 Grant's army had achieved its strategic goals. It controlled the Ohio, Tennessee, Cumberland, and Mississippi Rivers. Frank Leslie wrote, "The sturdy prowess of the western soldiers will be one of the most glorious traditions of the war. They fight for the rivers that are the life current of their prosperity, the natural highways to the sea. They fight with a heroism and an inspiration equal to the grandeur of the prize."

Chapter 4

1864
A Bridge: The Most Successful Effort

Eastern Battlefield

A new year marked the beginning of the fourth year of the rebellion. The Union armies were in their winter camps.

In the winter months the engineer soldiers anticipated they would return to the battlefront with the change of seasons. To prepare for the event, they spent their winter camp days training to increase their innovative and imaginative bridge-building skills.

On the morning of February 6, Companies A and C of the Engineer Battalion marched out of their camp in the rain and mud to Stevensburg, east of Culpeper, where in the afternoon they arrived and pitched tents in a field. At 4:30 p.m. the companies struck their camp and resumed their march. The chronicler of the event recorded at 1 a.m. in the morning of February 7 the engineer soldiers marched two and a half miles, and described the march: "The journey was worse than the 'Mud Scrape of 1863.' Fires were kindled to light the very dark road. The animals and men labored at moving the ponton train, but some ponton wagons became stuck every rod or two in knee-deep mud. One had to be abandoned. The mules were used up, and two died on the road. The chess wagons had to be unloaded and loaded again and again. Some of them could not be moved to get near the bank of the Rapidan River by morning. The infantrymen marching along to cross the river dispensed with the bridge, and after a detail of engineer soldiers fixed a road for them through the woods, they waded into the river. The engineer soldiers camped a mile back from the riverbank. Soon after they laid down on the ground, they heard the order to 'fall in.' The two engineer companies marched back to Stevensburg. They found the roads in awful condition. Some of the ambulances broke down three times. On February 8 they reached their winter camp looking much the worse for their short campaign."[1] Why the chronicler thought the march worse than the one of February 1863, he omitted placing his reasons on the record.

Training activities also intensified in the 50th New York Volunteer Engineer Regiment at Well's Ford as their daily schedule called for work and drill from reveille at 5:30 a.m. to taps at 9 p.m.

Additional instructions of Colonel Stuart, the regimental commander, directed company commanders "to be very particular to have every man instructed in the salute, both with and without arms. Also, to inspect knapsacks so articles of clothing not absolutely necessary were removed so as to provide space in the knapsacks for rations. The men should not be overburdened with superfluous articles." He also assigned Lieutenant Colonel Spaulding the duty to provide general supervision over all the ponton bridge trains, directing their fitting out, conducting frequent inspections, and issuing directions as necessary to engineer officers and noncommissioned officers to keep the trains in efficient order at all times.[2]

After a return to his company from leave at home in late February, Thomas James Owen wrote to his parents he was comfortable in his winter quarters by a fire in the fireplace the engineer soldiers of his company built for him while he was away. "Good to me to get back again," he wrote, "and meet happy smiles and warm shake of hand from my noble boys. Company in fine condition. Indeed, it takes away dread of soldier's life to have good men with him. Men he can feel towards as he would a brother. Colonel Spaulding glad to see me back. The company is preparing to cross Rapidan River. Unexpected but I am willing to go."

In a follow-up letter to his parents, Owen wrote, "There were 101 men in his company with 80 percent for duty. The company was without a chaplain," he wrote, but "it found ways to respect the holy day." He closed his letter with the remark, "I am enjoying winter quarters."[3]

Grant Appointed General in Chief

President Lincoln decided when the armies marched to the battlefield with the return of spring there would be new leadership at the army's headquarters in Washington. Grant's two standout victories in the past year at Vicksburg and Chattanooga catapulted him into the limelight. Lincoln judged him to be the general to win victories in the battles still to be fought to end the rebellion. He ordered Grant to report to Washington on March 3,

1864, and appointed him general in chief of the army with command over all the field armies. Grant also received instructions to prepare an integrated battle plan for the armies in the East, Southeast, and West. Congress confirmed Grant's appointment, and voted to raise him to the rank of lieutenant general.

Lincoln and Grant were in complete accord on the appropriate strategy to seek out the rebellious armies, to destroy them on the battlefield, and to scatter the soldiers to their homes. Grant appointed Halleck his chief of staff, continued Meade as commander, Army of the Potomac, and appointed Sherman to command the Military Division of the Mississippi, composed of the armies of the Cumberland, Ohio, and Tennessee.

Grant eschewed commanding the armies from a desk in Washington. He pitched his headquarters in the field in a tent next to Meade's Army of the Potomac's headquarters.

On March 18 Owen wrote to his parents his company was conducting drills with the ponton bridge trains. He also wrote, "Rumors of Rebs crossing the river to attack. Will not be for their interests to do so. Preparations ready to give them a Yankee welcome. Men have orders to be ready to fall in. Company filled up. Everything fine. Mumps and measles prevalent. Little said about Grant taking over. Expect to know him better before long. Hope he will do as well here as in west."[4]

On April 16 Owen wrote to his parents, "Today I became 2nd Lieutenant. Earned confidence of my captain and colonel. I hope I prove worthy of trust."[5]

March to Battle Begins

Grantism became a reality within sixty days of his assuming command. Grant ordered a movement of the armies against the enemy to start on May 4. Meade and Sherman began to carry out their orders.

Army of the James

Grant also issued orders to Major General Benjamin F. Butler's Army of the James, composed of the X and XVIII Corps, to march up the peninsula and attack Lee's soldiers posted before Richmond and Petersburg. On May 16, Butler's soldiers met defeat at Drewry's Bluff, eight miles below Richmond, when they attacked troops under command of General Beauregard. Butler withdrew his soldiers to a defensive position across the Bermuda Hundred peninsula. An alert Beauregard posted his soldiers in a defensive position on Butler's front. The battlefield became a stalemate. The alternative was a costly assault against the enemy's fortified line.

Ponton Bridge, Rapidan River

Butler anchored the right flank of his army on the James River, about one mile from the Howlett House and its left flank on the Appomattox River's high ground overlooking Port Walthall, west of City Point. There were strong garrisoned points at Wilson's Wharf and Fort Powhatan, on the James River, which protected the channel of the river at important points, and on the occupation of those points depended the secure supply line of Grant's armies.[6]

Engineers March Out

The Engineer Battalion under Grant's orders to march out left its camp at 8 a.m. with each engineer soldier carrying 30 rounds of ammunition, 3 days' cooked meat, 6 days' coffee, and 4 days' hard bread. The battalion arrived at Richardsville, eleven miles east of Stevensburg, 2 p.m., set up camp, and worked on repairing the roads leading to the Rapidan River.

The 50th New York Engineers also marched out of camp. The order of march placed the ponton trains in the forward echelon followed by headquarters, tool, cook, hospital, and forage wagons. The blacksmith forge and rear guard formed the rear echelon. The engineer soldiers were to act as pioneers to see that the roads were repaired for the ponton trains to pass on.

On its first day of march the 50th New York Engineers constructed ponton bridges across the Rapidan River as follows:

Ely's Ford, canvas pontons, 150 feet.
Ely's Ford, wooden pontons, 190 feet.
Germanna Ford, wooden pontons, 220 feet.
Germanna Ford, canvas pontons, 220 feet.
Culpeper Ford, wooden pontons, 160 feet.

Meade's army spent the first day on the march crossing the Rapidan River. On the next day Meade's soldiers engaged in a battle in a dense growth of shrubs, vines, and trees, appropriately called "the wilderness."

Because the battle required more riflemen, Meade, on May 6, ordered the Engineer Battalion's and 50th New York Engineers' soldiers to take positions on the line as infantrymen. At 4 a.m. the Engineer Battalion was on detail on the battlefield when the V and VI Corps fell back, and the engineer soldiers without their arms observed the enemy in the woods. On orders to "fall in" they moved on a new front of the V Corps to rifle pits where they had left their arms. The color guard kept the flag in place, rallying troops around it, earning the commendation of Brigadier General Charles Griffin, commander of the Third Division, who was active in restoring order on the battlefield. Griffin placed one engineer company in position as skirmishers, and the other two engineer companies supported an artillery battery on the right flank. The chronicler of the Engineer Battalion wrote in the records, "Day's service long to be remembered! On no occasion were good qualities of the battalion better displayed than their affair in the wilderness." At daylight on the seventh the enemy made a spirited attack on the left flank of the line, but the Engineer Battalion quickly repulsed it.[7]

Lieutenant Owen's diary reports his detachment was ordered into the line of battle at Old Wilderness Tavern and remained for twenty-four hours in rifle pits in back of the first line of battle. Fighting raged, he wrote, in front of his detachment all day. His soldiers constructed a defensive barrier.[8]

When Meade relieved the engineer soldiers from rifle duty on the line the next morning, he said he would never again call upon them for such duty, unless absolutely necessary, adding, the army could not afford to lose the services of the skilled engineer soldiers from death and wounds in battle.

Unwilling to incur costly casualties from striking a foe posted behind defensive works, Grant ordered the Army of the Potomac on the night of May 7 to march to the left flank. By such tactics he expected to position the Union soldiers in back of Lee's army's right flank so as to force the Confederate soldiers to give up ground and march out of their defensive positions. Lee, alert to Grant's tactics, countered with his tactics of marching his army southeast to Spotsylvania.

The Engineer Battalion took up the march at sunset. A remark in the records stated it was a tedious night march, picking a way through wagon trains, but there were no stragglers and all the men answered roll call.

When Grant's marching troops arrived at Spotsylvania in the morning they discovered Lee's entrenched army posted there. Grant ordered an attack. Lee's soldiers held off the attack, but with heavy losses. Casualties were 12,000 for the Confederate army and 14,000 for the Union army.

The two armies fought to a standstill; they faced one another from their static positions for two weeks. The Engineer Battalion became occupied supervising the building of earthworks, building a crib bridge over the Po River, and repairing roads. It reported that on the night of May 15 it had "its first night of undisturbed rest since crossing the Rapidan river." On May 17 it marched and camped at Anderson Place, "fine open country with exhilarating effect on men after thickets, entanglements, miserable roads." Two days later the battalion marched in the advance with the cavalry at Guiney's Bridge over the Ny River, which after its capture, the engineers repaired and stood guard as skirmishers.

A march to the North Anna River by the Army of the Potomac on May 23 to turn Lee's left flank failed. The army crossed the river on the twenty-fourth at Jericho Mills on a 160-foot canvas ponton bridge constructed by the 50th New York Engineers, and then two days later in the dark of the night the army recrossed to the north bank of the river as Grant abandoned a frontal assault on Lee's position.

At 4 a.m. on the twenty-seventh the Engineer Battalion started another march south. In an unfortunate occurrence the ration wagon broke down and it had to be abandoned, with the consequence of the battalion being without rations for three days. After a 12-mile march the battalion crossed the Pamunkey River at Huntley's, and stopped to repair and build the road. On the thirty-first the battalion's rations arrived. Each soldier, who did his own cooking, received three days' rations: 30 pieces of hardtack, 1 pound of cured meat, $1/2$ pint of ground coffee (tea for the sick), brown sugar, and pepper and salt. Soldiers reported the beef cattle herd, driven along day and night with the army's wagon trains, "became poor" for food. Some soldiers foraged and purchased food from citizens.

The sellers refused to take the soldiers' money, which, they declared, "They could not eat it." Hardtack thus became the medium of exchange.

During the month of May Lieutenant Owen had little free time to write letters. In a short one, he wrote to his father, "I have been in the saddle night and day." The thought of horseback riding prompted him to answer a question his father had raised earlier as to why he needed a horse. Owen answered that all Corps of Engineers' officers must be mounted. To inform his father he had been instilled with the military *esprit de corps* that each soldier's outfit stood out as the best, he wrote, "It [Corps of Engineers] is highest branch of service. The pay is better."[9]

In a letter Owen found time to write to his family on May 30, he reported he had been on the move for the past month, but had arrived within fifteen miles of Richmond. "Heavy fighting going on. I can hear the boom of artillery knocking at the gate of the doomed city." He added he marched south with the II Corps, and had built three 100-foot long canvas ponton bridges over the North Anna River. Near the end of the month he joined Sheridan's cavalry corps marching southeast to the Pamunkey River where on May 27 his detachment built a 180-foot long canvas ponton bridge over the river. In his closing remarks he mentioned: "Hard fighting. Feel confident of success. Communications opened to White House. Teams went for rations. Foraged some to keep men and animals in condition. There is any quantity of beauty and stuff. Do not allow men to pillage. They ought not to. When we need something we send out a party to bring it in. Company in good condition. We would sacrifice anything to put down rebellion.

"Now on peninsula. Believe McClellan did true way to Richmond. Month has been a bloody one. Army has done nobly. Lee driven out of favorite strongholds. I have me a good boy for a servant. He was a house servant and very handy, name is Albert. Hope to help you with money. Tell mother I am much better off than I ever was before since I have been in Army. Have a horse, a servant, good rations."[10]

After a seven-mile march on June 1, Grant's soldiers arrived at Cold Harbor. The engineer soldiers were immediately put to work opening roads through the pine timber. Fires were lighted to illuminate the road at night. Along the line of battle they assisted the infantrymen and artillerymen in the building of defense works, rifle pits, gun batteries, entrenchments, and a mine to blow up an enemy-held salient.

In a repeat of past failed tactics, Grant on June 3 ordered his soldiers to assault Lee's soldiers in their entrenched position at Cold Harbor. The futile attack, and consequent failure, netted Grant's soldiers 13,000 casualties against 3,000 for Lee's soldiers defending their dug-in position.

Grant declared in reaction to the Union defeat he was determined to "fight it out on this line . . . if it takes all summer." Contrary to the tactics that ended in defeat at Cold Harbor, Grant held fast to his belief in the tactics of skirting the enemy's flanks, forcing him out of his dug-in position, and battling on an open battlefield.

To break the stalemate and make real his tactical doctrine, Grant by June 6 had conceptualized his plan of operations to

Canvas Ponton Bridge, North Anna River

deploy the army out of its static position at Cold Harbor, march it to the Chickahominy and James Rivers, bridge and cross over them, and march toward Petersburg, twenty-two miles south of Richmond. A successful redeployment would force Lee out of his fixed position and cut his railroad connection for replacement soldiers and sources of supplies in the South.

The danger in Grant's tactics required the boldness of a tough-willed general. Grant possessed the qualities needed to impose his tactics. Firstly, he had to break off combat with a determined and alert foe, who knowing of his maneuvering for position, would hurriedly pursue him. The initiative had to be denied to Lee. Secondly, Grant had to redeploy 100,000 soldiers and the thousands of animal-drawn wagons transporting the army's supplies directly across the front of the enemy's position, to the left flank, southward through swamp and woodland, and finally bridge and cross the dangerous Chickahominy and James Rivers. The total Union movement had to be completed before Lee, who, when he discovered it, could hasten his soldiers south, place them into position in front of the advancing Yankees, and organize them for attack. In a preliminary act, based on his plan, Grant sent Colonel Comstock, of his engineer staff, to General Butler at the Army of the James, to ascertain what preparations were necessary for a quick crossing of the James River.[11]

Comstock required three days to complete his assignment to confer with Butler.

The records of the campaign fail to provide specific information on what action Butler took to assist the Army of the Potomac in its preparations to cross the James. Butler believed it to be Comstock's responsibility to make the necessary arrangements with his army's staff for the support the Army of the James could provide on the James' operation.

Butler did have the presence of mind to take one action. At 5:30 a.m., June 9, he telegraphed General Benham, the commander of the Engineer Brigade, at Fort Monroe, and informed him Comstock was at his field headquarters. He suggested to Benham he travel up the river at once to Bermuda Hundred. Benham replied, in essence, he took his orders from General Meade, and could not leave. He did acquiesce to say inasmuch as Comstock was a member of Grant's staff, Comstock could give him orders in Grant's name, and if Comstock ordered him to come to meet with him he would comply with that order.

Butler received information from Comstock to the effect the Army of the Potomac planned to cross the James River near the mouth of the Chickahominy River. He also knew he had on hand in his army 3,000 feet of ponton bridge equipage, the property of the Army of the Potomac. From the discussion with Comstock it did not occur to Butler to order the return of the equipage by its shipment down the river to the vicinity of City Point, which his soldiers had occupied as his army marched up the peninsula. To add to the complexity of the situation, on June 10 one of Butler's staff officers, for reasons not made of record, sent the ponton equipment back to Benham at Fort Monroe.

To implement Grant's battle orders the engineer soldiers, on their first task, supervised the work of the infantrymen in digging a trench line between the two contending armies to enable the rear echelon of the Union army to be protected as the frontal units marched away from Lee's entrenched soldiers. Without protection, Lee's army, discovering Grant's withdrawal, would pounce upon the remaining soldiers. Work on the trench line started on June 9, and the engineers and soldier working parties completed it within two days. The line, located about a mile north of Cold Harbor, extended from Elder Swamp to Allen's Mill Pond, between the Chickahominy and Pamunkey Rivers. On the night of June 12, after dark, soldiers of the Army of the Potomac's II and VI Corps occupied the trench line to protect other units as they marched out.

The march accomplished a difficult maneuver to the Army of the Potomac's left flank for the purpose of marching around the enemy's right flank. The units on the army's right flank vacated their defensive positions and marched in back of the units on their left flank in the trench line to the roads leading them to the Chickahominy River and the bridge sites to cross the river.

The scene shifted to the Chickahominy River where the 50th New York Engineers, under Colonel Spaulding's supervision, had arrived to commence building the bridges.

Sites selected for the crossing of the army were (1) Long Bridge, about twenty miles southeast of Cold Harbor; (2) Jones' Bridge, five miles down river from Long Bridge; and (3) Windsor Shades, four miles down river from Jones' Bridge. Terrain conditions at Windsor Shades made it necessary to change the bridge to Cole's Ferry.

(1) *Long Bridge.* Major George G. Ford commanded the engineers who built the bridge. Three officers were sent ahead to survey the crossing site. Ford started the wagons with the pontons moving to the river at 4 p.m., June 12. On the way he met the three officers he had sent ahead as they returned. They reported to him the information the V Corps' staff officers had told them there was only one channel in the river, about 100 feet wide, but upon examination they believed there were two streams separated by an island. Because of the Confederate sharpshooters on the south bank they could not approach close enough to sketch the exact terrain.

When Ford arrived at the riverbank, he found his most difficult job was to clear away the debris of the old bridge. Broad swamps bordered the approaches, and it became necessary to build the bridge near the narrow road leading to the destroyed bridge. Because the engineer soldiers were timid about crossing the stream to make a reconnaissance, Ford, with soldiers from the 3rd Indiana and 22nd New York infantry regiments, crossed the channel in a boat. He verified the truth of his officers' report about the two streams. The nearer stream measured about 100 feet wide; the island between about 250 feet wide; and the channel on the island's south side measured 60 feet wide.

When the second boat load of Indiana and New York infantrymen crossed the north stream, Confederate riflemen shot at them. The Union soldiers crossed the island to the south channel by edging their way over on fallen trees, and after a short skirmish forced the withdrawal of the Confederates. Bolstered by the presence of the infantrymen on the island, the engineer soldiers ignored the rifle fire and started to construct the 100-foot wooden ponton bridge over the north channel. One engineer soldier was killed by enemy rifle fire. Captain Frederick H. Pettes then formed some engineer soldiers of Company D and they dragged three pontons across the island. In two and a half hours they cleared away the debris and constructed a 60-foot wooden ponton bridge across the south channel.

With construction of the bridges completed, the cavalry crossed over to screen the crossing of the II and V Corps. The next day, the soldiers completed crossing the river at 1:30 p.m. The engineers dismantled the bridges, loaded the pontons on the wagons, and marched with the other soldiers to the James River.

(2) *Jones' Bridge.* The leading troops of the VI Corps arrived about noon on June 13 at the bridge site. There, too, Major Edmund O. Beers, the engineer officer in command, found an island about 240 feet wide divided the river into two channels. The north channel measured about 60 feet wide, and the one on the south side about 40 feet wide. The engineer soldiers first cleared away timber and the pile of debris the current washed up against the old bridge.

One company under Beers' command built a 60-foot canvas ponton bridge across the south channel. Another company built an adjacent 60-foot wooden ponton bridge across the main channel and a 40-foot wooden ponton bridge over the south channel. It took the engineers about an hour and a half to bridge both channels. The next morning the engineers constructed a third bridge, a trestle bridge built from timbers cut in the area.

The VI and IX Corps completed crossing the Chickahominy by 10 a.m., June 14. Colonel Spaulding then ordered the ponton bridges to be dismantled and the equipage taken to Charles City Court House, near the James River, to be used for a bridge there.

(3) *Cole's Ferry.* When the engineers arrived at Windsor Shades to build a ponton bridge for the supply wagons and the security guard to cross, Spaulding discovered the surrounding area to be marsh and swampland. The site could not be used unless the engineers build timber-trestle bridges and corduroy roads. The nature of the terrain left Spaulding with the job of finding a better place to build a bridge to cross the much-needed supply wagon trains.

According to Spaulding's map a better place seemed to be Cole's Ferry, about another eight miles down the river. Captain Walker V. Personius, Company G of the regiment, made a trip down river to examine the site, but he found the river much wider than shown on the available sketchy map. The Chickahominy was not a wide river, but in the area where it emptied into the James, it flowed through flat bottom lands where only a slight rise in the water increased the river to a width of 1,200 feet.

From his observations of the river, Captain Personius quickly concluded his pontons were insufficient to bridge the Chickahominy at that point. He reported his findings to the officer in charge of the supply trains. On June 14 when the information reached Major Duane, Meade's staff engineer officer, he ordered Spaulding to assemble all the wooden and canvas pontons in his regiment and build the bridge at Cole's Ferry.

After his arrival at Cole's Ferry, Captain Personius put his soldiers to work building a wharf made up of ponton boats on each side of the river. He also assembled some pontons into a raft and ferried small squads of cavalrymen, messengers, and supply wagons to the south side of the river.

Major Beers, who had supervised the bridge building at Jones' Bridge, arrived with his engineer soldiers at Cole's Ferry at one o'clock. Major Ford, who had supervised the bridge building at Long Bridge, and then marched to Charles City Court House, arrived at Cole's Ferry about five o'clock in the afternoon. Thus all the pontons of the regiment were in place at the Cole's Ferry site.

On the south side of the Chickahominy the engineers built a raised corduroy road across the marshlands, connecting to the bridge for a distance of 200 feet. They started to build the bridge from each shore, but when the engineers on both shores fastened all their pontons in place, an open space of thirty feet remained between the two working parties. Quickly improvising, the engineers detached the pontons from the north shore and connected

Cole's Ferry, Chickahominy, Raised Corduroy Road

Photographic File, U.S. Army Engineer School

them to the section jutting out from the south shore. To connect the ponton bridge to the north shore they then constructed a timber causeway with a corduroy road. The 1,240-foot long bridge opened for wagon traffic at 3 a.m. on June 15. The timber trestle and corduroy approaches were about 450 feet long. The supply trains proceeded to move from White House on the Pamunkey River to the Chickahominy.

The rear guard protecting the train of supply wagons crossed the Cole's Ferry Bridge late the next day. When the traffic cleared the bridge, the engineer soldiers dismantled it, formed the pontons into rafts, and towed them by the steamboat *James A. Stevens* down the Chickahominy River. When the steamboat reached the James River it turned upstream to deliver the ponton rafts to the site selected for building a bridge across the James River.

The delay in building the bridge at Cole's Ferry had a disastrous effect on Grant's plan for a rapid movement of the Army of the Potomac. The much-needed train of supply wagons arrived late. Also, the wooden and canvas pontons used at Cole's Ferry were to be used to build a second bridge across the James River, but they could not be used at the James until all the soldiers and wagon trains crossed the Chickahominy on June 16, and then the bridge taken apart, pontons, balk, and chess loaded on wagons and hauled to the James River.

In concurrent action at Butler's Army of the James, activity sprung to life on the bridging of the James River. As a result of Comstock's meeting with Butler, and the foresight of an alert engineer officer, Brigadier General Godfrey Weitzel, chief engineer Army of the James, steps were taken to assure the Army of the Potomac's successful crossing of the James. Weitzel issued orders on June 12 to First Lieutenant Peter S. Michie, a staff engineer officer, to examine the ground near Fort Powhatan for a bridge to cross the James.

The fort had been captured on May 28 by two infantry regiments of Butler's army as they marched up the peninsula. The fort had been employed by the Rebels to harass by artillery fire boats or naval vessels that sailed up the river. The Rebels failed to strengthen the fort with a large complement of guns, or post within it a strong force of soldiers. Butler's soldiers took hold of the fort as "part of the Union's grand operation on the river."[12]

With the ponton equipment available to the engineers at the James, the Fort Powhatan location was the nearest one to City Point, and a practicable place to build a ponton bridge. Also, the location was beyond the observation of the enemy. It also provided a favorable terrain to catch the enemy by surprise. If the Army of the Potomac crossed on the terrain occupied by the Army of the James at Bermuda Hundred, it would do so under the watchful eye of the enemy and face his weapons' fire.

The area Michie was assigned to survey was directly south of Charles City Court House where the James River made a turn to flow north to south. Douthat was on the east bank of that stretch of the river, and from that point the army's crossing would be from east to west. Later reports confirmed the army crossed from east to west, but other names were given for the crossing site, i.e., Douthad's, Wilcox's Landing, Fort Powhatan, or Wyanoke Point. Maps though relate the crossing occurred in the subject area.[13]

The James River narrowed at Fort Powhatan and Wyanoke Point (also called Neck), thirty-four miles below Richmond and fourteen miles below City Point. At that narrow point Lieutenant Michie examined three locations for the building of a floating bridge.

(1) At Fort Powhatan the river measured 1,250 feet wide. There were two approaches to the river's bank from the east, but they traversed 1,000 yards of marshlands. The approaches on the west side were in good condition and they led by a gradual ascent to a bluff where Fort Powhatan stood.

(2) A quarter of a mile upstream of the Fort Powhatan site the James River measured 1,570 feet wide. Michie on his survey there found two approaches from the east, but likewise over marshlands 800 yards in width. He found the approaches on the west side were in good condition.

(3) Michie on a survey at a point three-quarters of a mile above Fort Powhatan measured the James at 1,992 feet in width. The point's approaches on the east side were over sand and gravel beds.

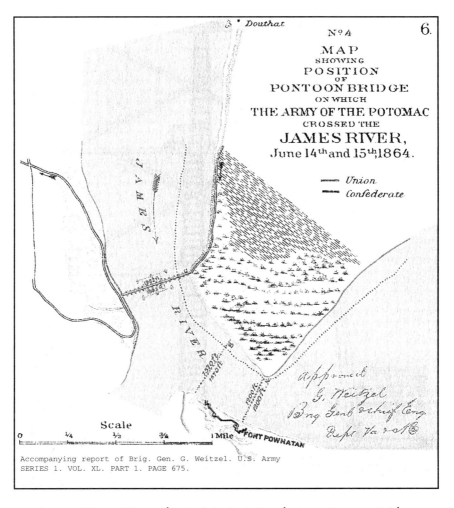

James River, Wyanoke Point, Fort Powhatan, Ponton Bridge

O.R. Atlas, Plate 68(6)

To build approaches on the western side, the engineers would need to clear away large trees, fill ruts and gullies, and construct a ramp up the bluff. A connecting road to the Petersburg and City Point Road would have to be constructed for a march route.

After reviewing Michie's surveys, Weitzel selected the third site (unnamed), three quarters of a mile above Fort Powhatan, as the most desirable one to construct a ponton bridge. On June 13 he sent a wire to Comstock at Grant's headquarters stating he would need thirty-six hours' notice to build the approaches to the bridge. Then, acting without awaiting Comstock's reply, Weitzel sent Michie back to the selected bridge site with the engineer soldiers to begin the cutting of the timber for the causeway landing to the ponton bridge.

In the afternoon a message arrived for Weitzel from Grant announcing the head of the column of the Army of the Potomac would reach the bridgehead at 10 a.m., June 14, the next day. Surprised, but alert to the situation, Weitzel pressed his engineer officers and soldiers to speed up the construction of the approaches. By nightfall an engineer work force had cut and trimmed about 1,200 feet of timber, in logs averaging 6 inches in diameter and 26 feet in length. The engineers brought down to the creek above Fort Powhatan about 3,000 feet of timber, formed rafts, and floated them to the James. Cypress logs, almost $3^1/2$ feet in diameter, were used in building approaches in the shallow part of the river.

Tired, swearing, and sweating in the humid heat the engineer soldiers, aided by work details from II Corps infantry units, worked in the mud late into the night and early morning. By 9:45 a.m., fifteen minutes before Grant's arrival time, the approaches stood in place on both sides of the river, including a 150-foot pier over the soft marsh on the east bank of the James.

Since the night of June 11, Grant's soldiers were on the march to the James River. The head of the II Corps' column reached Wilcox's Landing on the James at 5:30 p.m., two days later. Before dark all troops of the corps had taken up positions within the bridgehead and occupied the left flank of the defense line. By noon the next day, the VI Corps had arrived and occupied the center position of the line. The IX Corps arrived at 6:30 p.m. and took up its position on the right flank of the line. On the night of June 13 the V Corps, which had placed itself between the marching Army of the Potomac and the Confederate army to fight off any enemy attacks, withdrew its support to the cavalrymen and marched to the James. The V Corps joined the other corps the next day, June 14, and relieved the II Corps from the line to enable the latter to start the crossing of the James River on ferryboats.

Grant outfoxed Lee. Lee thought the 2nd Brigade of Wilson's cavalry division and the V Corps were marching south to join with Butler's army on the Bermuda Hundred peninsula, and then to attack Richmond. Lee in his response to the estimate of the tactical situation failed to discover the destination of the Union soldiers marching across the peninsula between the Chickahominy and James Rivers. At 9 p.m. on June 14, Lee sent a message to the Confederate secretary of war stating, "The enemy has disappeared."

Grant's soldiers completed a successful fifty-mile march to the James. They were free of their adversary. They were ready to cross the river, but, to their surprise, they camped idly on the river's bank because a bridge had not been built to enable them to cross the James.

On the march, Grant stopped at the headquarters of General Butler early in the morning of June 14 and issued to him a number of orders to start his army in motion:

(1) Major General William F. Smith was to march his XVIII Corps to Cole's Ferry to be ferried across the James to City Point to join the Army of the James' soldiers there. Smith would then march to Petersburg to seize the city before the arrival of Lee's troops.

(2) Grant also ordered Butler to contact Admiral Lee to send gunboats to Fort Powhatan to protect the army's bridge.

(3) Grant also informed Butler that Hancock's II Corps would be ferried over the James that night to reinforce General Smith at Petersburg.

Grant also telegraphed a message to President Lincoln on his operations.[14]

At the site selected for the bridge, Weitzel, early in the morning of June 14, sat anxiously waiting for the arrival of the pontons. To speed up construction of the bridge, he sent a dispatch boat down the river to look for the steamer towing the pontons up the river with instructions to tell the engineer officer in charge "to rush" his arrival.

Finally, after being en route for twenty-two hours and traveling at about three miles per hour, at noon the same morning, the steamer arrived at the construction site with the pontons. As fast as the pontons could be taken off the towlines, they were formed into sections and floated into position to form the bridge.

Early the same afternoon Duane arrived at the bridge site and relieved Weitzel of the task of supervising the building of the bridge. Weitzel willingly relinquished the job. Duane gave the Engineer Battalion's soldiers the command to build the bridge! Without hesitation they jumped into the slime and mud and water up to their shoulders, and by zeal and energy in one hour built a 200-foot abutment that reached out to the deep water. Upon completion of the task, the Engineer Battalion's soldiers were transported in pontons to the far shore.

A company from the 15th New York Engineers, which traveled up the James on the steamer with the pontons, and the 50th New York Engineers, who built the bridges on the Chickahominy, participated in the construction of the ponton bridge over the James River's channel. The heavy wooden pontons were formed into a bridge simultaneously from both shores. The Engineer Battalion's soldiers worked on the far shore and the 15th and 50th Volunteer Regiments' soldiers worked the near shore. Because the James River was tidal to Richmond with swift tidal currents, the pontons had to be fastened by guy lines on the up and down sides of the river. To provide guy-line anchorage for the pontons in the main channel where the river measured 85 feet deep, three schooners were anchored abreast above the bridge and also the same number below the bridge.

Late in the afternoon Benham arrived from Fort Monroe. He took over command of the engineer soldiers and supervised the completion of the bridge.

By midnight, after eight hours under construction, the bridge opened to traffic. It was constructed with 101 pontons, and 200 feet of trestle; a draw section made up of rafts 100 feet in length was built into the 2,200-foot-long bridge, with a width of 13 feet.

(A number of writers started and perpetuated the tradition the James River Bridge was the longest ponton bridge built during the Civil War. There is information reporting the earlier bridge built over the Ohio River at Paducah, Kentucky, in September 1861 deserves recognition as a longer bridge.)

At 12:45 a.m. on June 15 Benham received a message from Meade, written an hour earlier, stating the IX Corps should start crossing the bridge at once, but twenty minutes later another message arrived from Meade containing an order to hold up any troop movements over the bridge until "the big train gets nearer to us." The big train composed the animal-drawn wagon trains and animal herds from White House making their delayed movement down the roads and over the bridge at Cole's Ferry on the Chickahominy. Meade wanted his supplies near the army when it crossed over the James.

Meade, though, did state Benham was at liberty to send over the bridge trains and surplus artillery of the V, VI, and IX Corps. If Meade had not held up the crossing of the soldiers of the IX Corps,

Approach to James River Ponton Bridge

James River Ponton Bridge

General Grant Observing the Crossing of the James River

Porter, *Campaigning with Grant*

there would have been two corps of his army instead of one to march to Petersburg (the II had crossed earlier on ferryboats). Grant's orders to Meade were to the effect one corps was to remain on the east side "until the artillery and wagons are well over." Grant declared "expedition in the crossing is what is wanted."[15]

Finally, at six o'clock on the same morning the heavy traffic of the Army of the Potomac started crossing over the long bridge. The units that crossed were the V, VI, and IX Corps, and 3rd Cavalry Division, the Army Headquarters, and finally the army's wagon trains. The combat units crossed in fifteen hours.[16]

It was reported as General Grant stood upon the bluff on the bank of the river watching with unusual interest the busy scene spread out before him he was presented a sight which had never been equaled even in his extended experience in all the various phases of warfare. His cigar had been thrown aside, his hands were clasped behind him, and he seemed lost in the contemplation of the spectacle. The great bridge was the scene of a continuous movement of infantry columns, batteries of artillery, and wagon trains. The approaches to the river on both banks were covered with masses of troops moving briskly to their positions or waiting patiently their turn to cross. At the improvised ferries steamboats were gliding back and forth with the regularity of weavers' shuttles. A fleet of transports covered the water below the bridge, and gunboats floated lazily upon the stream, guarding the river above.[17]

The army wagon trains, vulnerable to attack and defenseless if a large Confederate force attacked them, moved all the way from White House on their circuitous route. They took thirty-one hours to cross their sixty-one-mile column over the bridge.

Making up the army trains were:

4,300	wagons
835	ambulances
34,000	horses
22,000	mules
2,800	head of beef cattle

Early in the morning on June 19 the engineer soldiers began the task of dismantling the bridge. The feat of its construction and the vast tonnage that crossed over the river on its roadway became history.[18]

Grant received a message from President Lincoln, "I begin to see it. You will succeed. God bless you all. A. Lincoln."[19]

A correspondent of *Harper's Weekly* reported on the army's crossing of the James' River Bridge:

"As we approach the ponton bridge we see distinctively huge bodies of infantry, cavalry, horses, artillery, and wagons moving across the bridge. They extend across the entire length of the bridge, and can be seen wending along from far away up the east bank of the James, enveloped in a dense cloud of dust, while on western bank is a part of the great body which has already effected its crossing.

"The army has been steadily marching for 50 hours. A brigade of infantry with possibly 1,000 cavalry horses and a battery of artillery has just gone over, and at this moment not more than 20 men are marching in units or couples across the bridge.

"Now comes a man leading a horse, now a cannon, now a dozen teamsters, now a battalion of negro soldiers. But a heavy body of troops of all arms is passing out of the woods filing to the bridge, and besides columns of infantry there are immense numbers of horses, long trains of wagons, numberless pieces of artillery and caisson.

"Now another body can be seen emerging from the woods on the river bank and passing on to the pontons, a long procession of beef cattle. They are in little detachments of 4, 5, or a half a dozen each, every detachment preceded and followed by two or more negro soldiers.

"Meridian is an hour gone and about a mile up the river a heavy volume of dust is sweeping southward.

"Forward march the long line of cattle. All the afternoon they advance and pour over the river. The movement is slow. I am told that in this whole mass there are but 2,500 head, or some six days supply for the Army of the Potomac.

"Below the bridge may be seen a fleet of transports which have been accumulating waiting for the bridge to be removed before they can pass to City Point, the new base of supplies. It should be mentioned here that Warren's corps protected the crossing of the trains.

"Our artist sketched Fort Powhatan just below the ponton bridge."[20]

An observer declared the sight of the bridge: "So light as scarcely to be capable of bearing a man on horseback."[21]

Impressed with the drama of the historic construction event, General Benham wrote in his report:

"My officers and men were scarcely allowed any sleep during this time for it was in anxiety not to say trembling that I saw the destinies of this whole army of our country even committed to this single frail bridge with the steamers and other vessels drifting against it, with most of its planking worn entirely through, and I dared not stop the living stream of men and matter to sheath it.

"By 7 p.m. on the 18th the last animals were over and I breathed free again. . . . The most successful effort on a large scale with ponton bridging that has ever occurred in our country, if it does not rival those in any other land."[22]

The building of the ponton bridges across the Chickahominy and James Rivers by the officers and engineer soldiers of the Engineer Battalion and the Volunteer Engineer Regiments marked an outstanding achievement. They worked strenuously under difficult conditions. They earned Benham's plaudits.

Butler's Engineers Build Bridges

To maintain the mobility of Grant's march on Petersburg, the engineers faced the tasks to build bridges on the James and Appomattox Rivers. In July the 1st New York Engineers built a ponton bridge made up of sixty-eight pontons across the James river, below Four Mile Creek, at Deep Bottom.[23]

On August 3, the same engineer regiment built a 560-foot-long bridge, made up of canvas pontons, at Broadway Landing on the Appomattox River, west of City Point. Soldiers who crossed the Deep Bottom Bridge marched south to cross the Appomattox River on the Broadway Landing Bridge on their march to Petersburg.[24]

Grant's successful crossing of his armies over the James River, and concentrating them at Petersburg, forced Lee to deploy soldiers from Richmond and Bermuda Hundred to reinforce his diminishing force at Petersburg. With Confederate defenses

GENERAL GRANT'S CAMPAIGN—THE PONTOON BRIDGE OVER THE JAMES RIVER, ABOVE FORT POWHATAN.—Sketched by A. R. Waud.—[See Page 419.]

James River Scenes: Fort Powhatan, Transports

Ponton Bridge at Deep Bottom, James River

weakened on its front, the Army of the James was able to deploy troops to Richmond and Petersburg fronts from its position on Bermuda Hundred peninsula.

The army's tactical movements required the engineers to build a number of bridges on the James and Appomattox Rivers.

During the night of September 28, one hundred 1st New York Engineers' soldiers built a 1,320-foot ponton bridge across the James River at Aiken's Landing near Varina Road. The bridge was constructed with sixty-seven pontons. The engineers completed the bridge after six and a half hours of work, early the next morning. From its bridgehead soldiers, redeploying to reinforce the soldiers at Petersburg, and their wagon trains, marched to Deep Bottom on the Appomattox.[25]

Lieutenant Owen's Foray with Sheridan

Sheridan's cavalry corps since the first of the month had been on a foray attacking the Confederates in the area of the Rapidan River. Lieutenant Owen, who had accompanied Sheridan with his detachment of fifty engineer soldiers and a wagon train of eight canvas pontons, began his march to return to the Army of the Potomac on June 6, and crossed the Pamunkey River at New Castle. On June 11 the cavalrymen engaged the Confederates near Gordonsville, successfully driving them off the field. With his supply of ammunition depleted and encountering a heavy enemy force on June 12, Sheridan ordered his corps to fall back. He then marched his corps due east, living off the land, to King and Queen Court House, arriving there six days later.

Farther south the same day at the James River the engineer soldiers dismantled the single, snake-shaped ponton bridge Grant's soldiers had used to cross over the river. Another means would have to be provided for Sheridan to cross when he reached the river's bank.

Concurrently with Sheridan's march, at Petersburg occurred the Union's attack against the Confederates after a three-day march to their lines. To counter the Union's attack, Lee quickly employed tactics to turn the course of the battle to his advantage. He had used the time the Yankees boldlessly dillied and dallied to redeploy his soldiers south of the James to reinforce General Beauregard posted in position behind fixed fortifications. The Union's head-on attack against the entrenched Confederate soldiers accomplished nought but casualties.

A siege operation became the accepted alternative at Petersburg.

Sheridan's cavalrymen, still moving south, crossed the Pamunkey River on June 19 to White House. According to Lieutenant Owen the cavalry corps and his engineer soldiers spent three days there organizing an 800-wagon train of supplies, which departed for the James River during the night of June 22–23. Owen further reported the cavalrymen had a difficult time fighting to protect the train from enemy raids. "The rebels seemed bound to have it, but because of good pluck of Yankees they failed."

The entire force of cavalrymen, engineer soldiers, and wagon trains began to arrive at the James on June 25. Owen used his detachment's pontons to build a dock to tie up the steamers assigned to ferry over the long train of wagons and Sheridan's cavalrymen.

In a letter home Owen wrote it was slow work for the next five days at the James, as the wagon train and the cavalrymen arrived, to load them on the steamers waiting to carry them over the river. On the twenty-ninth, Owen's detachment, bringing up the rear, crossed "the noble James," and marched to City Point where it arrived the next day at the cavalry corps' and his detachment's new camp. "It was like home," Owen added, "after being on a march for a month, several hundred miles in heat and dust of Virginia." He closed with the remark his detachment was glad to return to Grant's army, but to the important question as to when his soldiers would be paid no one could provide an answer.

As Owen's cavalry ponton train remained detached from the regiment, which was stationed on the line at Petersburg building defense works, Owen wrote home that on July 4 "with little to do" he journeyed to his company, [I], at the front "for a fine dinner, which did honor to its donors." He reported from the regiment's fortified position he observed the town (Petersburg) in the distance.

On the visit to his company, Owen observed static positions along the entire battle line where the contending armies faced one another from hastily built, strong fortifications. At some points the opposing soldiers were only separated by 100 yards. Under the supervision of the engineers the infantrymen dug deep trenches and built underground structures safe from fearsome artillery and mortar projectiles. The structures were also a means to dodge sharpshooters' bullets. Neither army seemed capable, much less willing, to assault the enemy's fortifications to force a breakthrough.[26]

How Owen and his detachment of engineer soldiers, posted in their static positions occupied themselves for the remainder of the year is revealed in Owen's insightful letters to his family.

On August 8 he wrote home he followed a busy routine, as the newly appointed quartermaster of the engineer detachment, keeping in operating order and repairing the ponton train, and looking after the government property in his charge. A large portion of the property consisted of 47 wagons, 18 pontons for 400 feet of bridging, 300 public animals, horses, and mules, which he remarked was "quite enough for one man."[27]

On August 28 he wrote: "Quiet—remarkably so. Rain cleared out flies. Still in our nice little camp. Animals doing well. Several ponton trains here. Put on alert for cavalry attack. Learned Weldon Railroad completely cut by Company I at front. Continual firing between enemies. Strength of army reduced by ETS (expiration of term of service), but what is left is of the true stamp. We all want peace but a union more. I do not like war or soldiering, but I could not think of abandoning the glorious cause we have undertaken until it is successful. I wish some at home would come down and help, but afraid they will have to be drafted. Pity wretches who wont help maintain their government. I'd rather be shot than scared to death."[28]

Owen wrote home on August 31: "I have been ordered to re-join Company I. No need for ponton bridge building jobs. Every-thing goes well. Pleased with my duties. That is my nature. I always try to make myself contented and pleased with anything that is my duty to be engaged in. I hope war will come to an end ere long."[29]

On December 1 from Poplar Grove Church, Owen wrote home: "The regiment has been brought together on a pleasant move, and spending time fixing up for winter. Winter houses built for us. Have beautiful camp. Nothing here compares with it."[30]

On December 9 Owen wrote home: "One canvas ponton train sent off on a mission. Unable to say where. Other trains sent back to City Point. My train is still here. Have a good log house, warm. Last night stormed, sleet, this morning ground covered with snow. Yesterday coldest day. We hold ourselves in readiness to go with V Corps. I wont speculate where. I think we will settle down for win-ter, pleases me. I feel deep interest in noble boys I have served with for so long."[31]

On December 10, from Poplar Grove Church, Owen wrote home: "Whole command ordered out and we on move. Rains made roads muddy but march went off well. Marched all night. At day-light at Nottoway river, 20 miles, IX Corps with us. Ordered to bridge river. Used 8 pontons. V Corps crossed from opposite side. They were out tearing up Weldon Railroad. Corps finished crossing at dusk. Took up bridge, camped till 2 a.m."

On December 16 Owen wrote home: "Started back to camp, arrived at noon. Unpleasant march on frozen ground. Bitter wind, could not keep warm. My most unpleasant day in service, but when arrived in camp and found good food and fires blazing away in our log huts we soon forgot cold."[32]

Winter Camp Chapel with Castle Insignia on Steeple, Built by
Engineer Soldiers

Library of Congress

Western Battlefront
Bridges on the Road to Atlanta

On May 6 Sherman closed the winter camp of the Military
Division of the Mississippi. The division consisted of General John
M. Schofield's Army of the Ohio, Thomas' Army of the Cumberland,
McPherson's Army of the Tennessee, and Major General George
Stoneman's cavalry force, and they were prepared to do battle. The
division's reported strength was approximately 105,000 soldiers,
and 50,000 animals. The division also reported a horse artillery
strength of 50 batteries, and to move the caissons and battery wagons, 4,668 horses.[33]

Sherman had fixed in his mind a clear awareness of his military situation. He also defined the mission, which he was setting
out determinedly to accomplish. A keen judgment and thorough
knowledge of military doctrine guided his decisions in combining
and integrating the marches of the three armies and the cavalry
forces. He also had the distinction to lead the largest command
ever of an American general on a battlefield.

Spring and its invigorating freshness raised the spirits of the
Union soldiers. They welcomed the change from the routine and
drabness of the uncomfortable winter camp life.

Sherman's orders from Lincoln, through General in Chief Grant, called for the engagement and defeat of Johnston's army. When Sherman set his military division in motion to begin its mission, Lincoln and Grant thought it a perilous undertaking to leave the separate armies' bases in Cincinnati, Louisville, and Nashville in jeopardy as they marched farther south. Their confidence in Sherman's ability in time overrode their doubts, and they refrained from any interference in his command decisions.

On the southward march the military division followed a route that paralleled the railroad network that reached Atlanta. Sherman needed the railroad to keep his armies supplied from the rear bases with the soldiers' and animals' needs and the materiel of battle.

Johnston also depended upon the railroad to bring supplies northward from Atlanta to his army on the battlefield.

The railroad from its terminal at Nashville delivered materiel to the supply depots opened along the route. At them supplies were unloaded into wagon trains for delivery to supply points.

The supply system became exceedingly important and entwined in the army's tactics. Sherman focused beyond the tactics to the planned strategy of the battle, to defeat Johnston's army in battle on the terrain approaching Atlanta. He recognized his army had the means in the railroad and the supply system to achieve victory. Further, he expected his soldiers, with the means at hand, to drive the foe from the battlefield.

To provide logistical support to his division, Sherman turned immediately to the maintenance of the single-track railroad operating hundreds of miles between supply depots and the line of battle. Its presence was threatened by attacks of enemy soldiers, guerrillas, and saboteurs. Thus Sherman, in need of 1,300 tons of supplies a day, reserved to himself centralized control of the railroad.

There were significant reasons for Sherman's actions on the railroad. If he had to depend upon the usual animal-drawn wagon trains, he would have had to have on hand 36,800 wagons, 220,800 animals to haul two tons twenty miles a day, which would have been impossible on the roads existing at the time. Added to the difficulty of supplying the above number of animals would be the animals and wagons needed to haul the forage for the wagon train animals, teamsters, and escorts. In time there would be the burden to the army of more wagons and animals hauling forage for the animals than subsistence for the soldiers. Such a burden would have developed into an intolerable situation. Sherman believed the railroad was the critical force in his operation, and its use was more cost effective. It also brought to the forefront the importance of the development of the railroad to the conduct of the war.[34]

Lee's and Johnston's strategy called for avoiding a head-on assault against their foes, employing defensive maneuvers. Johnston planned to implement the Confederate strategy with hit and run tactics to delay Sherman's march, to construct earthworks, and to disrupt the Union's use of the railroad. By such tactics he expected to draw Sherman's force away from Georgia, to watch for Union blunders to magnetize a war weary North to accept their cause to subdue the South to be futile, and to give up the armed conflict.

On May 6 the military division formed a sixteen-mile line at right angle to the railroad; Schofield on the east end, Thomas in the center, and McPherson on the west end.

Thomas and Schofield led their armies within two days up to Johnston's outposts of his defensively strong position at Dalton, approximately thirty miles south of Chattanooga. Johnston waited with his soldiers posted in carefully entrenched lines. If he had to retreat he would do so to succeeding prepared lines where he believed he had the advantage because one soldier on the defensive line equaled three to four on the attack. Johnston hoped for a failed assault by his enemy. He could then follow up with a successful counterattack.

Sherman, though, employed skillful tactics in the enemy-for-tified mountainous country. A problem he faced was knowledge of the topography and availability of current maps.

The three Union armies pressed Johnston on all fronts, and kept him occupied without an assault. Sherman decided against a fight for the strong defensive works at Dalton to avoid certain high casualties.

On May 8 Sherman ordered McPherson to march from his camp off to the right flank to occupy Snake Creek Gap Mountain Pass that led to Resaca, eighteen miles below Dalton. At the mountain gap McPherson intended to seize the railroad tracks behind Johnston's line. Sherman, from his assessment of the situation, recognized he could not dislodge Johnston from the mountain by a head-on assault. He ordered his commanders to keep up the pressure on the enemy. Johnston did not know the whereabouts of McPherson, then posted in his mountain position.

Thomas' and Schofield's pressure on Johnston prevented him from interfering with McPherson's flank march, but Johnston in time discovered the movement on his left. He knew if he did not post his soldiers in Resaca before Sherman posted his, the enemy's soldiers would be there in back of him. Johnston pulled his soldiers out of their positions at Dalton and marched them to Resaca and entrenched his soldiers in the high ground. He succeeded in arriving before McPherson because some of the Confederate militia were already there and able to block McPherson in a mountain pass. Instead of attacking, because of a problem known to Sherman at the outset of the march, lack of current maps to show the routes through the mountain, McPherson built entrenchments in front of Johnston and anchored both his flanks on the Oostanaula River. Sherman recognized the failure of his plan.

With his flank on the Oostanaula River, on May 14 McPherson marched his army to Resaca and occupied the west bank of Camp Creek expecting to establish a position on the railroad. Due to the inaccuracy of the topographical map, McPherson's engineer officer discovered the railroad curved eastward at Resaca. As the XIV and XX Corps of Thomas' army marched south to join McPherson's army on the left flank, the Confederate soldiers attempted to drive the Union soldiers back over Camp Creek, but they were repulsed. Union soldiers captured a hill commanding the railroad and wagon bridges on the Oostanaula. McPherson sent a force to seize and hold the south bank of the Oostanaula and to cover the laying of a ponton bridge. The bridge, laid with little opposition, was completed the next morning.

Johnston, with his soldiers' backs to the river, withdrew them over the Oostanaula during the night of the fifteenth. On withdrawing they set afire the railroad bridge, and then marched to Adairsville.

Sherman's soldiers entered Resaca the next morning, and his engineers and pioneers began repairing bridges to cross the remaining soldiers of Thomas' army at Resaca and Schofield's at Fites Ferry.

The Oostanaula was the first major river to block Thomas' march route. To enable the supply wagons to keep moving south, the pioneers started to prepare for the rebuilding at Resaca of the bridge of the Chattanooga and Atlanta Railroad, also called Western and Atlantic Railroad. Before they fled, the Rebels set the bridge afire. The pioneer crews were held up one day while they awaited the burnout of the fire. Three days after starting the bridge's rebuilding, 2,000 inventive pioneers rebuilt the 842-foot timber trestle bridge, with a height of 35 feet, and anchored on seven trestles.

The crossing of the Oostanaula River by the two foes brought them into approximately 35 miles of open country as far south as the Etowah River. Sherman sought such terrain to bring the enemy to open-field battle. Johnston, though, respected the soldierly qualities of the Union soldiers and Sherman's skill to lead them. He sought to deny Sherman his opportunity. He avoided risking a confrontation on an open battlefield against Sherman's soldiers quick to deploy to the flanks. Johnston decided to deploy his army to a narrow valley where Sherman could not employ his tactics on flank movements. On May 16 Johnston's soldiers reached a point south of Calhoun. The next day Sherman's soldiers marched to within a threatening position. Johnston ordered his soldiers on a march south heading for Cassville.

Sherman believed Thomas' Army of the Cumberland would be able to hold Johnston in his position while McPherson's Army of the Tennessee and Schofield's Army of the Ohio threatened the flanks.

Schofield's infantrymen, with the ponton train still at Resaca, forded the Conasauga at Fites Ferry, and the artillery and wagons were ferried over by flatboats. In waist deep water the soldiers stripped off their clothing and carried their arms and clothing above their heads, at the same time making sport of the soldiers' ludicrous activity. On the seventeenth Schofield's pioneers built a trestle footbridge for the infantrymen over the Coosawattee River which was too deep to ford, and again ferried artillery and wagons on a flatboat, the deployment requiring one day.

Schofield's and McPherson's armies were in place before Adairsville on May 17, but met enemy resistance and barricades. Sherman had anticipated a battle the next day to close out the campaign, but when the Union soldiers approached the enemy's lines in the morning they discovered them vacant. Johnston during the night divided his force, dispatching Generals Leonidas Polk and John B. Hood to Cassville and Hardee to Kingston. Schofield headed for Cassville where Johnston, who said to his soldiers, "the retreat is at an end," expected Hood and Polk to achieve a victory. In an attitude of dissension, Hood and Polk declared their positions untenable, and as a result Johnston redeployed his army to the Etowah River and crossed over it. Sherman took a risk in the deployment of his armies at Kingston and Cassville, but Johnston's decision placed in abeyance Sherman's expectations of a decisive battle and a hope for an end to the campaign.

Sherman still hoped to bring Johnston to battle north of the Etowah River with his soldiers deployed there, but he had to settle for forcing the Confederates' rear guard to Cartersville to cross the Etowah Bridge, which in doing so they foiled Sherman by setting afire the bridge.

Sherman issued orders to Colonel Wright to commence reconstruction of the railroad bridge over the Etowah River. Colonel Wright stated he did not receive General Sherman's orders until June 3. He arrived with his construction force at the bridge site on June 5. He commenced work on the sixth, and on the eleventh finished work on the bridge. Before a new trestle bridge could be built the work crews had to spend three days removing the old structure and cutting and dragging timber from nearby woods to the bridge site. The completed bridge provided Sherman with a 600-foot trestle-type bridge, made up of five trestles, and 67 feet high.

Instead of attacking Johnston at Allatoona, Sherman deployed the three armies on a march to the southwest in a wide-sweeping flanking tactic. When his armies stopped marching, they were in the enemy's rear area. Sherman's soldiers carried twenty days' food allowance in the wagons because Sherman ordered his commanders to cut their ties to the railroad to make the march. It was difficult to march while pulling wagons and animals through the mountains. The move to Dallas succeeded because Johnston abandoned Allatoona Pass.

The hills and wooded land prevented the three Union armies, stretched out for sixteen miles from Dallas to Marietta, to engage in one massive battle. There was dense undergrowth. Spring rains brought mud, and the wagons bogged down. The soldiers could not march in rapid flanking movements. With the bridge over the Etowah for the railroad completed, Sherman made Allatoona his forward base for supplies, but he still needed the railroad to bring the supplies forward.

The construction and upkeep of the railroad confronted the engineers and railroad construction crews with a constant challenge. The job of keeping the tenuous line of communications between Sherman's base and battlefield required inventiveness and hard work.

Sherman followed the railroad as a march route to battle, and Johnston followed it as a march route of retreat. The tactics of Sherman were to preserve and the tactics of Johnston were to destroy. Johnston, though, never destroyed enough of the railroad's bridges or tracks to keep the skillful Yankees from rebuilding the destructive work of the Confederates. There were attacks in northern Georgia and Tennessee to destroy the railroad bridges and tracks, but the engineer soldiers stationed along the line quickly repaired the damage.

Over the tracks of the Chattanooga and Atlanta Railroad rolled the supply trains. Every day each one of the one hundred thousand soldiers needed three pounds of food, but each of the fifty thousand animals needed fourteen pounds of hay and twelve pounds of grain. A thousand tons of supplies had to move forward every day.

The food for soldiers and animals moved down from Nashville. Soldiers consumed pork, bacon, salt beef, fresh beef, bread, flour, corn meal, beans, peas, rice, hominy, potatoes, mixed vegetables, coffee, sugar, salt, vinegar, and molasses. The railroad also brought the soldiers soap, candles, medical supplies, guns, ammunition, and one very important item, letters from home. The railroad cars also carried the wounded back to hospitals in Chattanooga and Nashville.

Each month the different engineer-pioneer work gangs working on the railroad system opened up 100 miles of track. By June, to bring all the supplies southward, there were 150 railroad engines and 1,647 cars running between Nashville and Allatoona.

In June the strength of Johnston's army declined to 75,000 soldiers and Sherman's military division increased to 113,000 soldiers. Both generals marched their soldiers through the mountains and forests, sparring for position. It was a reality of military tactics employed by two excellent tacticians. Sherman, aware of Lincoln's and Grant's orders to defeat Johnston's army, sought an all-out fight to gain the victory. He knew he commanded the numerically stronger army, which should assure him a battlefield victory.

At that period tactical operations shifted to the terrain between the Etowah and Chattahootchee Rivers. Sherman's line of communications was lengthened and Johnston's was shortened to a distance of twenty-five miles south of Kingston at Dallas. Sherman believed Johnston had forfeited his opportunity to take an aggressive offense. Johnston, though, from the mountains to the southwest observed the smoke of Sherman's soldiers' camp fires. He was uncertain where Sherman crossed the Etowah, but discovered the enemy's presence below the river. With Sherman's supply base remaining north of the river, Johnston ordered Wheeler to raid it with his cavalry, which he did, with a consequence to the Union army of considerable damage.

Johnston's soldiers were entrenched in a line on the Dallas road. To turn Johnston's right flank Schofield's army moved to the left flank of Sherman's military division to open the road to Allatoona. Sherman expected control of the road to open the line of communications with the railroad south of the Etowah River.

The soldiers on both sides of the line were fighting on difficult terrain, but they faithfully built the defenses the engineers laid out to protect themselves. Sherman recognized he faced three Confederate corps and it would be unwise to assault them. He continued to concentrate on Johnston's right flank on the Ackworth Road. The Confederate soldiers probed the Union army's strength, but were driven off with high losses.

On June 1 Stoneman's cavalry occupied Allatoona and covered the repair of the railroad tracks from Kingston. The next day

Sherman began a flanking attack on Johnston's left flank. Johnston decided he could not hold the line to New Hope Church. Two days later he deserted his line and retreated to a position between Lost Mountain and Brush Mountain near Kenesaw.

Colonel Wright started reconstruction work on the railroad bridge at Allatoona, and set the date of June 12 for it to be opened for traffic.

Sherman expected Johnston to establish his new line of defense at the Chattahootchee River, but his reconnaissance officers discovered the line to be at Marietta. Captain Orlando M. Poe then designed the fortified line to be erected by the pioneers to aid the infantrymen in Allatoona Pass near Ackworth.

Sherman's armies moved forward on June 10 through rough mountainous country, marching close to the railroad. Inclement weather set in and the rains turned the roads muddy, with chilly winds making the march uncomfortable for the soldiers. The next day the soldiers knew the Etowah Railroad Bridge was near completion when they heard the whistle of train engine "Big Shanty."

On the fourteenth the rain ceased. Sherman opened a series of attacks that forced Johnston out of his lines of defense at Gilgal Church and Lost Mountain, Mud Creek, and Marietta. On the night of the seventeenth Johnston, after a strong Union attack, retreated and took up a new impregnable position on Kenesaw Mountain. Two days later Johnston attacked the Union army's approach march, but the Union fire wreaked havoc on his soldiers. They returned to their entrenchments.

Suddenly, Sherman appeared to be confronted with a powerless and immobile position. The rains returned. There were transportation difficulties in maintaining the military division's supply levels. The railroad remained a target for enemy cavalry attacks that wrought heavy damages to equipment. On the battlefield the combat seemed to have reached a quietus with the enemy entrenched in Kenesaw Mountain. Sherman speculated if, as a solution, there might not be a weak spot on the line, a place where strength of position fostered carelessness in security, where a determined attack might break through. He proffered, "fortune favors the bold"; Kenesaw might be taken with attacks on other sections of the front. The alternatives were to wait or to break through the lines. Sap tactics would not be effective because as entrenchments were breached new ones would be built up in back of them.

Sherman sought action. He decided on an attack to break through the enemy's entrenchments.

On June 26 he ordered a demonstration to be made on the right of the enemy's line to attract attention. The next day the general advance started at 8 a.m. Schofield attacked near Marietta. Thomas assaulted the center of the line. McPherson attacked on the left of the enemy's line west and south of Kenesaw. The attack opened with a fifteen-minute artillery barrage on the enemy's left flank. Johnston's soldiers held their lines, inflicting 2,500 casualties on the Yankees. Sherman reported his soldiers demonstrated courage and steadiness to hold on to their entrenched positions in front of an enemy without intent to retreat. They acted intelligently to employ abatis, rocks, timber, and undergrowth to hold their position. Sherman concluded the breakthrough attempted by his soldiers had failed, and it would be futile to try another.

A period of rain followed the bloody battle, and again the ground turned into mud. The contesting armies bogged down. Sherman realized attempting another assault would be acting imprudently.

In the aftermath of the Kenesaw battle, Sherman decided to resume his tested and successful flanking tactics. Fortunately, a few days later the rain stopped, which permitted Sherman to order the supply wagons to move and Schofield to start his army marching. Schofield was able to maneuver his way to the west of Marietta and to cross Moses Creek. He kept marching until he positioned his army in the rear of Johnston's army and headed for Johnston's supply route extending back to Atlanta.

Chief Engineer Captain Orlando M. Poe's reconnaissance revealed that Johnston intended to make a stand upon a line from Ruff's Station to Ruff's Mill with flanks near Nickajack and Rottenwood Creeks. The six-mile line had been prepared by militia and contraband persons a few days before Johnston's army occupied it. The line was well built with infantry parapets, connecting salients, and emplaced artillery pieces.

On July 4, Union skirmishers forced Confederate soldiers into the defensive works on the main road and pressed against the works at all points, but not enough to silence the Rebel artillery. At daylight on July 5 Union skirmishers advanced and discovered Johnston's soldiers had withdrawn from their works.

Schofield's move forced Johnston to desert the mountains and move back to the banks of the Chattahoochee River. The Yankees took Marietta. Sherman hoped to catch Johnston as his mass of soldiers, animals, and wagons crossed to the south side of the river, but Johnston was clever enough to anticipate a trap. He threw up breastworks that Sherman feared to assault frontally. A rash attack against them would cost Sherman thousands of soldiers.

In a follow-up reconnaissance, Poe discovered the next line of defensive works to be in front of the railroad bridge and the several roads and ponton bridges at Pace's, Montgomery's, and Turner's Ferries, forming an extensive *tête-de-pont*, which consisted of a system of square redoubts, in defensible positions, connected by infantry parapets. A few of the redoubts were prepared for artillery. The left of the line rested upon a large seven-gun redoubt near the mouth of Nickajack Creek, and the right upon another redoubt prepared for eight guns, and situated near the Chattahoochee River, about one mile above the railroad bridge. Opposite that point the entrenchments on the south side of the river began and extended in a continuous line for eight miles almost to Island Creek. The railroad bridge at its southern end was protected by three batteries of irregular shape, and one redoubt. The line, owing to the care bestowed upon its construction and the nature of its approaches, was by far the strongest Sherman's soldiers encountered on their march.

Sherman decided to cross the Chattahoochee River on the left flank. Strong demonstrations were carried out on the right flank to give Johnston the impression the tactical movement was to be made in that direction, and that Sherman's soldiers would cross the river at a point below the mouth of the Nickajack Creek. The points selected for the crossing were at Roswell Factory and Phillips' Ferry.

McPherson's Army of the Tennessee which had been demonstrating on the right flank suddenly turned and marched to Roswell where it crossed the Chattahoochee River without Confederate opposition on a trestle bridge built by the XVI Corps pioneer soldiers from material collected at the site.

The Army of the Ohio rapidly made a movement to send a small force of soldiers across the river on a dam at Phillips' Ferry, surprising a force of the enemy posted there, and capturing an artillery piece. The Union force then constructed some light works to serve as a bridgehead.

Colonel George P. Buell's 58th Indiana Infantry pioneers on July 8 carried canvas pontons to Soap Creek and launched them filled with infantrymen. The pontons moved down the creek into the Chattahoochee River, crossed, and debarked the soldiers without a loss. The Confederates opened with artillery fire and moved their battle line to the riverbank, but Union soldiers drove them back.

Buell's pioneers then threw two canvas ponton bridges over the river to enable the remainder of the Army of the Ohio to cross its soldiers to the far side.

The 58th Indiana Infantry pioneers replaced the canvas ponton bridges with trestle bridges as a means to preserve the canvas pontons, even though it required considerably more labor to build trestle bridges with wood, but wood was in a greater supply.

Another ponton bridge was built at Powers' Ferry two miles below Phillips' Ferry. The IV Corps crossed there and formed a junction with Schofield's army. One division of the IV Corps marched quickly down the south bank of the Chattahoochee to Pace's Ferry. Buell's 58th Infantry pioneers then built two ponton bridges to enable the XIV and XX Corps to cross the river.

In the face of Sherman's soldiers crossing the Chattahoochee River and establishing a secure lodgement, Johnston crossed his entire army to the south side of the river on county, railroad, and ponton bridges. All his bridges were removed and the county and railroad bridges were burned.

The passage of the Chattahoochee River by Sherman's soldiers had been accomplished with a loss of less than a dozen soldiers.

Sherman reported in two months he had pushed his foe back 100 miles. Johnston reported he held his opponent to a two-miles-a-day advance, kept his army intact, and incurred a low number of casualties. The farther Sherman pushed Johnston south the longer he extended his supply line and gave Johnston a shorter supply line and more space to his destruction-bent cavalry to roam in back of the Union army's Chattanooga and Atlanta Railroad lifeline.

Sherman in planning his next march to achieve the victory for the Union had to avoid a route that exposed his flank to the enemy to be able to recross the Chattahoochee River and wreak havoc on the railroad. The tasks for Sherman were (1) to pursue Johnston's army and force it into battle, (2) to start work on rebuilding the railroad bridge at the Chattahoochee, (3) cut the Atlanta to Augusta Georgia Railroad at Decatur, and (4) to cut Johnston's communications with Richmond to obtain reinforcements. Sherman decided to take the long route near the Chattahoochee on the left flank. Orders were issued to Schofield to move his army to Decatur, McPherson to cut the railroad at Decatur and Stone Mountain, and Thomas to seek out and hold at bay Johnston's army until the military division deployed into position.

In a surprise action on July 17, Confederate President Jefferson Davis gave in to the outcry against Johnston for his defensive tactics and relieved him of command of the Army of the Tennessee. The next day General John B. Hood assumed command of the army. He was a reputed combatant and promised to trade blows with Sherman on the open battlefield. The Confederate army he assumed command of had been reduced to 60,000 soldiers. It would be no match in an open battle with Sherman's 100,000 Yankee soldiers.

Sherman became well aware in the assessment of the change in command he would be confronted with aggressive action by Hood, but he was confident his battle-proven soldiers would defeat the aggressor.

Sherman remained concerned about the fragile supply line and turned to solidifying the Chattanooga and Atlanta Railroad. He ordered Colonel Wright on August 2 to build a timber-trestle bridge over the Chattahoochee River to replace the one destroyed by Johnston's retreating army. Every available pioneer and railroad construction worker was thrown into the construction job.

Work pressed onward on the Chattahoochee Bridge from dawn on August 2 to dusk. Working in the hot sun, pioneers chopped down trees in the nearby woods, lopped and logged them, and then hauled the cut pieces to the bridge site where they were shaped into needed pieces. As the uprights for each section were erected, bridge workmen climbed the shaky ninety-foot poles, measured the cross pieces, and then fastened them in place with spikes made on the ground.

As the framed trestles rose higher and higher, and farther and farther out into the river, workmen shinnied the thin frames, erected hoists, and manipulated sticks into position as they were hoisted on blocks and tackles. It became a scary experience to stand on the unsupported structure high in the air.

Some workmen and pioneers lacked the iron nerve and equilibrium to climb around the trestles. Looking down into the river from their high work site, a number of pioneers and workmen froze in their steps. When the trestle framework was completed, pioneers walked out on the bridge roadway and laid the cross ties and railroad rails.

Some railroad construction engineers believed that a trestle bridge more than one story high was impossible to build. The Chattahoochee Railroad Bridge, and railroad trestle bridges constructed in Virginia, changed that belief. The trestle bridge the railroad construction workmen and pioneers built over the Chattahoochee with four million feet of timber looked frail, but the bridge builders erected a sturdy one four stories high on ninety-foot high trestles, 780 feet long, and they completed the bridge on August 6 in a record time of four and a half days. At noon a train moved over the bridge to within three miles of Atlanta. Colonel Wright recorded, "No night work was done upon it whatever, but the men worked from daylight till dark with one hour intermission at noon for dinner. At the capture of Atlanta, then the pioneers completed the railroad into the city on September 3, a day after General Henry W. Slocum's soldiers took possession of the city. General Haupt, who managed the military railroad construction service in the east, said it was the greatest feat of its kind."[35]

The pioneers and railroad construction workmen built six other trestle bridges on the Chattahoochee River for the supply wagon trains. Each one was approximately 350 feet long. To build one of the bridges, a pioneer officer answered Sherman it would take four days. "Sir," Sherman reportedly said to him, "I give you forty-eight hours or a position in the front ranks."

On July 18 soldiers of McPherson's and Schofield's armies crossed Nancy's Creek. A day later a small force of soldiers of Thomas' Army of the Cumberland crossed Peachtree Creek and dug in. Hood offered battle with orders to his soldiers to make it a decisive one. His soldiers fought Thomas' soldiers fiercely. Thomas' determined army took the blows without flinching and pushed the Rebels back to their entrenchments around Atlanta, suffering 1,700 casualties, but inflicting 4,400 on Hood's army.

Poe's reconnaissance confirmed that the Confederate soldiers were posted in a well-built line of entrenchments around Atlanta capable of providing strong defense. The line consisted of open batteries for artillery connected by infantry parapets with accessories of *abatis* and *chevaux de frise*.

On July 22, the battle erupted between the armies of Sherman and Hood. Sherman was only three miles from the Confederate entrenchments. On a wide-sweeping move to Decatur, McPherson cut the Georgia Railroad entering Atlanta on the east side and perched his soldiers on a high hill overlooking the city. Hood was determined to push off the Union soldiers. He started a flanking movement at night and at the same time had other forces engage Thomas and Schofield to prevent them from moving to McPherson's assistance. McPherson discovered the attack and rode out to place his soldiers in battle position to meet Hood's oncoming attack, but in his movement he rode into a Confederate patrol. One of the members of the patrol shot McPherson when he refused to surrender.

The battle that cost McPherson his life continued and intensified with Hood gaining ground. He made a gap in the Union line and began to march his soldiers through it. Fortunately, Schofield's army arrived on the field and began to pour artillery shells into the oncoming enemy soldiers. The destructive metal slowed them down, and as the barrage continued they gradually retreated to their entrenchments. The Confederates' withdrawal signaled the end of the battle. Hood lost 8,000 soldiers and Sherman 3,700. With the arrival of nighttime, the Union army was firmly posted in its position on the south bank of Peachtree Creek. Three of Sherman's four

Chattahoochee River Railroad Trestle Bridge

objectives were achieved: (1) the opening of the railroad bridge, (2) driving the Confederates into their entrenchments, and (3) cutting the railroad at Decatur.

After Poe reported on July 23 on his reconnaissance of the enemy's entire line in front of the military division's soldiers, Sherman stated he would not attempt to assault the enemy line that could be observed because of the cost in lives.

Sherman instructed Poe to insure that the lines occupied by his soldiers were of such a character they could be held against sorties, and to put them forward at all points where it could be done conveniently. He stated his tactics would be to attempt to reach the enemy's line of railroad communications at or near East Point, about six miles from Atlanta, the junction of the Atlantic and West Point Railroad and the Macon and Western Railroad to continue to Atlanta on a single track. The movement he hoped would either result in a general engagement, with the chances greatly in the Union's favor, or in the evacuation of Atlanta. He also directed Poe to select a line on the Georgia Railroad where the Union's left flank could post and command the railroad.

Sherman's Cavalry

Sherman ordered a cavalry division at daybreak on July 26 to clear the ground around Turner's Ferry on the Chattahoochee, approximately ten miles north of Atlanta. The pioneers constructed a ponton bridge at the ferry, and communications were established between the cavalry forces on the south bank of the river with the forces on the north bank. Hood attacked on July 28 on Lick Skillet Road, but suffered his third repulse.

During the month of August, Sherman's soldiers spent their time operating on the Confederates' line of communications to cut them as a means to bring permanent immobility to Hood's army. On August 13, Sherman decided to transfer his military division, except the XX Corps posted at the Chattahoochee River Railroad Bridge, around Atlanta to a position on the railroads running south from East Point.

On August 25 he started a daring tactical march from his base of supplies and marched his forces to Jonesboro, south of Atlanta. From there he decided to follow up the march with a foray around Atlanta. On September 1 the Army of the Cumberland was concentrated so as to connect from the left of the Army of the Tennessee to the railroad, about two miles north of Jonesboro, with the IV Corps destroying the railroad as it advanced. The Army of the Ohio commenced the destruction of the Macon and Western Railroad at Rough and Ready. About 4 p.m. the XIV Corps assaulted and carried the right flank of the enemy's line, which consisted of the usual batteries connected by infantry parapets. The approach of night prevented the capture of the entire Rebel force. Sherman's force was then squarely upon Hood's line of communications.

The Union soldiers destroyed the Atlanta and West Point Railroad, approaching from the southwest, and cut the Confederates' important supply line from Alabama and Mississippi. Hood attempted, but failed, to block the Union army's march. Sherman's soldiers burned ties and twisted rails. They then turned to the east and destroyed the Macon and Western Railroad that entered Atlanta from the south.

The march of Sherman's military division had been so rapid Hood's soldiers exhibited confusion. They thought the Yankee soldiers had abandoned the fight. Suddenly they heard thunder from the south. They learned of Sherman's approach. Hood faced the fact the Yankees had completely cut all the railroads leading into Atlanta. It was harvest time, which meant his soldiers were in Atlanta without food, and also a transportation system to bring the food into the city. He peremptorily decided to abandon the city.

On September 2, General Henry W. Slocum's XX Corps in its bivouac at the Chattahoochee railroad bridge, packed its impedimenta and marched into Atlanta.

Hood completely misjudged Sherman's deployment of his soldiers, which when it became public news, was applauded as boldly conceived and systematically conducted. Some persons hailed Sherman's achievement as a signal the end of the war was in sight. An engineer officer declared, "Sherman did not sacrifice the position of numbers. Such constitutes the solid foundation for the highest military reputation."

Captain Poe wrote in his war diary the engineer and pioneer soldiers were popular in the Union army marching to Atlanta. Their skill helped the armies to keep moving south along the railroad tracks. Their labor and skillfulness in building bridges adaptable to the terrain amazed the fighting soldiers.

"I doubt whether the history of war can furnish more examples of skill and bravery," Sherman wrote about his engineer and pioneer soldiers, "than attended the defense of the railroads from Nashville to Atlanta in 1864."

In his report on the Atlanta campaign, Poe stated he had gone into detail on the operations "in order that they may be clearly understood, deeming it peculiarly the province of the engineer to call attention to such brilliant maneuvers as those which enabled us to pass a river, too deep to be forded, in the very face of the enemy with a loss of less than a platoon of men, and those which placed six army corps upon the enemy's line of communications, in opposition to a single corps."

Number of Bridges

On bridge-building tasks, Poe listed the following accomplishments of the military divisions' engineers-pioneers:

Ten canvas-ponton bridges built across the Chattahoochee River with an average length of 350 feet.

Seven trestle bridges built across the Chattahoochee River from material cut from the riverbank; five double and two single tracked; each with an average length of 350 feet.

Six bridges built over Peach Tree Creek with an average length of eighty feet.

Five bridges built over Flint River with an average length of eighty feet.[36]

Sherman Revises the Strategy

After the occupation of Atlanta, Sherman instructed Poe on September 3 to make a reconnaissance of the lines occupied by the Confederates during the Yankees' advance against Hood with the intent to modify them for the defensive use of Sherman's soldiers.

Poe observed the Confederate defense network to be about twelve miles in extent, and estimated it to be larger than what could be occupied by a Union garrison force. He made a reconnaissance within the network to ascertain whether a shorter one could be constructed to house a garrison force. He examined a three-mile line of the high points nearest the center of the city. He concluded the construction of a new defensive line would require the destruction of many of the city's buildings.

When Poe reported his findings, Sherman approved the proposed interior line and ordered its construction. Sherman, though, immediately countermanded his orders because he decided he wanted to wait until there was a necessity for a defense system.

Poe also took steps to increase the efficiency of the engineer organization to meet the possible new workload.

To comply with his earlier orders the 1st Missouri Engineers marched from Jonesborough and on August 31 reported for duty with the military division in the field.

Poe ordered the engineer officer of the Army of the Cumberland to transfer the 1st Michigan Engineers and Mechanics Regiment from its posts on the Chattanooga and Atlanta Railroad to the front at Atlanta. The regiment, with eight of its companies, arrived at the end of September.

With the cessation of the fighting around the captured Confederate city, Sherman ordered a month's rest for his war weary soldiers. He also ordered General Thomas and his Army of the Cumberland to Nashville to secure the city and to counter General Forrest's cavalry raids in Tennessee. Sherman did not order any rest for his engineer-pioneer soldiers.

At the end of September, Sherman ordered Poe to start the new line of fortifications around Atlanta. Poe then set the entire engineer-pioneer force to work constructing the profiles and revetments. Work details made up of 2,000 soldiers were assigned from the infantry regiments to assist the engineers-pioneers.

On October 5, Poe reported to General Sherman that a new two-mile line on the south side of the city was in a defensible condition. Work continued on the new defenses by the Michigan and Missouri engineer regiments, but the work details from the infantry regiments diminished; thus work proceeded slowly. A reason for the work slowing down was the impression of the soldiers there would be no requirement for the defense line.

"Much care had been bestowed upon the several redoubts," Poe reported, "and the finish put upon each one was excellent."[37]

The soldiers in the defense works around Atlanta were correct in their estimates. Hood decided not to attack the Union army while it was posted behind protected fortifications. He chose the easier target, the supply line with miles of railroad tracks running through unprotected wilderness. The 400 miles of railroad track connecting Sherman to Nashville became an enticing target. The alert and aggressive Hood did not waste any time in mounting his attack. The isolated attacks alarmed Sherman. He could not afford to be in Atlanta with a disruption of a single supply line.

Hood attacked Allatoona on October 5, ripping up railroad tracks and burning the ties. A week later he made another damaging raid at Dalton.

After Hood's second successful attack, Sherman decided to rid his military division of the menace plundering in the rear echelon. He set out from Atlanta with a striking force.

Hood, aware he had forced Sherman out of Atlanta, believed he could maneuver Sherman to the wilderness of northern Georgia where on favorable terrain he was confident he would defeat him in open field battle. With Forrest cutting up the railroad and threatening Nashville, Hood had high hopes after the defeat of Sherman to move north to the Ohio River or perhaps march east to join Lee.

Sherman sought out Hood for battle but he found him to be an elusive foe. The two foes maneuvering for the favorable tactical situation failed to come to battle. In late October they turned away from one another.

Sherman returned to his Atlanta fortress entrusting the task to defeat Hood to Thomas. To reinforce Thomas he ordered Schofield to Nashville with the XXIII Corps. Hood decided to turn his attention to a better prospect for a decisive battle, which would be the defeat of General Thomas' army in Nashville.

Sherman's march back to Atlanta signaled the abandonment of his strategy to engage and destroy the Confederate Army of the Tennessee, which had been one of the central objectives of the strategy at the outset of Grant's spring campaign. Hood's army remained intact, although with a diminished number of soldiers, and Sherman decided he could not afford the time to engage in a chase to seek battle. A new strategy of an entirely different nature for the corps remaining in Sherman's military division had been in the making to bring a decisive end to the rebellion. Sherman had been discussing with President Lincoln and General Grant the first operation to implement the strategy, a march to Savannah, which targeted the destruction of the Confederates' productive capacity to conduct further military operations.

Dismantling of Atlanta

Before turning his attention to the tactics to carry out his new mission, Sherman issued Poe two orders:

(1) On November 1 work to be stopped on the defense system of Atlanta.

(2) On November 7 he ordered Poe "to take charge of the destruction with engineer troops all railroads and property belonging thereto; all storehouses, machine shops, mills, factories, &c, within the lines of the enemy's defenses of Atlanta."

Poe laid out to the commanders of the 1st Michigan and 1st Missouri engineers just what tasks were assigned to them, and selected for them the buildings and works for destruction.[38]

On November 9 Poe telegraphed Sherman, "I am ready to do the work assigned to me, and will act the instant I get your orders to do so."

On the morning of November 12, Sherman directed Poe to proceed with the work of destruction, and added "be careful not to use fire, which would endanger other buildings than those set apart for destruction."

The engineer regiments were divided into detachments under picked officers, each of whom received a written order as follows:

"You will please take the detachment now under your orders to the first high chimney (stating locality and buildings) and throw it down and continue the work along (stating the route) until you reach (the point designated as the limit of work for this detachment), being careful not to use fire in doing the work, since it would endanger buildings which it is not intended to destroy."

Poe personally supervised the 1st Michigan and 1st Missouri engineers' work of destruction and its thoroughness.

If any engineer soldier craved destructive tasks, Atlanta provided him his heyday.

An infantry soldier, watching the destructive work of the engineer soldiers, enviously wrote in his diary, "The pioneers were having all the fun."

After battering the walls of buildings, toppling smokestacks, breaking up furnace arches, knocking steam machinery to pieces, and punching holes in the boilers, the engineers used fire and powder to destroy the remnants of the buildings. The railroads within the limits of the old Rebel defenses were destroyed by tearing up the iron and setting afire the ties. Poe devised an iron cant hook his engineer soldiers employed to tear up the rails. The engineers heated the torn-up rails over a pile of burning ties, and then with a cant hook at each end twisted them around their horizontal axis. The length of railroad track destroyed in that manner, within the limits of the city, reached out about ten miles. The depots, car sheds, machine shops, and water tanks were also destroyed. When Poe's work crews finished their work, Atlanta had been stripped of its railroads to or from Carterville, Fairburn, and Lovejoy. Nothing of the slightest value could be found in Atlanta to supply any military needs of the contending armies.

On November 15, fire was applied to the city's heaps of rubbish. Poe reported he stood upon the ground in person to see that the engineers carried out their work in the prescribed and orderly manner, and unhesitatingly he vouched for the results.

Many buildings, though, in the business part of the city were destroyed by lawless persons, who, defying Sherman's orders, sneaked around in blind alleys and succeeded in firing many houses.[39]

Building Bridges to Ward Off Hood

After Hood turned his soldiers away from Sherman's soldiers, he made a reassessment of the tactical situation in northern Georgia and the disposition of the Union army.

He was aware of Thomas' army deploying to Nashville, and Schofield marching his corps there to reinforce Thomas. Hood decided his best opportunity would be to assault Schofield on his march route north. He set out to engage Schofield in battle. When Schofield wired to Thomas the information Hood was pursuing his army, Thomas sent him orders to fight a delaying battle to Nashville where defensive works were being built to position his soldiers.

Hood marched on and made contact with Schofield's soldiers below Columbia, Tennessee, but Schofield fought Hood off and crossed the Duck River on a hastily constructed ponton bridge, and headed for Franklin.

Marching north on the road to Franklin, Schofield studied his map and recognized a ponton bridge train would be required when he reached the Harpeth River. He sent a messenger ahead to Nashville to inform Thomas of his need for pontons. The pioneer company had abandoned the pontons at the Duck River (twenty-four miles below the Harpeth River) because Hood's arrival there did not allow the pioneers time to remove them from the water.

When Schofield arrived with his troops in the area of Franklin and at the Harpeth River, he expected to find in response to his message to Thomas a ponton bridge train awaiting him there, but the train had not arrived at the river. In his first action, Schofield sent an immediate message to Thomas stating he was "worried about the lack of pontons for the county bridge was gone and the ford in the river hardly passable."

In his second action he placed his soldiers in battle positions on the south bank of the Harpeth River and gave them orders to hold Hood until a bridge could be built over the river to cross them and the animal-drawn wagon trains.

Three bridges had crossed the Harpeth River at Franklin:

(1) The Nashville Turnpike Bridge was destroyed early in the war and never rebuilt.

(2) The county bridge, a timber trestle, was a frail structure compared to the turnpike bridge. It did have the built-in advantage of being placed lower on the riverbanks and having easy approach routes.

(3) The third bridge over the river was a railroad bridge.

The three bridges, though, at an earlier time were set on fire by the Confederates.

The situation for Schofield's pioneer officer (unnamed) called for a feat of assessment, of ingenuity, of adaptability, and the conceptualization of an expedient to provide the army with mobility. Engineer-pioneer officers had accomplished such feats since the onset of the rebellion. That was the time to accomplish another bridge-building feat.

The pioneer company commander discovered the county bridge had not been entirely destroyed by fire. After his assessment of the situation, he reported to Schofield he could rebuild the bridge. Schofield instructed him to start work on the rebuilding job. The pioneer officer, based on his mental conceptualization of an expedient, instructed his pioneers to saw off the burnt tops of the upright supporting posts close to the water. On top of the posts he had them fasten new beams and then on top of the beams fasten floorboards. He intended the rebuilt bridge to be a temporary structure until the arrival of the pontons. As the situation developed, the pioneers' improvised bridge was found to be strong enough to hold the loaded wagons sent across to test its strength. The floor of the roadway was so close to the water the soldiers thought it was a ponton bridge. Some official reports called it a ponton bridge. Because the roadway was close to the water level, soldiers crossed over it with the water splashing on their feet.

Late in the afternoon the ponton train arrived at the river, but the pioneers' rebuilt county timber bridge was holding the load so well Schofield decided not to have his pioneers spend the time building a ponton bridge. The only extra work needed to use the county bridge was to change the grade on the north bank of the river to make it easier for the horses, mules, and oxen to climb up the bank with their wagon loads.

The pioneer officer also adapted the railroad bridge over the Harpeth to the movement of wagon trains. Nearby barns, sheds, and houses were torn down and the planks collected were used to put a solid roadway on top of the railroad ties. Then the wagon trains used the bridge to cross the river.

When Hood attacked Schofield at the Harpeth River at 4 p.m. on November 20, the wagon trains, animals, and artillery had already crossed the river. They were on their way to join Thomas in his anticipated battle with Hood.

After successfully achieving the victory over Hood at Franklin, Schofield said nothing other than the intelligent and energetic rebuilding of the Harpeth River bridges by the pioneers had made possible the saving of the wagon trains and the army. In an oft-repeated performance the well-led pioneers demonstrated the skill and imagination to turn a battle at a crucial time into a Union victory.[40]

Even though Schofield's soldiers were able to hold off Hood at the Harpeth until the army crossed safely with its wagons, Hood persisted in returning to the attack and battled Schofield's soldiers as they withdrew to Nashville. Determinedly, Hood pursued the Yankees with the expectation to engage the entire force entrenched at Nashville. Even with a force diminished by casualties, he refused to back away from battle with his enemy.

In the interim of Schofield's and Hood's marches, Thomas prepared his position to meet the Rebel attack. When Schofield's corps arrived at Nashville, Thomas' soldiers welcomed the soldiers to the safety of the city's defense works with hot coffee.

Thomas had his army in readiness on December 10 to attack Hood's army, but the attack was gainsaid by the occurrence of a sudden change in the weather. It turned cold, and rained. The rain turned to sleet and ice. The ground was slippery and hard. The weather and terrain immobilized Thomas' army.

Finally, the weather in Nashville cleared up on beautiful, sunny December 15. Thomas ordered his soldiers to the attack. He sent General James Wilson's cavalry on a sweep around Hood's left flank. Schofield's infantrymen charged Hood's infantrymen straight on. Hood's soldiers, unable to muster some semblance of order to recoil from the attack, instead instinctively faded away from their foe's charge. The relentless attack of Thomas' soldiers became overpowering. Hood's soldiers could not muster the sense of duty to raise a feeble resistance. They were driven from the battlefield. The massive Union attack became a rout of the enemy and scattered the Rebels to the four points of the compass in Tennessee, Alabama, Georgia, and Mississippi. It became the first battle in the rebellion where an army was so completely demolished and defeated that its soldiers were never rounded up by their officers to be regrouped into an army to return to the battlefield.

For the Union's soldiers, Nashville was a glorious end to the fighting in the western theater. The victory epitomized Lincoln's long sought strategy to defeat the rebellious soldiers, scatter them to their homes, and bring the bloody fratricide to an end. The long-suffering wait for the president began to show evidence of an ending at the battle of Nashville.

The March to Savannah

With desolate Atlanta strewn with ashes and Thomas in Tennessee victorious over Hood, Sherman became offensive-minded. He directed his energy to implementing his new task to destroy totally the Confederates' war-making ability and resources. "I can make Georgia howl," he declared as he issued the order to his army to march southeast to Savannah.

On the march Sherman cut his army off from the line of communications reaching back to Nashville and Chattanooga. Thus, in the changing tactical operation, maintenance and safety of the gigantic railroad system that supplied the army on its march to Atlanta ceased to be useful and important. In the fluid dynamics of war, the key to mobility switched to the animals and wagon trains.

Sherman issued additional instructions to his soldiers to load their wagon trains with ammunition, twenty days' supply of breadstuffs and military impedimenta, three days' forage of grains, and forty days' supply of meat in the large herd of cattle to accompany the army. He further broadened his instructions, "by a judicious system of foraging" the army would maintain the specified levels of supply in the wagon trains by living solely upon the country which, he pointed out, abounded in corn, sweet potatoes, and meats. Marching at the end of the harvest season, the soldiers with such a license to forage looked forward to harvesting on the farms many crops to satisfy their appetites and raw forage for their animals.

To facilitate his task, Sherman regrouped the estimated 60,000 infantrymen and 5,500 cavalrymen in his military division around Atlanta into two wings, left and right.

(1) *The Left Wing.* Under the command of Major General Henry W. Slocum the left wing was made up of the XIV and XX Corps, with the engineer and pioneer support provided by the 58th Indiana Volunteer Infantry, commanded by Colonel George P. Buell, with ten companies, for a total strength of 775 officers and enlisted men.

(2) *The Right Wing.* Under the command of Major General Oliver O. Howard the right wing was made up of the XV and XVII Corps, with engineer support provided by the 1st Missouri Engineer Regiment, commanded by Lieutenant Colonel William Tweeddale.

In the four corps of the wings there was a pioneer corps in each of the divisions with an average strength of 100 white pioneers and 70 Negroes.

The 3rd Cavalry Division under command of Major General Hugh J. Kilpatrick and the 1st Michigan Engineers and Mechanics Regiment, ten companies, with an authorized strength of 150 engineer soldiers, commanded by Colonel J. B. Yates, were assigned to Sherman's headquarters.

General Kilpatrick received his orders from General Sherman.

Colonel Yates received his mission assignments from Sherman's staff engineer officer, Captain Poe.[41]

In the switch of the army's means of mobility, the railroads lost their importance and the emphasis on them shifted from preservation to destruction.

On the march to Savannah Sherman's force would steal a march upon an area of approximately twenty-nine percent of Georgia's area of cross-formed terrain obstacles of about ten major rivers, numerous smaller rivers, creeks, and streams.

If it could be visualized in the entirety, the huge mass of soldiers, animals, wagons (and the followers it attracted along the way of Union and Confederate deserters and freed Negroes) moving in columns extending from left-right flanks for approximately sixty miles on primitive dirt roads, paths, and across farms and fields, and over bridges and culverts on the watercourses running south to southeast, would appear as the network of human columns on lines moving east and the watercourses on lines flowing south.[42]

The composition of the Georgia terrain presaged a prodigious amount of construction work to be expected of the engineer-pioneer soldiers to provide roads and bridges to guarantee the army's mobility.

The size of the engineer and pioneer units' wagon trains and supply of hand tools projected a picture of their expected work. In reality, the two engineer and 58th Indiana pioneer regiments and the pioneer units in the divisions lacked the manpower to perform all the tasks. To prepare the terrain for the army's march the infantrymen would also be called upon to labor corduroying roads, building defense works, building small timber bridges, removing obstacles, and destroying enemy engines of war. The daily rate of miles marched was set by the ability of the soldiers and animals to overcome the obstacles that blocked their path.

Fortunately, Company A of the 1st Missouri Engineers, which marched on the right flank, provided for posterity a daily record in its morning report about the progress of its march and its activities.

A reader, following Company A's itinerary, is presented a plausible picture of the typical daily movement of the company and its work to move Sherman's force on the left and right wings, amidst laborious and exhausting tasks. The soldiers were not on a forced march, but Sherman and his subordinate commanders structured the march with a mission and enforced discipline, and it became a toilsome and herculean one. Sherman estimated his soldiers would march an average of ten miles a day, and the records indicate they approximated Sherman's expectations.

The Right Wing. With the XV and XVII Corps, and the 1st Missouri Engineers, the right wing left Atlanta on November 15 heading for Jonesborough and McDonough. Its instructions were to make a feint on Macon, cross the Ocmulgee River at Planter's Mills, and rendezvous at Gordon in seven days. Company A, Missouri Engineers, with four officers and seventy-two enlisted men, put down its first ponton bridge on a major river, the Ocmulgee, on November 17. The company spent three days there aiding troops and animals to cross; upon the completion of the task the engineers took up the bridge. The next three days they spent marching to Clinton.

The Left Wing. The XX Corps, with a detachment of four companies, 220 pioneers of the 58th Indiana Infantry under command of Lieutenant Colonel Joseph Moore, also left Atlanta on November 15 heading for Decatur, Stone Mountain with orders to tear up the railroad from Social Circle to Madison, and to burn the railroad bridge over Oconee River east of Madison. From the river the XX

Corps' orders directed it to turn south and be at Milledgeville in seven days. On November 20 Colonel Moore's detachment constructed its first ponton bridge, 220 feet in length, across Little River, twelve miles north of Milledgeville.

General Sherman left Atlanta on November 16 with the XIV Corps heading for Lithonia, Covington, Shady Dale, and on a direct march to Milledgeville. Colonel Buell with six companies of the 58th Indiana Infantry and 440 feet of ponton bridging provided pioneer support. On the second day, after a twenty-mile march, Buell's pioneers constructed two ponton bridges, each one 120 feet in length, over the Yellow River east of Atlanta.[43]

The next afternoon one of the Yellow River bridges was taken up, the pontons hauled to the Ulcofuhachee River, and a bridge built across the river. On the nineteenth Buell's pioneers dismantled the two bridges they had built on the two rivers.

On November 20 General Kilpatrick with his cavalrymen on the right flank made a feint south on Macon, driving the Georgia militia, the largest force in Georgia to oppose Sherman's army, into their entrenchments. His cavalrymen also spent two days tearing up the railroad. The enemy reappeared in front of Kilpatrick's cavalrymen from their entrenchments on November 22, but his cavalrymen forced them to scatter.

On November 22 Sherman's soldiers in the two wings met their targets. The right wing reached Gordon, and the left wing reached Milledgeville.

Right Wing. The itinerary in the morning report of Company A, Missouri Engineers, noted the engineer soldiers had marched ninety-three miles and bridged one major river in seven days. Company K of the regiment, as it approached Sherman's first target area, found it appropriate to enter some comments in the morning report about the November weather, something no other unit found fit to do:

November 18	Fair.
November 19	Cloudy, cool showers.
November 21	Cold, rainy
November 22	Marched 13 miles to Clinton—execrable roads, frequent snow squalls. Teams stalled in road where remained all night.
November 23	Clear, cold. Extricated wagons frozen mud, 6 miles Gordon, Georgia.[44]

Left Wing. The 58th Indiana Regiment reported its detachments built four ponton bridges over three major rivers.

At the rendezvous Sherman met with his wing and cavalry commanders and issued orders for the next leg of the march.

Right Wing. General Howard received orders to march east with the right wing from Gordon and destroy the Georgia Central Railroad as far as Tennille Station, south of Sandersville.

Left Wing. General Slocum's orders were to march his wing to Sandersville.

Sherman ordered Kilpatrick to march east with his cavalrymen and break up the branch of the Georgia Central Railroad operating from Millen to Augusta. Upon completion of the task, he was then to enter Millen, seek out the reported prisoner of war camp with imprisoned Union soldiers located there, and achieve their release.

On November 24 Moore's pioneer detachment constructed an eighty-foot-long bridge over Buffalo Creek. He reported at the bridge site, "I also repaired five bridges at this point by repairing the trestles that had been burned off, and using balk and chess for covering. These bridges were 300 feet in length. I also repaired two bridges at the same flat or swamp, 120 feet in length, using timber procured from the woods, making the whole length of bridging at this point 560 feet."

Sherman accompanied the XX Corps from Milledgeville to Sandersville. On the twenty-fifth he approached the town and found the bridge across Buffalo Creek burned. Colonel Buell's detachment also arrived after a five-day march and built a ponton bridge and a small trestle bridge over the creek in three hours. Kilpatrick's cavalrymen entered the town the next day and skirmished with Wheeler's cavalrymen, who offered little opposition.

Right Wing. Company A, Missouri Engineers, spent three days from November 25 to 27 on the Oconee River putting down a ponton bridge, aiding in the crossing of soldiers, and taking up the bridge.

Across the Oconee River the surroundings and terrain changed considerably for the Union soldiers. They found themselves in a much more rural area. There were multitudinous creeks, branches, and streams branching off the Oconee, Ohoopee, Cannouchee, and Ogeechee Rivers to cross by bridging and wading.

At Sandersville, Sherman shifted his command post to the right wing and accompanied the XVII Corps south to the railroad at Bartow. The XV Corps moved to the XVII's right to turn the enemy's flank. At Bartow, Sherman learned Kilpatrick's cavalrymen reached the Augusta Railroad at Waynesborough and learned further the Confederates had removed the Union prisoners of war from Millen to another location. Thus failed the rescue mission Sherman had "set his heart on."

Sherman ordered Howard to fight Wheeler's cavalry if he offered battle.

Kilpatrick joined up with the left wing's XIV Corps at Waynesborough, and the combined Union force encountered Wheeler at Thomas Station, attacked his cavalrymen, and drove them from three lines of barricades. The Confederate cavalrymen fled over Brier Creek, leaving behind a burning bridge.

The XVII Corps destroyed the railroad to the Ogeechee River at Millen, the last major river to cross before Savannah. On December 2 Company A, Missouri Engineers, arrived at the river and put across a ponton bridge. On December 3 soldiers of the corps crossed, and the engineer soldiers took up the bridge three days later.

Left Wing. On November 28 Moore's pioneer detachment reached the Ogeechee River at 1 p.m. and discovered the bridge across the river burned, plus seven others that crossed a swamp three-quarters of a mile in width. A bridge 110 feet in length was constructed over the river. The pioneers also were put to work to cut a new road across the swamp, which they had to corduroy from the river through the entire swamp.

During the night of November 29 Moore's pioneers built two small trestle bridges 65 feet in length across Big Creek, three miles south of Louisville.

Attesting to a further change in the terrain as the Union soldiers started on the final leg of the march to Savannah, Moore wrote in his report, "From the Ogeechee river on we had no more ponton bridges to lay, but we traveled through a country that was very level and swampy, and I had detailed daily 100 of my men under charge of Captain William E. Chappell, of this regiment, to march in advance as pioneers to corduroy swamps and repair bridges, and clear out the timber which had been felled in the roads at every swamp by the enemy. There were a good many small bridges built, not, however, worth reporting."

The XX Corps crossed the Ogeechee River four miles north near Buck Head Creek, and the XIV Corps at Lumkin's Station.

Right Wing. The morning report of Company K, 1st Missouri Engineers, relates when the company approached the Ogeechee River it completed a march of 205 miles, with an average daily march of 12.81 miles. "March as a general thing well conducted," it further reported, "Men in good spirits, but many of them being unused to marching found it difficult to keep up. The teams of the ponton train were in such poor condition that it was almost impossible at times to advance and several wagons were abandoned."[45]

The 1st Michigan Engineers, who on the march spent most of their labor on the destruction of the railroads, from November 27 to 29 destroyed Georgia Central Railroad and wagon bridges over Williamson's Swamp from Tennille Station to the Ogeechee River.

At the river they also destroyed the long railroad bridge. Captain Poe reported the regiment performed indefatigable and valuable, as well as skillful service, in the destruction of railroad rails, constructing bridges, and corduroying and repairing roads.

Once the two army wings passed Millen, Sherman ordered them to march in a southeast direction to Savannah, where they were to arrive in four days.

Left Wing. The XIV and XX Corps marched in a narrow area between the Ogeechee and Savannah Rivers, which required the soldiers to close up the extended formation.

Right Wing. The XV Corps marched in the same area of the left wing, on its right flank, and on the east side of the Ogeechee River. The XV Corps marched on the west side of the Ogeechee River.

On the approach march to Savannah, Sherman's soldiers again found a noticeable change in the terrain; they found it difficult to march on the marshy terrain. There were many streams and marshes, bordered by rice fields, favorable to the enemy's defense works.

The enemy also placed obstructions of felled trees where roads crossed creeks, swamps, and narrow causeways. Captain Poe reported the well-organized Union engineer and pioneer companies removed the obstacles in "incredibly" short time.

The Georgia militia and Confederate soldiers under General William J. Hardee, defending Savannah, began to offer stiff resistance as Sherman's army approached within fifteen miles of Savannah. They placed obstructions on the roads, erected earthworks, and emplaced artillery. Sherman's soldiers easily turned the obstacles and drove the enemy into his lines at Savannah.

On December 10 the two wings of Sherman's army arrived in the area of Savannah.

There were five approaches to the city by narrow causeways. Two approaches were railroads, and three were dirt roads. The railroads were broken up, preventing supplies from being transported into the city. Sherman's observations revealed the city would have to be invested from the north or west.

He sent Kilpatrick's cavalry on a reconnaissance mission to Fort McAllister and to open communications with the Union fleet expected to be standing by in the sound. It was necessary for Company A, Missouri Engineers, to rebuild a ponton bridge on the Ogeechee for the cavalrymen to return to the west side of the river. Fort McAllister was southeast of the river, and the cavalrymen had to maneuver around the marshlands eastward along the riverbank to the fort.

Poe conducted reconnaissance south of the Cannouchee River. Fortunately, he located a plan of Fort McAllister. Other reconnaissances were made along the entire extent of the Confederate front. The line was entrenched in the usual manner and the defenses were strengthened by closing the sluice gates at the Savannah River and building dams across Salt Marsh Creek to provide a body of water in front of the entire Confederate line.

On December 11, Sherman issued the order to attack Fort McAllister. The fort stood as the remaining obstacle to the army's communication with the naval fleet in Ossabaw Sound.

The Confederates burned the road bridge over the Ogeechee River below the mouth of the Cannouchee River, known as King's Bridge. Company A, Missouri Engineers, and the 58th Indiana Infantry reconstructed the bridge, according to Poe, in "incredible" time in a "substantial" manner to enable the Second Division, XV Corps to cross early in the morning of December 13 to assault Fort McAllister. By 5 p.m. the division's soldiers successfully carried the fort at three points. The task, Sherman reported, "was accomplished in a handsome manner."

Sherman sailed down the Ossabaw Sound on December 15 to meet Admiral John A. Dahlgren on the *Harvest Moon*. The Union forces were joined. Two days later Sherman asked General Hardee to surrender Savannah, and Hardee refused the next day. Sherman issued orders to his staff and commanders to set up siege guns. The detailed work to set them up became unnecessary. Sherman received a message on December 20 to the effect the enemy had evacuated Savannah. Hardee crossed his soldiers over the Savannah on a bridge of flatboats, abandoned a large number of guns and a quantity of war material, and blew up the ironclads. Victorious, Sherman entered the city two days later and declared that he had accomplished the object of capturing the city and controlling the harbor and the Savannah River. He ordered Captain Poe to examine the enemy's works.[46]

In his report on the campaign, Colonel Buell, 58th Indiana Infantry, inscribed a number of interesting comments:

My command, consisting of about 900 men and 600 mules, started from Atlanta with four days' forage and twenty days' rations. My men and mules lived well throughout the whole campaign and had been in Savannah several days before we drew from the U.S. Government. My entire command was in better condition when it arrived in Savannah than when it left Atlanta.

I would state that great credit is due to officers and men of the regiment for the manner in which they conducted themselves throughout the entire campaign. Although many times, after a hard day's march, they had bridges to build or roads to repair, they were always on hand. Praise is likewise due my officers and men for the good discipline retained throughout the entire march.[47]

Sherman sent a message to Grant that his army had taken possession of Savannah, 12,000 bales of cotton, arsenals, ammunition, railroad equipment, and had captured 800 prisoners of war. "We," he added, "are in magnificent position here."

On his next march, Sherman announced, he would move north via Columbia and Raleigh, but he did not believe the Georgia militia would follow Hardee to South Carolina.

To President Lincoln, Sherman sent a message stating he was presenting to him Savannah as a Christmas present.

In his report of the Savannah campaign, Sherman wrote the offensive against the enemy's resources destroyed east and west 100 miles of the Georgia Railroad and Georgia Central Railroad. Also, the army consumed, in the region of the country thirty miles on either side of a line from Atlanta to Savannah, corn, fodder, sweet potatoes, cattle, hogs, sheep, and poultry, and carried away more than 10,000 horses, mules, and a countless number of slaves.

"Damage," Sherman's report states, "amounted to 100 million dollars." He lessened the total amount by reporting twenty million dollars of property became a beneficial possession to the Union, and the remainder became simple waste and destruction and a hard specie of warfare. "Such consequences," Sherman lectured, "brought home sad realities of war to those who had been directly or indirectly instrumental in involving the Union Army in its attendant calamities."

On the conduct of his army's soldiers, Sherman said, "They were a little loose in foraging. They did some things they ought not to have done. Yet on the whole they supplied wants of the army with as little violence as could be expected and as little loss as I calculated."

Speaking of the rank and file soldiers, Sherman declared, "They are confident in themselves. They desire no compliment from me, but I must say when called upon to fight, march, wade streams, make roads, clear out obstructions, build bridges, make corduroy and fascines, tear up railroad tracks they have done it with alacrity and a degree of cheerfulness unsurpassed."

Particularly, Sherman made the point the rank and file performed the tasks he described, which were traditionally tasks performed by the engineer-pioneer soldiers.

The Savannah campaign engineer-pioneer tasks were beyond the capacity of the three regiments and pioneer corps present. The engineer-pioneer soldiers did, according to Captain Poe's report, "perform immense labor." The work done by engineer-pioneer and infantry soldiers under engineer officers' directions in the campaign totaled:

Ponton bridging built—3,460 feet,

Trestle bridging built—1,700 feet,

Roads corduroyed (estimated)—60 miles,

Roads destroyed (estimated)—240 miles,

Roads surveyed and mapped—1,700 miles.

The 1st Missouri Engineer Regiment and the 58th Indiana Infantry Regiment alone hauled the ponton trains and constructed ponton bridges up to a length of 800 feet.

In the larger picture, as Sherman emphasized, the rank and file had to pitch in with their manual labor and hand tools to adapt the terrain to the marching army of approximately 60,000 soldiers, thousands of animal-drawn wagons, and herds of beef cattle. They built small trestle or log bridges, corduroyed roads, and built and removed obstacles. Most of the work they performed escaped tabulation or a description in the records.

Sherman's army battled as a dynamic force. It performed toilsome tasks to keep up the mobility of soldiers, animals, and wagons at an average rate of ten miles a day for forty-one days on an approximate 284-mile deployment from Atlanta to Savannah. To march the soldiers had to construct their engines of war, and conversely carry out Sherman's army's mission to destroy the enemy's engines of war. They also marched within the presence of and fought off the enemy in the campaign, which classified in the records totaled 45 skirmishes, 2 actions, 1 affair, and 3 engagements, and incurred casualties numbering:

Killed—5 officers, 58 enlisted men.

Wounded—13 officers, 232 enlisted men.

Missing—1 officer, 258 enlisted men.

Confederates captured—77 officers, 1,261 enlisted men.[48]

Mustering Out of Michigan Engineers

At the same time the Atlanta campaign reached a conclusion, so did the three-year term of service of Colonel Innes and a number of members of the 1st Michigan Engineers and Mechanics Regiment. They served honorably and faithfully. They demonstrated in their service to the Union many exemplary human qualities and construction feats. Colonel Innes personified the skill of a leader and an engineer as he molded the regiment into an outstanding organization.

At the end of 1864 when many members of the regiment completed their term of service and the time to muster out approached, Innes expressed concern for the soldiers with time to serve who would remain in the regiment. In a letter to the governor of Michigan he reported, "Our regiment's term of service expires soon and 350 men are to be mustered out. I have no sympathy with consolidating in other regiments without maintaining our engineer regiment status. I ask immediate permission to recruit. I tremble for those left behind, they will be like a church without a bishop and will be nobody's child" (his favorite expression for a situation beyond his control).

A positive sense is conveyed in the reading of Innes' regimental records. He developed in his tenure an *esprit de corps*, high morale, mutual respect, and camaraderie. On his being mustered out his soldiers gave him tokens of their appreciation. "I accept with pleasure the chair you sent me," he wrote to Company D. "Sincere thanks returned. An elegant gift. I will send to my home and properly preserve, not only because it is a relic of the nobly won Lookout Mountain but specimen of handiwork of my own regiment. Therefore value double and most 'hily' [*sic*] prized." To those soldiers who made him a desk, he expressed his appreciation and remarked, "credit to any worker in wood," the occupation of many members of his regiment.

Innes left to posterity an image of himself, and of the high caliber of the volunteer engineer officers who served in the Union army, in his farewell message to his regiment on being mustered out in Atlanta:

> Your colonel is leaving his command by virtue of expiration of term of service and takes opportunity to tender to officers and enlisted men of 1st Michigan his thanks for many favors and kindnesses bestowed on him during past three years, expresses sincere regret that circumstances will not admit of his remaining in the army.
>
> The regiment will be left in hands of able and qualified officers who will conduct it successfully through the campaigns which await the future. The original members are quitting ranks of regiment 'to gather with their friends around the family hearthstone' in full enjoyment of peaceful and quiet scenes of home life. An entire regiment well organized, disciplined, and equipped will still be left in field. To officers and enlisted men left we commit the welfare of the regiment.To you is intrusted the fair fame which as a regiment your departing fellow soldiers have helped to win and by you it can and must be sustained.
>
> The regiment has won for itself a name which will live and be respected long after we shall of been gathered to our 'fates.'
>
> You may always look back with pride upon your soldier life and know that while serving your country honestly and faithfully you were at the same time erecting for yourselves a monument which time cannot destroy. For the lamented dead we drop the

tear of sorrow. They willingly laid down their lives to preserve inviolate the honor of their country and though their graves are scattered over the hills and valleys of the sunny south they will be ever present with us in our memory.

The readiness with which you answered your country's call gave proof of your own true patriotism.While the spirit rules the hearts of the people, rebellion will surely find rebuke. Our country's flag must float over not a part of but the whole land with its stripes untarnished and its stars undiminished and while the war must result only in the restoration of the Union and the preservation of our Nationality let us hope that such a result may soon be realized and our hearts made glad at no distant day by the joyful tidings that strife is at an end.[49]

Chapter 5

1865
Where Right and Glory Led

Sherman's Goldsborough Campaign

Before Sherman could celebrate his December 20 victory on the surrender of Savannah, he had to bring to fruition Lincoln's wish "to skin the remainder of the lion." The uncompleted mission to defeat the last vestige of the Confederate army would require a continuation of the fighting. Confederate States' President Davis restored General Johnston to a field command. A number of his soldiers of the routed Army of the Tennessee returned to join him in battle. Johnston determinedly returned to the battlefield to do better in his second engagement with Sherman.

To complete the skinning of the lion, Grant and Sherman agreed on the course for Sherman's army to march north through the Carolinas, and Virginia, and join the Army of the Potomac.

Brevet Brigadier General Orlando M. Poe, Sherman's chief engineer officer, wrote the midwinter campaign would be made through a country famous for its 500 miles of swamps to be crossed at right angles, at a season of the year when they were flooded with water, and generally regarded as impassable for troops. Soldiers derided the swampy countryside as the worst marching terrain in the country. The engineer department, Poe reported, was organized with great care, anticipating a constant demand for bridges to insure the army's mobility. The ponton trains were put in perfect order. Every officer and soldier belonging to the engineer organization was duly impressed with the importance of the part the engineers were to take in the march to build bridges and roads.[1]

Sherman's army for the march consisted of:

(1) *Left Wing:* The left wing consisted of the XIV and XX Corps and the 58th Indiana Volunteer Infantry, under command of Lieutenant Colonel Joseph Moore, with an aggregate strength of 650 men, including teamsters and all other men detailed from other infantry companies, and a ponton train of 85 wagons to haul a ponton bridge of 1,000 feet.

(2) *Right Wing:* The right wing consisted of the XV and XVII Corps and the 1st Missouri Volunteer Engineers, under command of Lieutenant Colonel William Tweeddale.

(3) *Unassigned:* 1st Michigan Volunteer Engineers and Mechanics, under command of Colonel J. B. Yates. The regiment's duties were assigned by General Poe.

Left Wing. On January 20 Moore's 58th Indiana regiment with the XX Corps marched out of Savannah on the Springfield road. Heavy rains fell just as the march commenced, muddying the roads and impeding the soldiers' movements. Moore marched his regiment eight miles and camped. He received orders from headquarters to postpone the march because of the rain.[2]

With an easing of the rain on January 25, the left wing resumed the march. Along the way Moore's pioneer soldiers corduroyed swamps. On the night of the twenty-seventh they built a low wooden bridge 450 feet long across a swampy creek, two miles northeast of Springfield, on the Sister's Ferry Road.

On January 28 the regiment arrived at Sister's Ferry and went into camp, their first objective point, in advance of the XX Corps which was moving up the Savannah River on the South Carolina shore. Colonel Moore conducted a reconnaissance for a suitable site to build bridges. During the night the XIV Corps commander, Major General Jefferson C. Davis, arrived. In the morning, after examining the area, he ordered built a 250-foot ponton bridge at the ferry site across the Savannah River. The march on the road to the bridge, for a distance of two and a half miles, was over a low, wet bottom until it reached the upland. At the time of the left wing's arrival at the river the country from the ferry to the mainland was entirely overflowed, ranging in depth from one to six feet.

Heavy timber, felled by the enemy, blocked the road. The high water made a laborious and tedious job for the soldiers to move forward. Besides the obstacles which impeded the clearing of the road, working parties were frightened by torpedoes secreted under the fallen timber. One exploded, wounding two soldiers severely. As the work progressed, fifty other torpedoes were disarmed, preventing further injuries. To clear the road the infantrymen of the XIV and XX Corps furnished a high number of work details. High water held up completion of the opening of the road until February

3. When the soldiers completed crossing the river on February 6, the pioneers took up the ponton bridge, and on the seventh marched on the Brighton Road to Barnwell and the Saluda River.[3]

Right Wing. The right wing met with similar terrain obstacles. The 1st Missouri Engineers built a ponton bridge across Whale Branch, and fully corduroyed one-quarter of the road leading to Pocotaligo. On February 1 the movement from Sister's Ferry and Pocotaligo commenced, but the enemy endeavored to hold the line of the Salkehatchie without success. On February 4 the XV Corps reached Beaufort's bridge and found it destroyed, the enemy having evacuated his works there. The pioneers rebuilt twenty-two bridges scattered over a mile of swamps, averaging twenty-five feet in length, during the night, and corduroyed the entire road through the swamps.[4]

During the night of February 9 the engineers built a ponton bridge at Binnaker's, South Fork Edisto River, and the infantry drove the enemy soldiers away from their position at the crossing. The engineers built another ponton bridge on the river at Holman's, and the Union right wing crossed by the evening of February 11. The wing then marched directly upon Orangeburg. The enemy opposed the crossing of the North Fork of the Edisto River, but the Union soldiers forced away the Confederates. Three ponton bridges were built, one on the main Orangeburg Road, and two others at Shilling's Bridge. The XVII Corps occupied Orangeburg and destroyed the railroad.

The Right Wing then directed its march toward Columbia, and after some opposition at Thomas' Creek and Congaree Creek, where on February 16 the enemy was found well entrenched at a point opposite the city. The enemy also burned the bridges over the Saluda, Broad, and Congaree Rivers. The right wing engineers built a ponton bridge at the Saluda River Bridge, near a factory, and a portion of the XV Corps crossed during the night.

Left Wing. The wing arrived on the sixteenth at the Saluda River at Zion Church, some seven miles above Columbia, and during the night Colonel Moore's pioneers built a bridge across the river, spanning 400 feet, for the wing's soldiers to cross. At 1 a.m. the next day Colonel Moore received orders to send two companies of pioneers with 200 feet of ponton bridging to the XV Corps near Columbia, to splice the bridge there in order for it to span Broad River. At 7 a.m. Major William A. Downey, with the pontons collected within the XIV Corps, began to march to the Broad River Bridge. Downey and his detail reached the river at 11 p.m. and worked on completing the bridge, but as he brought only twenty-one pontons, and the bridge required thirty-one pontons to span the stream, he had to leave the bridge unfinished until another portion of the ponton train arrived.

Ponton Bridge, South Fork, Edisto River

On February 18 a detachment of the 58th Indiana took up the bridge at the Saluda River and marched to Broad River, at the mouth of Watereer Creek, arriving there at 2 a.m. on the morning of the next day after passing on a bad road through swampy country. The detachment then finished the bridge partially constructed by Major Downey's detachment. The river's width measured 640 feet. After being assisted by the left wing pioneers, the right wing then crossed to the north bank and occupied the city.

On the twentieth, a day after completion of the Broad River bridge, the 58th's pioneers received orders to take up the bridge. They completed their task at 10 p.m., and then departed on an all-night march. They reached the camp of the XX Corps at 5 a.m. on the morning of the twenty-first. There they halted for two hours, and after being fed, resumed their march on the Winnsborough Road.[5]

General Poe reported the greater part of the city of Columbia was burned during the previous night. Many reasons were given for the flagrant violation of General Sherman's orders, but, as Poe conjectured, it was principally because some citizens gave liquor to the soldiers after their arrival and they became "crazily drunk" and beyond control of their officers. The burning cotton, fired by retreating Rebels, and the presence of a large number of escaped prisoners, he added, excited the intoxicated soldiers to the first acts of violence, and with the momentum escalating, further violence could not be restrained.[6]

By the orders of General Sherman, General Poe undertook the destruction of all the railroad shops, depots, and city gasworks in Columbia. The Michigan Engineers provided the work parties to carry out the tasks.

Right Wing. The march resumed on February 20. The wing's XVII Corps with the Michigan Engineers continued their work destroying the Columbia and Charlotte Railroad from Columbia northward, while the XV Corps continued the destructive work from Columbia toward Kingsville. The railroad was thoroughly destroyed from Columbia to White Oak Station, forty-four miles.

Sherman's entire army concentrated at Winnsborough. The Left Wing assisted in the destruction of the railroad on to the north.

Left Wing. On February 22 the wing and the cavalry marched on the road to Rocky Mount, reaching the Catawba River at 5 p.m., where Colonel Moore's pioneers constructed a 660-foot ponton bridge across the river during the night. The bridge was laid just below the rapids. At the time the water level was low and the current slow, but during the night of the twenty-third a heavy rain occurred. For the next two days the XX Corps' soldiers and cavalrymen crossed the bridge. The hill on the opposite bank being steep, and becoming almost impassable from the increasing rain, and mud, the trains' crossing progressed slowly. The river continued to rise and the current became rapid. Colonel Moore had to place heavy timbers on the lower ends of the pontons to prevent them from sinking or filling with water. During the next day about two-thirds of the train of the X Corps, which had completed a march west from the Department of North Carolina to join Sherman's army, crossed and stopped at dark on account of the hill on the opposite bank. The heavy rain continued. At 7 p.m. Moore sent an order to the quartermaster in charge of the remainder of the train to cross the bridge immediately. The teams were soon ready at the bridge, but ground conditions slowed the movement. At midnight a 400-foot section midway of the bridge span broke loose and washed away in the strong current. On the morning of the twenty-sixth the 58th's pioneers took out the remainder of the pontons and were making hasty preparations to span the river at a point about 500 yards below when orders were received from General Davis, XIV Corps, to suspend operations until further orders. Climatic conditions changed on February 27. The pioneers then laid their second bridge, 680 feet in length, in an area where the current was less rapid. By 11 p.m. they completed the bridge and the soldiers commenced crossing. At night on the twenty-eighth, with the entire Right Wing across the river, Moore ordered the bridge taken up.[7]

Right Wing. From Winnsborough the wing marched to Peay's Ferry. The 1st Missouri Engineers built a ponton bridge over the Catawba River. After much trouble arising from high water, rapid current, and muddy roads the Right Wing was transferred to the eastern bank of the river. Traffic started crossing on the morning of February 23 and required four hours to complete the crossing of the bridge. The bridge extended 700 feet in length; a section of about 200 feet was totally lost from wear and tear. On the arduous tasks of the bridge builders to bridge the Catawba River, General Poe wrote, "There are but few of us who will not remember the labor, hardships, and exposures of the 23d, 24th, 25th, and 26th of February."[8]

The two wings of the army marched to Cheraw, and were concentrated there on March 3 without much opposition.

Left Wing. The wing marched to the Great Pedee River, arriving 11 p.m. on March 5 at Haile's Ferry. During the bridging of the river by the 58th Indiana regiment, Colonel Buell, the regimental commander, relieved Colonel Moore who became incapacitated with rheumatism. Colonel Buell started construction of the bridge at 1 p.m. at the 920-foot-wide river. The regiment only had 820 feet of pontons in its train; Buell was compelled to construct a trestle bridge for the last 100 feet. Buell's pioneers worked all

night, but on account of the rapid current and considerable difficulty in fixing the anchors the construction took longer. The pioneers finished the bridge at 3 p.m. on March 7, and the wing
completed its crossing. The next day, after taking up the bridge,
the detachment moved out with General James D. Morgan's Second Division; it marched some twenty miles and turned into camp
at 10 p.m.[9]

All the bridges on the road to Fayetteville were destroyed by
the retreating enemy, but each one was quickly replaced with a
ponton or trestle bridge by Sherman's engineer and pioneer soldiers. Sherman completed the concentration of his army at
Fayetteville with opposition on a small scale, but the enemy's cavalry remained in the area at a safe distance. In the town Sherman
observed the Confederates had greatly enlarged the capacity of the
old United States Arsenal. He assigned to Poe the special duty to
undertake its destruction.

The Michigan Engineers immediately began the work to batter
down the arsenal's masonry walls, to break to pieces all machinery
of whatever kind, and to prepare the two large magazines for explosion. The machine shops, foundries, and timber sheds were soon
reduced to a heap of rubbish. At a concerted signal, fire was applied
to the heaps, to all wooden buildings and piles of lumber, and to the
powder trains leading to the magazines. A few hours sufficed to reduce every combustible item to ashes. The high wind prevailing at
the time scattered the ashes. The only remains of the repossessed
arsenal were a few piles of broken bricks. Poe stated much of the
destroyed machinery had been seized from the old arsenal at Harpers Ferry by the Confederates at the beginning of the rebellion.[10]

After spending two days in Fayetteville and building two 400-
foot ponton bridges over the Cape Fear River, Sherman's left wing
soldiers and wagon trains on March 13 commenced crossing the
river. The bridges were in use for two days before being dismantled
as the left wing, together with the cavalry, moved out of the town
on the Raleigh Road. The supply trains of the cavalry and of the
wing, under escort of one division from the XIV Corps and one from
the XX Corps, after marching about eight miles on roads in terribly
bad condition, turned to the eastward, taking the main
Goldsborough Road according to Sherman's orders. The cavalry
and the other four divisions continued on the Raleigh Road until
they encountered the enemy at Taylor's Hole Creek.

Marching northward, Sherman had expectations of a more
aggressive resistance by Johnston's soldiers than he had met so
far to Fayetteville, and he expected the encounter at the creek would
become the reality of Johnston's army's first defensive battle. Early

the next morning the Union soldiers were ordered to take the initiative and attack Major A. Burnet Rhett's brigade of South Carolina Heavy Artillery. They quickly dislodged the Rebels from their entrenchments. Sherman's soldiers pressed on in pursuit and soon encountered Johnston's soldiers in a considerable force entrenched at the crossroads south of Averasborough, their lines extending from Cape Fear River to Black River. At that point the peninsula between the two rivers marked its narrowest point. Darkness had set in by the time commanders made a proper disposition of their soldiers for a Union attack. Before daylight the next morning, the seventeenth, the enemy withdrew from its bivouac. Discovering the enemy had left the battlefield, soldiers of the XX Corps pursued the Rebels as far as Averasborough.

The corps' arrival at Averasborough developed the intelligence the enemy had retreated in the direction of Smithfield. Sherman's army resumed its march along the main road leading to Goldsborough.

Right Wing. On the morning of March 19, Sherman's right wing approached to within two miles of the army's left wing. The enemy took a position at a safe distance from Sherman's soldiers, and destroyed all the bridges to the north in advance of the head of the right wing. Intelligence officers inferred the Rebels did not intend to offer any serious opposition to the wing's march.[11]

Sherman ordered his right wing to march from Lee's Store direct to Goldsborough, and the left wing to march to reach the same point via Cox's Bridge. The fortuitous tactical move of the two wings precipitated the second confrontation with Johnston, who, when marching his soldiers down the Smithfield Road and nearing Bentonville, learned Sherman had split his two wings, and ordered his soldiers to attack. Their attack of Sherman's left wing won a temporary advantage over the wing's leading division. The left wing's other three divisions, its cavalrymen, and the 1st Michigan Engineer Regiment were deployed into battle positions and repulsed the desperate enemy attack. Johnston knew by daylight the next morning the right wing of Sherman's army would march to the battlefield to close up with the left wing. The wing completed that tactical maneuver by marching all night on the same road the left wing occupied, but from the opposite direction, fighting off the enemy's opposition, and reached the rear of his lines. General Johnston's line of soldiers at once doubled back, and General Sherman's left and right wings joined. The next day the First Division, XVII Corps, succeeded in marching to within 200 yards of the bridge over Mill Creek, on the Smithfield Road, and the XV Corps carried and held the entire line of the enemy's skirmish pits in front. The enemy again withdrew during the night. The right wing pursued its foe two miles beyond Mill Creek.

The wagon trains meanwhile had continued their movement toward Goldsborough, and the soldiers who followed crowded into the town on the two ponton bridges built over the Neuse River at Cox's Bridge and the two near the county bridge. General Schofield with his XXII Corps had occupied the town earlier (after being brought from Nashville to Wilmington by railroad train).

With the capture of Goldsborough, Poe declared, "The most wonderful campaign of the war was ended," without elaborating in what respect it was the most wonderful.[12]

Poe, in his final report of the march, mentioned some pertinent engineer subjects:

"Supplies of all kinds were very badly needed, and, amongst the rest, the canvas covers of the ponton boats needed renewal. In the train attached to the right wing this was particularly the case, since many of the covers had been in the water an aggregate of 60 days. Attention is especially directed to this train, because the material had been hauled from Nashville to Goldsborough upon wagons and had been in constant use, and yet the train was serviceable. Indeed, all that was required to make it perfectly efficient was a new set of covers.

"Fully one-eighth of the whole army was without shoes, and nearly as badly off for the other articles of clothing, having now marched through the heart of the enemy's country, over swamps and through forests, nearly if not quite 500 miles, occupying 60 days of time, during which they drew but little more than their sugar and coffee from the government, gathering subsistence for themselves and animals from the enemy's country.

"Still our route at its best involved an immense amount of bridging of every kind known in active campaigning, besides some 400 miles of corduroying. The latter was a very simple affair where there were plenty of fence rails, but in their absence involved the severest labor. We found that two good fences furnished enough rails to corduroy a strip of road as long as one of them so as to make it passable. I estimate the amount of corduroying on the campaign at fully 100 miles to each army corps, making an aggregate of 400 miles. This is a moderate estimate. This kind of work was rarely done by the cavalry, since their trains moved with the infantry columns. The right wing built 15 ponton bridges, having an aggregate length of 3,720 feet, rebuilt 25 wooden bridges, an aggregate length of 4,000 feet. The left wing built 12 ponton bridges, having an aggregate length of 4,000 feet, thus making for the army a total of 11,720 feet, or in excess of two miles.

"In corduroying, the entire available force of the army was employed: engineers, pioneers, and infantrymen."[13]

On April 10, Sherman's army marched forward on the road to Raleigh, and his soldiers met with feeble resistance from Johnston's soldiers. Engineer and pioneer soldiers were called upon at once to perform their duties to corduroy and build bridges. On April 11 four ponton bridges were laid across the Neuse River. After two more days of marching, Sherman's soldiers entered the city of Raleigh without any opposition.[14]

Meticulously, the pioneer corps of the XVII Corps collected and consolidated by hand statistics of the extensive and impressive amount of work they labored on during the campaign from Pocotaligo, South Carolina, to Goldsborough, North Carolina, from January 30, 1865, to March 24, 1865, which appears in the following table.[15]

Description of work done.	First Division.	Third Division.	Fourth Division.	Total.
Corduroy built ....yards..	13,135	24,753	32,975	70,863
Bridges built....................................do...	133	303	439	875
Rafting prepared................................do...	190	....	....	190
Side roads cut...................................do...	25,980	53,836	17,675	97,491
Obstructions of fallen timber cleared.............do...	150	650	150	950
Infantry foot bridges............................do...	....	....	....	1,760
Half-destroyed bridges repaired ....number..	....	....	....	11
Batteries built a................................ do..	6	2	5	13
Breast-works built..............................yards..	5,096	4,140	3,505	12,741
Railroad track destroyed.........................do...	27,280	25,440	35,200	87,920
Railroad culverts destroyed...................number..	8	7	8	23
Trestle-work destroyed ....yards..	....	....	300	300
Cars destroyed.................................number..	....	....	3	3
Car wheels destroyed............................pairs..	150	....	....	150

a Containing in all forty-seven embrasures.

Work Done by XVII Corps during the Period January 30, 1865, to March 24, 1865.

Army of the Potomac

A new year arrived with the engineer soldiers quartered in their winter camps near Petersburg. Their daily camp life remained active as they trained and performed engineer tasks.

From the 50th New York Engineers' camp at Poplar Grove, Lieutenant Owen early in the year wrote a letter home reporting his time in the comfortable winter camp passed pleasantly. He added he had little news about the army, but he could say the weather was cold and rainy; the ground turned into ankle deep mud. Later in the month his letter home stated, "Everything goes nicely, the rebellion is crumbling away, and the Johnnies coming in every day."[16]

Army of the James

On January 5 Lieutenant William R. King, Corps of Engineers, received the assignment to build a permanent bridge across the James River near Varina, and where Varina Road ended at the river. On the far side the bridge connected to Curl's Neck. The existing September-built ponton bridge had to be replaced because of the damage caused by the freshets, floating ice, and driftwood in the river.

On January 25, King reported some progress on the bridge, but there were delays because of unfavorable weather.

He completed the pile bridge on February 19 and removed the remnants of the ponton bridge.

He wrote in his report the work was supervised in detail by Captain James W. Lyon, 4th Rhode Island Volunteers, an assistant engineer, "who deserved great praise for the rapid and workmanlike manner in which it was executed."

The bridge was 1,350 feet long, 21 feet wide, and about 9 feet above low water. The bays were 15 feet wide, and each one was supported by 3 piles. As the water in the channel was about 25 feet deep, some of the piles were cut 150 feet long; the greater number being 30 and 40 feet long. Because of the hardness of the river bed it was impossible to drive piles more than 8 or 10 feet, and it was also found unnecessary to drive them farther, as they would break off instead of pulling out.

In order to form ice-breakers and prevent lateral motion of the bridge, an inclined brace was placed above each row of piles, the larger end being spiked to the cap and the other end chained to a pile fifty or sixty feet above the bridge, the pile being sawed nearly through before driving, and so arranged as to break off just above the chain. Near the draw similar braces were placed on the lower side also to give additional strength.

The roadway was constructed in the ordinary manner, with caps, stringers, and three-inch planks. The draw was constructed of three wood lighters, which were all that could be obtained at the time. The bays being very wide, light trusses were used to prevent sagging. The ends of the draw were connected with the bridge by aprons which allowed for rise and fall of the tide. These were entirely lifted from the bridge by ropes and levers when the draw was to be opened, and the latter was maneuvered by means of a small chain which passed over a windlass on the draw, and when the draw was opened it sagged down to allow vessels to pass over it.

"It may be proper to state that the entire cost of this bridge to the government was $750, the labor, including sawing of plank and hewing of timber, having been performed by enlisted men. But for the delays caused by freshets and the nonarrival of the boats for the draw, the bridge would have been completed within 15 days from the time it was commenced."[17]

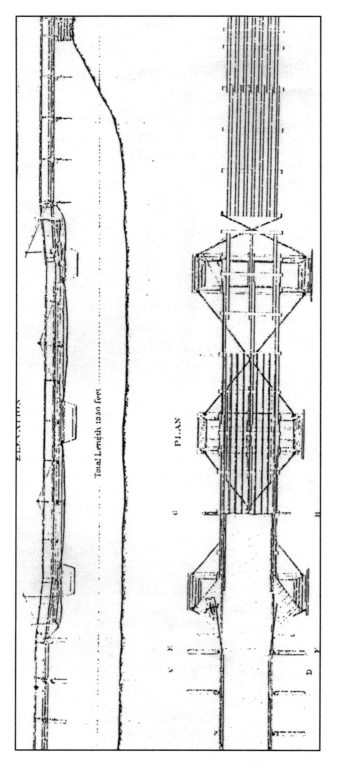

ELEVATION

Total Length 1350 feet

PLAN

Pile Bridge, James River near Varina

O.R., Atlas, Plate 76(6)

On February 7 Owen wrote home, "nasty snow during the night." In a letter two weeks later, he wrote the peace question had died out and there would be more fighting "ere little men see folly of ways." Bearing his soul to his parents, he declared, "Fight if we must, those who survive it will never repent time spent in so serious a cause. Must have Union and abolition of slavery. I feel same warmth in cause. My duty is to help what little I can."[18]

Opening Acts of Final Battle

At the top command level Lee and Grant brooded over the stalemate. The inaction delayed the achievement of the sought after victory. They turned over in their minds how to extricate their soldiers from the massive and intricate network of inactive defensive works to a more favorable active battlefield position.

Lee thought out his tactics to achieve his victory. Orders would be issued to his soldiers to leave their inactive positions, slip away from Grant's soldiers on the right flank, and march to North Carolina to join Johnston's army. The newly combined Confederate force would then seek out, battle, and defeat Sherman's army. After such a victory, the Confederate soldiers would march north and on equal terms engage Grant's soldiers in battle.

Grant's thoughtful ruminations reminded him his soldiers in defensive fortifications defied his tactical doctrine to avoid static positions. Yet, he knew from battle experience the folly to assault head-on the enemy's fortified position. He subscribed to the tactics to maneuver to the flanks, slip around enemy lines, and, as his soldiers' movement rolled up a flank, they would engage and defeat the enemy.

To give his tactics reality and to develop an expedient to end the stalemate, Grant decided to extend his battle line to the west and to erect more defense works to protect the soldiers on the extended line. As his army possessed more manpower than Lee's army, he could afford to take such action. Lee, with less manpower, countered Grant's tactics by thinning out his line, thus increasing its vulnerability.

Eventually, Grant believed, the Union deployment to the flank and breaking through a weakened enemy line would force Lee into battle in the open where he would be an unequal match for the superior Union army.

To implement the tactical plan, Duane, Grant's chief engineer officer, issued orders to Major M. Van Brocklin, on February 5, to march a detachment of four companies of the 50th New York engineers, to Vaughan Road near its crossing of Hatcher's Run. There the detachment was to repair the road and to build corduroy bridges over the small streams. The next day Duane issued orders to Van Brocklin to build an additional bridge over Hatcher's Run. Van Brocklin's engineer soldiers collected and carried the timber for the bridge from the woods, and finished a bridge, 250 feet in length, over the run in two days.[19]

Spring freshets washed away the corduroy bridge Van Brocklin had built across Hatcher's Run. He received orders to build a substantial and permanent replacement.

By March 15 Van Brocklin completed construction of a permanent bridge over Hatcher's Run, 285 feet in length above the high water mark, supported by eleven cribs each 16 feet long, 6 feet wide, and from 2 to 6 feet high. The roadway of the bridge consisted of two tracks each 8 feet in width, separated by longitudinal timber, firmly pinned to the corduroy flooring. A day was also spent repairing the corduroy of Vaughan Road. Company C, 50th New York Volunteer Engineers worked on the bridge assisted by work crews from the V Corps.[20]

Lee made his first tactical move to implement his plan to withdraw from his defensive position. It was his first offensive attack since the one a year ago at the Wilderness, a hundred miles to the north. At dawn on March 25 his soldiers launched an attack on Fort Stedman, with the objectives to cut off the railroad that supplied Grant's soldiers and to open a march route to the South.

Lee's soldiers' initial attack carried the railroad tracks. When the Union soldiers mounted their counterattack, the Confederate soldiers, unable to sustain their attack, exhausted their last full measure and will to continue the battle. By noon the Yankees forced the Rebels back into their lines, where, they discovered, their revered general had grasped an illusion.

The glorious moment and initiative passed to Grant to accelerate his battle plan. He issued orders to his infantrymen to march to the west to turn Lee's right flank. Lee's soldiers made an effort to contest their foe's advance.

To carry out Grant's orders for the coordinated movement of the armies, on March 29 the marching column of the Army of the James, consisting of the XXIV and XXV Corps, under the command of the newly appointed commander, Major General Edward O. C. Ord, occupied the left of the Army of the Potomac on an entrenched line anchored on Hatcher's Run.

On the following day the Army of the James' XXIV Corps made an advance across Hatcher's Run and captured a Rebel picket line, and secured a position beyond Armstrong's House on the 800 yards of the Rebel line of works.

The engineer force with the army consisted of seven companies of the 1st New York Volunteer Engineer Regiment. Its equipment consisted of a tool train of ten wagons, a ponton train of thirty-two wagons, which carried spare chess, 380 feet of bridge equipment, and forage.

The engineers built their first ponton bridge over Hatcher's Run, to enable the XXIV Corps to cross the run and make contact on the right with the entrenched VI Corps of the Army of the Potomac. The engineers made attempts during the night to build entrenchments, but the ground being saturated with water from recent heavy rains lacked a firm support.[21]

Colonel Ira Spaulding, 50th New York Volunteer Engineers, reported he left winter camp near Petersburg on March 29. He left one company with the wagon trains, and Major Van Brocklin's detachment accompanied Major General Gouverneur Warren's V Corps with a ponton train consisting of twelve pontons, and one company accompanied Major General Andrew A. Humphreys' II Corps, with a train of eighteen pontons.

At Hatcher's Run Spaulding observed a ponton bridge had been built for troops to cross, and the log bridge for the passage of trains. The crossing at the run was found to be in a difficult condition because of the rapidly rising stream and the almost impassable roads. He set his engineers immediately to work crossing the bridge and moving upon the Old Stage Road where they repaired the worst places and assisted the trains. At midnight he permitted his soldiers to rest in a bivouac.

At 4 a.m. the next morning Spaulding's engineers restarted the work on the crossing of Hatcher's Run. The stream rose so rapidly during the night as to threaten the log bridge. It became necessary to raise the abutments of the ponton bridge about four feet, and to build a corduroy bridge nearly a 100 yards in length to the hill on the south side of the run. Rain came down incessantly, and only by constant and severe labor of the engineer soldiers was the road kept passable for the trains.[22]

The chronicler of the Engineer Battalion wrote in the records on March 29 the army was in motion to force the enemy from its position at Petersburg by a turning movement and to assure the success of Sheridan's cavalry. The record states the battalion moved out at 2 a.m. and performed the duties to repair and keep roads open, and at night there was heavy rain. On the next day the Engineer Battalion reported they were occupied on the same tasks, corduroying roads beyond Hatcher's Run, the rain continued, and the soil was like quicksand without a bottom.

Lieutenant Owen wrote home, "There is a big move going on. Heavy firing before Petersburg. You may expect to hear great news. The rebellion is in its last reel, within few months will fall prostrate before the victorious armies of U.S. Grant."[23]

On April 2, soldiers of the Army of the James attacked the Confederates at Fort Gregg, and after a desperate engagement successfully drove them off and occupied their works. The Army of the Potomac soldiers also attacked along the line, and they occupied vacated positions entirely surrounding Petersburg. To ward off attacks, Lee was forced to thin out his soldiers on the lines in an attempt to hold his position. Faced with a hopeless situation, Lee made a late night decision to evacuate Petersburg and Richmond, and started marching to the west.

Alerted to Lee's move, Grant ordered a pursuit of the enemy.

The Army of the James made quick preparations for a rapid march. It started to march out on March 3 at 5 a.m. on Cox Road, parallel to the South Side Railroad. A detachment of the 1st New York Volunteer Engineer Regiment marched ahead to repair roads and bridges, and another remained with the ponton train at the alert with the army's headquarters.[24]

Major Van Brocklin with his 50th New York Volunteer Engineers detachment marched in support of the Army of the Potomac. His detachment built a ponton bridge over Hatcher's Run, near Perkins' House, and also one over Gravelly Run near Friends' Meeting House. As the army marched, the detachment also engaged in tasks of building and repairing corduroy roads. Colonel Spaulding gave Van Brocklin orders to keep the bridges in operation until all the trains on the Old Stage Road had crossed his bridgehead.[25]

General Benham, Grant's chief staff engineer officer, reported he entered Petersburg early in the morning as the armies were marching out, and observed three or four principal bridges over the Appomattox River destroyed or in flames. He sent orders at once for the 15th New York Engineers Regiment to report to reconstruct them, and he reported, during the day before 4 p.m., Colonel Brainerd, regimental commander, "with most praiseworthy activity had almost entirely rebuilt the principal bridge, ready for passage of the artillery, and repaired the railroad bridge, for rapid passage of infantry, and by early next morning, as directed by General Grant, had ready a third temporary bridge at the upper part of the city across the river at a most difficult point." The work on the bridges completed, the regiment returned to City Point the next day.[26]

A detachment of the 1st New York Engineers, under Major W. R. King, marched into Richmond on April 3 to help in extinguishing the fires consuming the city. It also constructed a ponton bridge 2,400 feet in length across the James River to connect

Ponton Bridge, James River at Manchester

Manchester and Richmond. It was the third longest ponton bridge built by engineer soldiers during the rebellion.[27]

Lieutenant Owen wrote home on April 5, "Much news, so many victories. Yesterday (4th) President Lincoln visited Richmond."[28]

At Farmville on April 7, Colonel Michie, staff engineer officer of the Army of the James, wrote, "We had the honor of having our ponton trains first up by a detachment of the 1st New York Volunteer Engineers, so that we were enabled to build a bridge over the Appomattox river to pass over the trains and artillery of the II and VI Army Corps, Army of the Potomac, although the ponton trains of that army were better equipped, lighter loaded, and possessed other advantages over the ponton train of our army."[29] (This event occurred to the dismay of the 15th and 50th New York Engineers who had performed arduous bridge-building duties for the army, but missed the opportunity to build a bridge at the last battle of the campaign.)

Colonel Spaulding, 50th New York Volunteer Engineers, reported he arrived at Burkeville at 10 p.m., and received an order from army headquarters to move a train of eighteen pontons to Farmville with sufficient engineer soldiers to build a ponton bridge. "At 10:45 p.m.," he recorded, "I started with three companies. From Rice's Station to Farmville the roads were very bad indeed and required a large amount of work to provide passage of our own and other trains.

"At 9:30 a.m. April 8th my trains reached Appomattox river at Farmville. Major Van Brocklin immediately began to build a ponton bridge across the river to take the place of the one that had been in place but had deteriorated from the heavy traffic that passed over it. At the same time I sent an order to Burkeville for the rest of the regiment to join me, which reached me 2 a.m. on April 9th.

"Leaving a detachment in charge of the bridge at Farmville, I marched the balance of my train at 9 o'clock a.m. on the 9th toward Appomattox Court House and late in the evening the main portion of my ponton trains were within about one mile of army headquarters. There I learned of Lee's surrender."[30]

Colonel Michie reported on April 8 at daylight the XXIV Corps, Army of the James, moved from Farmville, taking the road running nearly with the South Side Railroad, and made a forced march of nearly thirty-three miles before midnight, resting for a few hours on the railroad where Sheridan had captured several cars loaded with bacon and corn. At 3:30 a.m. April 9, the infantry moved again and at 8 a.m. were in action on the extreme left of the army. The leading soldiers of the XXIV Corps went into action on the double quick, and delivered the volley which staggered and drove back the advance of the enemy, who had at that

Ponton Bridge, Appomattox River

moment gained some temporary advantage over the cavalry. The action lasted until 10 a.m. when a truce was granted preliminary to the surrender.[31]

Lieutenant Owen reported the arrival of the news of Lee's surrender at his detachment's camp at Poplar Grove. "Salute of guns fired. I turned out my men to give three cheers." He remarked to his parents he was ready "to bid farewell to this inhuman life, but proud we participated in crushing the wicked rebellion."[32]

Victory Celebrations

With the surcease of battlefield combat, Meade's soldiers received orders to march to Washington to parade in a victory celebration.

Before Meade's army could take up the march, it had to deploy from the battlefield and reform at a staging area. There remained bridges to be built by the engineers to enable the army to collect itself. Some units had been dispersed throughout southwestern Virginia. To reform, the army bridges were built by the 50th New York Engineers over the Staunton and Appomattox Rivers.

Because there would be rivers to cross on the army's deployment to Richmond, and on to Washington, the engineers were in the forefront of the march route to build the necessary bridges. Colonel Spaulding reported his engineer regiment on April 10 started on a march to Burkeville.

Spaulding's regiment reached Manchester, south of Richmond on the James River, on May 5 after marching the last forty-two miles in twenty-five hours, about one and two-thirds miles in an hour. On the march to that point the engineer soldiers marched about four miles a day. The regiment left on May 7 for a two-day march to the Rappahannock River. On May 18 it left Fredericksburg for the forty-eight-mile march to Washington where it arrived on the twenty-first at the engineers' camp near the Navy Yard.[33]

The chronicler of the Engineer Battalion recorded when the battalion left its last battlefield near Farmville for Washington, it moved out "in rags and tatters, shoes held together by thongs, canvas trousers in shreds and hats and blouses tattered and torn." Another entry related when the engineer soldiers arrived in Fairfax County (Occoquan River), "they were ordered on a forced march of 15 miles in a day [for four days to reach the Potomac River], it was most severe march engaged in by the battalion."[34] An ironic comment for soldiers who in four years of arduous service marched up and down the Maryland-Virginia countryside. There were soldiers in the war who averaged ten miles a day and on some days marched sixteen to twenty-two miles.

A veteran engineer soldier, ruminating on his regiment's marches on the vast expanse of the battlefields from river bank to river bank, posed the question, where had his regiment marched? and in his answer declared the regiment marched "where right and glory led!"

General Johnston Surrenders

Sherman's army remained in Raleigh for three days after the April 26 signing of the surrender document by Sherman and Johnston.[35]

On April 29 Sherman's victorious army marched out for Washington. The 1st Michigan Volunteer Engineers and 1st Missouri Volunteer Engineers accompanied the army because there was still a need for them to build bridges. They built their first bridge on the Neuse River, at Powell's Bridge, northeast of Raleigh, 200 feet long. Other bridges they built were:

May 3, Roanoke River, at Robinson's Ferry, 740 feet.

May 13, Pamunkey River, at Littlepage's Bridge, 200 feet. The Pamunkey River was extremely swollen, the water overflowing the southern bank to the depth of two and a half feet when the army arrived in the morning. The river continued rising during the day. The ponton bridge was built and some wagon trains moved over in the afternoon, but by the next morning the water was so high it became necessary to build a trestle bridge about thirty yards in length to approach the pontons.

May 18, Occoquan River, 280 feet.

May 19, Sherman's force of XV and XVII Corps, after marching with surprising celerity, arrived in Alexandria.[36]

Victory Parade

On May 24 the nation celebrated the Union army's victory in the nation's capital city. Proud soldiers passed in review. General Meade marched at the head of the Army of the Potomac, and he was followed by the Engineer Battalion. General Sherman marched at the head of the Military Division of the Mississippi, and he was followed by the 1st Michigan and 1st Missouri Volunteer Engineer regiments.

A concurrent celebration occurred in Nashville. General Thomas' victorious army marched for the last time under his watchful eye in a colorful victory parade.

The victory parades closed out, an inchoate nostalgia already present, the engineer and pioneer soldiers packed their axes and headed home to resume their axemanship and mechanical skills. They left on the battlefields the monuments of their manual labors and skills.

Last Bridge

With the rebellion formally ended, Major King and his 1st New York Volunteer Engineers, awaiting the process of being mustered out of the army, achieved one more significant feat of bridge construction on the James River.

In June General Barnard assigned Major King and his engineer soldiers the task of replacing, on the James River, the 2,400-foot ponton bridge they had built when they entered Richmond on April 3 with a permanent bridge, at a site called Mayo's Bridge, connecting Richmond and Manchester.

The following is an extract from his report on the new bridge's construction, and the plan he adopted for its completion:

"Dimensions, entire length of bridge, 1,396 feet; width, including sidewalks, 31 feet; width of carriage way in clear, $19^1/_2$ feet, number of bays, 18; width of bays, 69 to 78 feet; height of piers at low water, 20 feet."[37]

James River Bridge at Mayo's

Date.	No. of bridge.	Length.	Kind of boat.	Location.	River.	Officer in command of train.	Remarks.
[1862.		*Feet.*					
Sept. 28	1	800	Wooden	Harper's Ferry	Potomac	Captain Spaulding	
Oct. 20	2	1,500	...do	Berlin	...do	...do	
21	3	80	...do	...do	Chesapeake and Ohio Canal.	...do	
Nov. 22	4	280	...do	Occoquan	Occoquan	Major Spaulding	
Dec. 11	5	440	...do	Fredericksburg	Rappahannock.	...do	Lacy house.
11	6	420	...do	...do	...do	Captains McDonald and McGrath	Lower crossing.
12	7	440	...do	...do	...do	Major Spaulding	Lacy house.
1863. Apr. 20	8	420	...do	U. S. Ford	...do	...do	
20	9	400	...do	...do	...do	...do	Part French pontoons and part Waterman boats.
May 6	10	400	...do	Franklin's Crossing.	...do	...do	
7	11	400	...do	...do	...do	...do	
July —	12	800	...do	Harper's Ferry	Potomac	Lieutenant-Colonel Spaulding.	
	13	1,500	...do	Berlin	...do	...do	
	14	80	...do	...do	Chesapeake and Ohio Canal.	...do	
	15	1,500	...do	...do	Potomac	...do	
Oct. 11	16	180	...do	Kelly's Ford	Rappahannock.	Major Beers	
11	17	180	...do	Beverly Ford	...do	...do	
18	18	100	...do	Ball's Ford	Bull Run	Captain Hine	
18	19	100	...do	Mitchell's Ford	...do	Captain McDonald	
18	20	120	...do	Blackburn's Ford.	...do	Lieutenant Beers	
18	21	120	...do	McLean's Ford	...do	Captain Folwell	
Nov. 8	22	180	...do	Rappahannock Station.	Rappahannock.	Captain McDonald	Above railroad bridge.
8	23	190	...do	Norman's Ford	...do	Captain Hine	Below railroad bridge.
9	24	180	...do	Rappahannock Station.	...do	...do	Do.
26	25	180	...do	Culpeper Ford Gold Mine.	Rapidan	...do	
26	26	170	...do	...do	...do	Captain McDonald	
Dec. 4	27	180	...do	Rappahannock Station.	Rappahannock.	...do	
4	28	140	...do	Welford's Ford.	Hazel	Captain Hine	
1864. Apr. 29	29	180	Canvas	Kelly's Ford	Rappahannock.	Captain Folwell	
May 4	30	150	...do	Ely's Ford	Rapidan	...do	
4	31	190	Wooden	...do	...do	Major Brainerd	
4	32	220	...do	Germanna Ford.	...do	Captain McDonald	
4	33	220	Canvas	...do	...do	Captain Van Brocklin.	
4	34	160	Wooden	Culpeper Ford	...do	Captain Palmer	
7	35	190	...do	Ely's Ford	...do	Captain McDonald.	
10	36	420	...do	Fredericksburg (lower crossing).	Rappahannock.	Major Brainerd	
10	37	50	Canvas		Po	Captain Van Brocklin.	
10	38	50	...do		...do	...do	
18	39	440	Wooden	Fredericksburg (Lacy house).	Rappahannock.	Major Beers	
23	40	160	Canvas	Jericho Mills	North Anna	Captain Van Brocklin.	

Ponton Bridges Built by 50th New York Volunteer Engineers

September 1862–May 1865 (Part 1)

Date.	No. of bridge.	Length.	Kind of boat.	Location.	River.	Officer in command of train.	Remarks.
1864.		*Feet.*					
May 24	41	100	Canvas	Railway bridge	North Anna	Captain Folwell	
24	42	100	...do	...do	...do	...do	
25	43	100	...do	Above railway bridge	...do	...do	
25	44	80	Wooden	Quarles' Mills	...do	Major Beers	Besides pontoon, 200-feet crib bridge.
26	45	160	...do	Jericho Mills	...do	...do	
26	46	100	...do	Below railroad bridge	...do	Captain McDonald	
26	47	100	.. do	Above railroad bridge	...do	...do	
27	48	180	Canvas	Hanovertown	Pamunkey	Captain Van Brocklin	
27	49	164	.. do	...do	.. do	Captain Folwell	
28	50	146	...do	Mrs. Nelson's	...do	...do	Or Mrs. Hundley's.
28	51	140	Wooden	....do	...do	Major Beers	
28	52	180	...do	Hanovertown	Pamunkey	Captain McDonald	
28	53	180		Dunkirk	Mattapony	Captain Personius	
June 1	54	188	Canvas	....do	...do	Captain Van Brocklin	
3	55	160	...do	New Castle Ferry	Pamunkey	...do	
5	56	150	...do	...do	...do	Captain Folwell	
12	57	100	Wooden	Long Bridge	Chickahominy	Major Ford	Main channel.
12	58	60	...do	....do	...do	...do	South branch.
13	59	60	Canvas	Jones' Bridge	...do	Captain Folwell	Main channel.
13	60	40	...do	....do	...do	...do	South branch.
13	61	60	Wooden	....do	...do	Captain Palmer	Main channel.
13	62	40	...do	....do	...do	...do	South branch.
14	63	1,240	Wooden and canvas.	Coles' Ferry	...do	Lieutenant-Colonel Spaulding.	
19	64	100	...do	Dunkirk	Mattapony	Captain Folwell	
23	65	60	...do	Jones'Bridge	Chickahominy	...do	Main channel.
23	66	40	...do	...do	...do	...do	South branch.
Dec. 7	67	152	...do	Freeman's Ford	Nottoway	Brevet Major Van Brocklin	
9	68	56	...do	Near Hicksford	Three Creek	...do	
11	69	152	...do	Freeman's Ford	Nottoway	...do	
11	70	152	...do	...do	...do	Major Folwell	
1865.							
Mar. 29	71	65	...do	W. Perkins' house	Hatcher's Run.	Brevet Major Van Brocklin	
29	72	55	...do	Quaker road	Gravelly Run	...do	
Apr. 8	73	90	Canvas	Farmville	Appomattox	...do	
12	74	90	...do	...do	do'	...do	
22	75	100	...do	Genito Bridge	...do	Major Folwell	
24	76	315	...do	Clark's Ferry	Staunton	Brevet Major Van Brocklin	
27	77	270	...do	Roanoke Station	...do	Major Folwell	
29	78	350	...do	Moseley's Ferry	...do	Brevet Major Van Brocklin	
30	79	50	...do	Roanoke Station	Little Roanoke.	...do	
30	80	270	...do	...do	Staunton	...do	
May 8	81	400	...do	Franklin's Crossing	Rappahannock.	Major McDonald	
17	82	300	...do	Clark's Ferry	Staunton	Brevet Major Van Brocklin	
20	83	100	...do	Goode's Bridge	Appomattox	...do	
21	84	90	...do	Richmond, Va	Canal	...do	
24	85	180	...do	Littlepage's Bridge.	Pamunkey	...do	
28	86	65	...do	Near Guiney's Station.	Po	...do	

Total number of bridges.. 86
Total length of bridges..feet.. 21,248
Equal to...miles.. 4.022

Ponton Bridges Built by 50th New York Volunteer Engineers

September 1862–May 1865 (Part 2)

What campaign.	Pontoon bridge built.	Trestle bridge built.
	Feet.	Feet.
Atlanta campaign	3,500	3,330
Savannah campaign	3,460	1,700
Goldsborough campaign	7,720	4,000
March to Washington	a 3,000	
Total	17,680	9,030
Total ....miles..	3.35	1.7

a Estimated.

Bridges Built by Engineers, Military Division of the Mississippi
1864–1865

In Retrospect

Civil War commanders and staff officers possessed a penchant to compile statistics on the activities of the war in their areas of responsibility.

The statistics on the bridges the engineer officers left to posterity might strike a reader as void of detail. They do, though, project an awareness of an enormous amount of mental activity expended on planning and manual labor exerted on the construction of the bridges. They may also be difficult to comprehend in human terms, but they relate the accomplishment of a tremendous amount of needed bridge construction. They also exemplify the progress made in technology at that period of the country's history.

There are, in addition, many reports of newspaper correspondents whose writings on bridges enable readers to create mental images of unique structures. There are also letters and diaries of engineer officers and soldiers in the ranks who wrote of the bridges in whose construction they took part. Many times due to the intense activity of building a bridge on the battlefield, the engineers were unable to record the details of building a bridge in the official records. This is particularly true on the building of the bridge at Paducah. We are indebted to newspaper correspondents for the details on that historic bridge.

Fortunately, we have visual presentations of many of the bridges constructed in the war prepared by artists who sketched them and photographers who photographed them on the spot as they travelled about with the armies in the field, witnessing the engineers' "inventive genius," or their advancement of technology.

245

Accolades

Many accolades, written and verbal, were expressed on the innovative and imaginative bridge-building feats by the engineers.

In the forefront, President Lincoln, after a visit to a railroad bridge General Haupt built in May 1862, across Potomac Creek in Virginia, marveled at its remarkable construction, "with nothing in it but bean poles and cornstalks." General Haupt, in his wartime service, became a leading contributor to the technology of railroad construction.

General Grant remarked in 1863 that whenever a requirement arose on the battlefield for practical mechanical work, officers and soldiers were always available to handle a job at hand.

General Barnard, chief engineer officer of the Army of the Potomac, expressed an incisive observation on the work of his bridge builders. He attributed the success of their work to the quality of the fertile American genius they possessed to construct expedients. He qualified his observation to add genius itself could not provide for an object which was not understood in the context of an assigned mission.

What he essentially said was the impressive feats of the bridge builders were their understanding of the object on which they were to focus. In a battle situation they stood on a riverbank, and upon being given orders to provide a bridge, they focused on and conceptualized for the army's mobility the necessary expedient, a bridge. Their bridge plan from their conceptualization took form as a mental image, then they set the engineer soldiers to work to build it with the resources in the area.

General Barnard reinforced his point in his report on the close of the Peninsular Campaign, 1862. At lower Chickahominy River the Army of the Potomac passed over a ponton bridge his engineer soldiers built "of the extraordinary length of 650 yards. A feat," he added, "scarcely surpassed in military history at the time." The general, at that time, correctly called it a feat of technology, but the feat was exceeded a number of times during the war.

In the early days of the war, Captain Pike understood the object to be the need for a bridge for General Grant to cross his soldiers, and their wagon trains, over the Ohio River to capture Paducah. He conceptualized and formed a mental image of his plan for a bridge. As he brought his planned bridge into reality, he supervised his pioneer soldiers in the collection of the necessary materials and in the construction of a record length floating bridge built of coal barges.

Captain Patterson also perceived on three occasions the object of the need for a bridge. The first occasion was a chasm in the

Cumberland Mountains. Later in the Vicksburg campaign he perceived the object to build a bridge over the North Fork of Bayou
Pierre, and later one over the Big Black River. On each occasion by
the use of his imagination and trees and brush he built the needed
bridges. He, too, in his wartime service became a leading contributor to the technology of bridge construction.

Captain Stewart R. Tresilian in a like experience built a floating bridge out of cotton bales to span the Big Black River.

Colonel Spaulding, through the experience he gained in his
wartime service as commander of an engineer regiment, wrote, for
the record, by the spring of 1864 the bridge trains of the Army of
the Potomac, and the engineer soldiers in charge of them (which
were pre-thought-out objects of the fertile American genius possessed by Corps of Engineers' officers), "were more perfectly arranged than any bridge trains before organized in America." He
based his conclusion on the fact that, from the crossing of the
Rapidan River in the spring of 1864, to the closing of the war, no
bridge material was ever lost, destroyed, or abandoned to the enemy, nor were any soldiers ever kept waiting for the construction of
a bridge. He concluded the ponton bridges built were "monuments
of the skill and industry of the officers and enlisted men of his
regiment."

Colonel Innes, of the Michigan engineer regiment, echoed Colonel Spaulding's accolade to his engineer soldiers when he completed his term of service in the army. He concluded the ponton
bridges his regiment built were "monuments to noble and fruitful
exertions."

General Poe mentioned in the records the creditable service of
the 58th Indiana Infantry regiment, which early in the Atlanta campaign had been detailed by General Sherman to engineer duty and
equipped with canvas ponton trains. "Under the tutelage of their
efficient commander, Colonel George P. Buell, the soldiers became
very valuable for all purposes required at their hands, comparable
to the engineer regiments (of Michigan and Missouri) in bridge building skills." The detail of the 58th Indiana also reinforced what General Grant stated, when there was a need for soldiers to do a
mechanical task, they were present to do it.

Major Van Brocklin, 50th New York Volunteer Engineers, who
in the closing days of the war built a number of ponton bridges for
the army's march from Petersburg to Farmville, wrote in the records:
"I desire to mention Company C, 50th New York Engineer Regiment, by long experience in handling canvas pontons and the zeal
it uniformly manifested in the discharge of its duties has well merited the honor they are entitled to: the recognition as the number
one company of pontoniers in the service."

The engineers recorded well their beliefs and jealousies of their achievements by their skills and manual labor with hand tools, and how they upheld in those prideful achievements the fertile American genius of practical engineering.

The engineer officers' accolades express metaphors. Their metaphors, in turn, speak of technology, which, in turn, speaks of the exertion of the energy of the human mind, the catalyst of technology.

Notes

CHAPTER 1

1. Merlin E. Sumner, ed., *The Diary of Cyrus B. Comstock* (Dayton, Ohio: Morningside House, Inc., 1987), p. 227.

2. Gilbert Thompson, "The Engineer Battalion in the Civil War," *Occasional Papers*, Engineer School, U.S. Army, No. 44 (1910): p. 49.

3. Ibid., p. 49; *American Military History 1607–1953, ROTC Manual 145–20* (Washington, D.C., Department of the Army, GPO, 1956), p. 192.

4. Ivor D. Spencer, "Rubber Ponton Bridges—in 1846," *The Military Engineer*, 37, 231 (January 1945), p. 26.

5. The War of the Rebellion, *A Compilation of the Official Records of the Union and Confederate Armies* (Washington, Government Printing Office, 1891), ser. 1, vol. 2, pp. 328–29 (hereinafter cited as *O.R.*).

6. Ibid., p. 317.

7. Ibid., p. 323.

8. Ibid., p. 332.

9. *American Military History 1607–1953*, p. 204.

10. *O.R.*, ser. 1, vol. 2, pp. 328–29.

11. Ibid., p. 323.

12. Ibid. p. 203.

13. Ibid., p. 766.

14. *O.R.*, ser. 1, vol. 5, pp. 24–25.

15. Ibid., p. 25. In spite of McClellan's decision, there were records in the early months of the Civil War of some volunteer engineer-pioneer companies in the field being equipped with India rubber ponton bridges. A few remained in use and were employed in the course of the war to build floating bridges, i.e., Eastern Branch of the Potomac River, Maryland; Big Black River, Mississippi; Arkansas River, Arkansas; for information on the India rubber ponton bridge, see George W. Cullum, *Description of a System of Military Bridges with India Rubber Pontoons* (New York: D. Appleton & Company, 1849); Ivor D. Spencer, "Rubber Ponton Bridges—in 1846,"

The Military Engineer, 37, 231 (January 1945); Adrian G. Traas, *From the Golden Gate to Mexico City*, Washington, D.C. GPO, 1993.

16. Ibid., p. 25.

17. Ibid., p. 617.

18. Ibid., pp. 617–18.

19. Ibid., pp. 619–20.

20. Don Pedro Quaerendo Reminisco, *Life in the Union Army or Notings and Reminiscences of a Two Year's Volunteer* (New York: 1864), p. 41.

21. 15th New York Volunteer Engineer Regiment, *Book Records, Regimental Orders Book*, August 1, 1861, Record Group 94, National Archives, Washington, D.C.

22. 50th New York Volunteer Engineer Regiment, *Book Records, Regimental Consolidated Morning Report*, September 1861, Record Group 94, National Archives, Washington, D.C.

23. Thomas Wolff, "Pioneers of the Army—A Survey of the History of Military Engineering and Modern Requirements," *The Scientific American Supplement*, 80, (October 1915), pp. 226–27.

24. *O.R.*, ser. 1, vol. 33, pt. 1, p. 596.

25. *O.R.*, ser. 1, vol. 27, pt. 3, p. 1017.

26. Arnold Gates, ed., *The Rough Side of War, The Civil War Journal of Chesley A. Mosman, First Lieutenant 59th Illinois Volunteer Infantry Regiment* (Garden City, N.Y.: The Basin Publishing Co., 1987), pp. 233–42.

27. George W. Cullum, *Description of a System of Military Bridges with India Rubber Pontoons* (New York: D. Appleton & Company, 1849), p. 27.

28. Radnitz is not listed in the General Index, *O.R.* The officer apparently was Captain John Rziha, 19th U.S. Infantry, as printed on plate 6, Official Atlas, *O.R.*

29. *Frank Leslie's Illustrated Newspaper*, 28 September 1861, vol. 12, no. 306, pp. 310–11.

30. *Harper's Weekly*, 26 October 1861, vol. 5, pp. 684–85.

31. Michigan Engineers and Mechanics Regiment, *Regimental Books. Letters Book, Regimental Consolidated Morning Report*, October–November 1861, Record Group 94, National Archives, Washington, D.C.; Microform, Michigan Engineers and Mechanics Regiment, *Daily Activities Cards*, December 1861, M594, roll 4007, National Archives, Washington, D.C.

32. Missouri Engineer Regiment, *Book Records, Descriptive Book*, October 1861, Record Group 94, National Archives, Washington, D.C.

CHAPTER 2

1. *O.R.*, ser. 1, vol. 1, p. 41.

2. *History of 1st Engineers Battalion During the Civil War*, Unpublished Manuscript, File 391, Entry 100, RG 98, National Archives, Washington, D.C., p. 49.

3. Ibid., p. 50.

4. *O.R.*, ser. 1, vol. 5, pp. 48–49.

5. Reminisco, *Life in the Union Army*, p. 31.

6. *O.R.*, ser. 1, vol. 5, pp. 44–49.

7. *O.R.*, ser. 1, vol. 7, p. 102.

8. Ibid., ser. l, vol. 5, pp. 18, 41, 50.

9. Ibid., ser. 1, vol. 11, pt. 1, p. 158.

10. 15th New York Volunteer Engineers, Company H, *Book Records, Morning Report Book, April 1862*, RG 94, National Archives, Washington, D.C.

11. *O.R.*, ser. 1, vol. 11, pt. 1, p. 14.

12. Ibid., p. 15.

13. *Harper's Weekly*, May 16, 1862, p. 182.

14. *O.R.*, ser. 1, vol. 11, pt. 1, p. 10.

15. Ibid., Atlas, plate 17, p. 1.

16. James L. Nichols, *Confederate Engineers* (Tuscaloosa, Ala.: Confederate Publishing Company, Inc., 1957), p. 98.

17. *O.R.*, ser. 1, vol. 11, pt. 1, p. 143; Atlas, plate 7, 1.

18. Ibid., p. 144.

19. Ibid., p. 51.

20. Ibid., pp. 31–32.

21. Ibid., p. 28.

22. Ibid., p. 144.

23. Ibid.

24. Ibid., p. 112.

25. Ibid., p. 511.

26. Ibid., p. 113.

27. Ibid., p. 143.

28. Ibid., pp. 113–14.

29. Ibid., pp. 52–54; Atlas, plate 17, p. 1.

30. Ibid., p. 32.

31. Ibid., p. 117.

32. Ibid., p. 167.

33. Ibid., pp. 60–65.

34. Ibid., pp. 118–19.

35. Ibid., pp. 67–71.

36. Ibid., p. 123.

37. George W. Cullum, *Biographical Register of Officers and Graduates of the United States Military Academy* (Boston: Houghton-Mifflin and Co., 1891.)

38. *O.R.*, ser. 1, vol. 12, pt. 3, p. 813.

39. Francis A. Lord, *Lincoln's Railroad Man: Herman Haupt* (Rutherford, N.J: Fairleigh Dickinson University Press, 1969), pp. 69–74; Karl A. Von den Steinen, "Military Bridging in the American Civil War," *Mines Magazine* (November–December 1938), p. 15.

40. *O.R.*, ser. 1, vol. 12, pt. 1, p. 281.

41. Ibid.

42. Von den Steinen, "Military Bridging in the American Civil War," *Mines Magazine* (November–December 1938), p. 15.

43. Miller, *Photographic History of the Civil War.* vol. 5, p. 280.

44. Jno. J. Boniface, *The Cavalry Horse and His Pack* (Kansas City, Mo.: Hudson Kimberly Publishing Company, 1903), p. 15; *O.R.*, Atlas, plate 85, p. 5.

45. *O.R.*, ser. 1, vol. 12, pt. 2, p. 12.

46. *O.R.*, ser. l, vol. 21, pt. 1, pp. 48, 793.

47. *History of 1st Engineers Battalion During the Civil War*, p. 67.

48. Gilbert Thompson, "The Engineer Battalion in the Civil War," p. 60.
49. Ibid., p. 47.
50. Ibid.
51. Ibid., p. 148.
52. Ibid., p. 149.
53. Ibid.
54. Ibid., p. 795.
55. Oliver Otis Howard, *Autobiography*, p. 317.
56. Kenneth P. Williams, *Lincoln Finds a General*, p. 507.
57. *O.R.*, ser. 1, vol. 21, p. 51.
58. Ibid., p. 21.
59. Ibid.
60. Ibid.
61. Ibid.
62. *History of 1st Engineer Battalion During Civil War*, p. 68.
63. William A. Neal, *An Illustrated History of the Missouri Engineer and 25th Infantry Regiment* (Saint Louis: Donohue and Henneberry Printers, 1889), pp. 41–42; *O.R.*, ser. l, vol. 8, pp. 81–90, p. 435.
64. Mark M. Krug, ed., *Mrs. Hill's Journal–Civil War Reminiscences*, (Chicago: R. R. Donnelley & Sons Company, 1980), pp. 70–92.
65. William F. Patterson, *Letters and Papers*. Manuscript Division, Library of Congress, Washington, D.C.
66. *O.R.*, ser. 3, vol. 2, p. 805.
67. R. V. Johnson and C. C. Buel, *Battles and Leaders of the Civil War*, p. 491.
68. *O.R.*, ser. 1, vol. 36, pt. 1, pp. 247–48.
69. Miller, *Photographic History of the Civil War*. vol. 5, p. 211.
70. *O.R.*, ser. 1, vol. 16, pt. 1, p. 725

CHAPTER 3

1. *O.R.*, ser. 1, vol. 21, pt. 1, pp. 47–48, 84–87, 99.
2. Gilbert Thompson, "The Engineer Battalion in the Civil War," *Occasional Papers*, Engineer School, U.S. Army, No. 44 (1910), p. 133.
3. Andrew H. Humphreys, *From Gettysburg to the Rapidan* (New York: Charles Scribner's Sons, 1883), p. 176.
4. Francis A. Lord, *Lincoln's Railroad Man, Herman Haupt*, pp. 206–8.
5. Reminisco, *Life in the Union Army*, p. 40.
6. *50th New York Volunteer Engineers, Regimental Orders Book.* May 3, 1863, RG 94, National Archives, Washington, D.C.
7. *15th New York Volunteer Engineers. Book Records. Regimental Orders Book*, May 5, 1863, RG 94, National Archives, Washington, D.C.
8. Thompson, "The Engineer Battalion in the Civil War," p. 78.
9. *O.R.*, ser. 1, vol. 27, pt. 1, p. 15.
10. Ibid.
11. Ibid., pp. 226–27.
12. Ibid., p. 143.
13. Thompson, "The Engineer Battalion in the Civil War," p. 80.
14. Ibid.

15. Ibid.
16. *O.R.*, ser. 1, vol. 27, pt. 3, p. 484.
17. Ibid., p. 22.
18. Ibid., p. 67.
19. Ibid., pp. 22–24.
20. Ibid., p. 23.
21. Lord, *Lincoln's Railroad Man.* p. 221.
22. *O.R.*, ser. 1, vol. 27, pt. 3, p. 522.
23. Ibid., p. 620.
24. *O.R.*, ser. 1, vol. 27, pt. 1, p. 83, 105, 109–10.
25. Ibid., pp. 307–10.
26. *O.R.*, ser. 1, vol. 27, pt. 2, p. 172.
27. Ibid., p. 299.
28. *O.R.*, ser. 1, vol. 27, pt. 1, p. 17.
29. Ibid., pt. 2, p. 300.
30. Ibid., p. 301.
31. Ibid., p. 991.
32. *O.R.*, ser. 1, vol. 27, pt. 1, pp. 307–10.
33. Ibid., p. 302.
34. Thompson, *The Engineer Battalion*, p. 181.
35. *O.R.*, ser. 1, vol. 24, pt. 1, pp. 370–90.
36. MOLLUS, Minnesota Commandery, Brigadier General John B. Sanborn, "The Campaign Against Vicksburg," 1890, pp. 116–18.
37. MOLLUS, Ohio Commandery, Brigadier General A. Hickenlooper, "Our Volunteer Engineers," Robert Clarke & Co., 1890, p. 308.
38. General U. S. Grant, *Personal Memoirs*, vol. 1, p. 437.
39. MOLLUS, Illinois Commandery, William B. Jenney, "Personal Recollections of Vicksburg," 1899, vol. 3, p. 247.
40. *O.R.*, ser. 1, vol. 24, pt. 2, pp. 187–89.
41. MOLLUS, Ohio Commandery, Colonel Manning F. Force, "Personal Recollections of the Vicksburg Campaign," Detroit, Ostler Printing Company, 1888, pp. 293–95.
42. *O.R.*, ser. 1, vol. 24, pt. 1, p. 14.
43. Ibid., p. 55.
44. Ibid., p. 56.
45. MOLLUS, Illinois Commandery, Brigadier General William E. Strong, "The Campaign Against Vicksburg," 1894, pp. 320–26.
46. *O.R.*, ser. 1, vol. 24, pt. 1, p. 601.
47. Colonel Force, "Personal Recollections of the Vicksburg Campaign," p. 294.
48. Grant, *Personal Memoirs*, p. 480.
49. Brigadier General John B. Sanborn, "The Campaign Against Vicksburg," p. 117.
50. *O.R.*, ser. 1, vol. 24, pt. 1, p. 145.
51. Ibid., pp. 145–46.
52. *Reports of Adjutant General*, Kentucky, p. 494; Captain William F. Patterson, Kentucky Company of Mechanics and Engineers, *Daily Activity Cards*, May 3, 1863, Microform M 397, roll 472, National Archives, Washington, D.C.

53. MOLLUS, Ohio Commandery, Brigadier General A. Hickenlooper, "Our Volunteer Engineers," vol. 3, 1890, p. 309; *O.R.*, ser. 1, vol. 24, pt. 1, pp. 203–6.

54. *O.R.*, ser. 1, vol. 24, pt. 1, p. 716.

55. Patterson's *Letters and Papers*, Manuscript Division (MD), Library of Congress (LC).

56. Colonel Force, "Personal Recollections of the Vicksburg Campaign," p. 294.

57. *O.R.*, ser. 1, vol. 24, pt. 1, pp. 148–51.

58. Ibid., pt. 2, pp. 650, 725.

59. Ibid., pt. 1, p. 601.

60. Ibid., p. 125; John D. Billings, *Hardtack and Coffee*, pp. 383–84.

61. Ibid., pp. 125, 755, 203–6; Captain William F. Patterson, Kentucky Company of Mechanics and Engineers, *Daily Activities Cards*. May 17, 1863, Microform M 397, roll 472, National Archives, Washington, D.C.; Patterson's *Letters and Papers*, MD, LC.

62. Brigadier General A. Hickenlooper, "Our Volunteer Engineers," p. 308.

63. A. Hickenlooper, "Our Volunteer Engineers," p. 309; *Harper's Weekly*, June 27, 1863, p. 1; *O.R.*, ser. 1, vol. 24, pt. 1, pp. 203–6.

64. William E. Strong, "The Campaign Against Vicksburg," pp. 328–30.

65. Brigadier General James H. Wilson, *Under the Old Flag*, pp. 204–6.

66. Ibid., p. 208.

67. *O.R.*, ser. 1, vol. 24, pt. 1, pp. 54–55.

68. Ibid., p. 56.

69. *O.R.*, ser. l, vol. 24, pt. 1, p. 37.

70. A. Hickenlooper, "Our Volunteer Engineers," p. 310.

71. *O.R.*, ser. 1, vol. 24, pt. 1, p. 38.

72. Ibid., pp. 57, 59.

73. Ibid., p. 44.

74. Sanborn, "The Campaign Against Vicksburg," p. 118.

75. *O.R.*, ser. 1, vol. 30, p. 650; William B. Jenney, "Personal Recollections of Vicksburg," p. 248.

76. Ibid., vol. 23, pt. 2, pp. 550–53; Charles Lanman, *The Red Book of Michigan—A Civil, Military, and Biographical History* (Detroit: Smith & Co., 1871), p. 233; Francis F. McKinney, "The First Regiment of Michigan Engineers and Mechanics," *Michigan Alumni Quarterly Review*, 62 (1956); pp. 142, 145.

77. *O.R.*, ser. 1, vol. 30, pt. 1, p. 34.

78. Ibid., pt. 1, p. 39.

79. *O.R.*, ser. 1, vol. 29, pt. 1, p. 150.

80. Ibid., pp. 148–82.

81. *O.R.*, ser. 1, vol. 30, pt. 1, p. 78.

82. Ibid., pp. 33–39, 50–52, 78.

83. *O.R.*, ser. 1, vol. 31, pt. 1, pp. 41–42, 77–78, 929.

84. Ibid., p. 729; *O.R.*, ser. 1, vol. 30, pt. 1, pp. 685, 697, 835; Stephen Z. Starr, *The Union Cavalry in the Civil War*, vol. 3, p. 290.

85. *O.R.*, ser. 1, vol. 30, pt. 2, pp. 675–76, 683, 819–21; F. T. Miller, *Photographic History of the Civil War*. vol. 3, 1957, pp. 160–64; *Confederate Veteran*, 24, No. 9, September 1914, pp. 11–12.

86. MOLLUS, Michigan Commandery, Henry S. Dean, "The Relief of Chattanooga," Detroit, Ostler Printing Company, 1888, p. 133.

87. *Harper's Weekly*, vol. 7, no. 361, November 28, 1863, p. 764; *O.R.*, ser. 1, vol. 31, pt. 2, p. 123.

88. *O.R.*, ser. 1, vol. 31, pt. 2, pp. 52, 73–75, 123.

89. Mark M. Krug, *Mrs. Hill's Journal—Civil War Reminiscences*, p. 253; *O.R.*, ser. 4, vol. 3, p. 910.

90. Ibid., p. 278.

91. *O.R.*, ser. 3, vol. 5, pt. 3, pp. 934–36; Francis F. McKinney, "The First Regiment of Michigan Engineers and Mechanics," *Michigan Alumni Quarterly Review*, 62 (1956); pp. 146–47.

92. Arnold Gates, *The Rough Side of War*, pp. 140–56.

93. *O.R.*, ser. 1, vol. 31, pt. 2, p. 73.

94. *O.R.*, ser. 1, vol. 30, pt. 1, pp. 40, 77–78, 216–35; Atlas, plate 49.

CHAPTER 4

1. Thompson, *The Engineer Battalion in the Civil War*, p. 76.

2. 50th New York Volunteer Engineer Regiment, *Book Records, Regimental Orders and Letters Book*, February 1864, RG 94, National Archives, Washington, D.C.

3. Dale E. Floyd, ed., *Dear Friends at Home. The Letters and Diary of Thomas James Owen*, pp. 21–22.

4. Floyd, *Dear Friends at Home*, p. 30.

5. Ibid., p. 32.

6. *O.R.*, ser. 3, vol. 5, p. 183; Atlas, plate 77, p. 3.

7. Thompson, *The Engineer Battalion in the Civil War*, p. 83.

8. Floyd, *Dear Friends at Home*, p. 38.

9. Ibid.

10. Ibid., p. 40.

11. Horace Porter, *Campaigning with Grant*, (New York: The Century Co., 1897), p. 136.

12. *Frank Leslie's Illustrated Newspaper*, no. 452, p. 151; *O.R.*, Atlas, plate 68.

13. *O.R.*, Atlas, plate 74.

14. Horace Porter, *Campaigning with Grant*, p. 136.

15. Reid, "Another Look at Grant's Crossing of the James," p. 306.

16. Porter, *Campaigning with Grant*, p. 137.

17. Ibid., p. 138.

18. *O.R.*, ser. 3, vol. 4, pp. 796–97.

19. Ibid., p. 138.

20. *Harper's Weekly*, vol. 8, no. 392, pp. 392, 419.

21. Reid, "Another Look at Grant's Crossing of the James," p. 309.

22. *O.R.*, ser. 3, vol. 4, pp. 796–97.

23. *O.R.*, ser. 1, vol. 40, pt. 1, p. 680; Atlas, plate 125, p. 11.

24. *O.R.*, ser. 1, vol. 42, pt. 1, p. 661; *O.R.*, ser. 1, vol. 46, pt. 2, p. 1169; Atlas, plate 67, p. 7 and plate 76, p. 3.

25. *O.R.*, ser. 1, vol. 42, pt. 1, p. 661; *O.R.*, ser. 1, vol. 46, pt. 2, p. 1169; Atlas, plate 67 and plate 76, p. 3.

26. Floyd, *Dear Friends at Home*, p. 44.

27. Ibid., p. 49.

28. Ibid., p. 66,

29. Ibid., p. 55.
30. Ibid., p. 66.
31. Ibid., p. 67.
32. Ibid., p. 69.
33. Ibid., ser. 1, vol. 38, pt. 1, p. 63.
34. Lord, *Lincoln's Railroad Man: Herman Haupt*, p. 261.
35. *O.R.*, ser. 3, vol. 5, pp. 950–52.
36. *O.R.*, ser. 1, vol. 38, pt. 1, pp. 61–85.
37. Ibid., pp. 138–39.
38. *O.R.*, ser. 1, vol. 44, p. 56.
39. Ibid., pp. 57–58.
40. Ibid., ser. 1, vol. 45, pt. 1, p. 42.
41. Ibid., ser. 2, vol. 44, p. 59.
42. Ibid.; Atlas, plate 69, p. 5, and plate 101, p. 21.
43. *O.R.*, ser. 1, vol. 44, p. 60.
44. 1st Missouri Engineer Regiment, Company A, *Book Records, Company Morning Report Book*, November 1864, Record Group 94, National Archives, Washington, D.C.
45. 1st Missouri Engineer Regiment, Company K, *Book Records, Company Morning Report Book*, November 1864, Record Group 94, National Archives, Washington, D.C.
46. *O.R.*, ser. 1, vol. 44, pp. 57, 61.
47. Ibid., pp. 160–62.
48. Ibid., pp. 60–61.
49. 1st Michigan Engineers and Mechanics Regiment, Book Records, Regimental Letters Book, December 1864, Record Group 94, National Archives, Washington,D.C.

CHAPTER 5

1. *O.R.*, ser. 1, vol. 47, pt. 1, p. 169.
2. Ibid., p. 426.
3. Ibid., pp. 426, 429.
4. Ibid., p. 171.
5. Ibid., p. 427.
6. Ibid., pp. 170–71.
7. Ibid., p. 427.
8. Ibid., p. 173.
9. Ibid., p. 427.
10. Ibid., p. 172.
11. Ibid.
12. Ibid., p. 173.
13. Ibid.
14. Ibid., p. 175.
15. *O.R.*, ser. 1, vol. 47, p. 384.
16. Floyd, *Dear Friends at Home*, p. 71.
17. *O.R.*, ser. 3, vol. 5, pp. 377–83; Atlas, plates 76, 77.
18. Floyd, *Dear Friends at Home*, p. 75.

19. *O.R.*, ser. 1, vol. 46, pt. 1, p. 160.

20. Ibid., pp. 162–63.

21. *O.R.*, ser. 1, vol. 5, pp. 193–94.

22. Ibid., pp. 642–43.

23. Floyd, *Dear Friends at Home*, p. 89.

24. *O.R.*, ser. 3, vol. 5, p. 194.

25. *O.R.*, ser. 1, vol. 46, pt. 1, p. 643.

26. Ibid., p. 641.

27. *O.R.*, ser. 3, vol. 5, p. 193.

28. Floyd, *Dear Friends at Home*, p. 82.

29. *O.R.*, ser. 3, vol. 5, p. 1166.

30. *O.R.*, ser. 1, vol. 46, pt. 1, pp. 643–44.

31. *O.R.*, ser. 3, vol. 5, p. 195.

32. Floyd, *Dear Friends at Home*, p. 82.

33. *O.R.*, ser. 3, vol. 5, p. 199.

34. Thompson, *The Engineer Battalion in the Civil War*, p. 156.

35. *O.R.*, ser. 3, vol. 5, p. 199.

36. Ibid.

37. Ibid., p. 195.

Glossary

Abatis. An obstacle of trees with bent or sharpened branches directed toward the enemy, now often interfaced with barbed wire.

Artificer. One who is skilled or clever in devising ways of making an article (for profession or trade); an inventor; skillful or artistic worker; craftsman. Mil. A skilled and specialized mechanic.

Balk. A crossbeam or girder to support roadway of floating bridge.

Barbette. A platform or mound of earth, within a fortification, from which guns may be fired over the parapet instead of through embrasures.

Bastion. Fort. A projecting portion of a rampart or fortification that forms an irregular pentagon attached at the base to the main work.

Bateau. A double ended flat-bottomed rowboat used on rivers in Canada and the northern United States. A ponton (pontoon) of a floating bridge.

Battlement. A parapet or cresting, originally defensive, but later usually decorative, consisting of a regular alternation of merlons and crenels. Also called embattlement.

Blockhouse. Mil. A fortified structure with ports or loopholes for gunfire, used against bombs, artillery, and small arms fire.

Bombproof. A structure of such design and strength as to resist the penetration and the shattering force of shells, usually built in part beneath the level of the ground.

Breastwork. Fort. n. A hastily constructed defensive work, usually breast high.

Chess. One of the planks forming a roadway of a floating bridge.

Cheval-de-frise (pl. Chevaux-de-frise). A portable obstacle, usually a sawhorse, covered with projecting spikes or barbed wire, for military use in closing a passage, or breaking in a defensive wall.

Contraband. An African-American slave who escaped to or was brought within the Union army lines.

Corduroy. n. A road constructed of logs laid together transversely across swampy ground. v. To form a road or the like by laying logs transversely. To make corduroy road.

Crenel. Any of the open spaces between the merlons (solid part between two crenels) of a battlement.

Éclat. Brilliance of success, reputation.

Embrasure(s). In fortification, an opening as a loophole or crenel, through which missiles may be discharged.

Engineer. A person versed in the design, construction, and use of engines or machines, or in any of various branches of engineering. A member of military service specially trained in engineering work.

Engineering. n. Science concerned with putting scientific knowledge to practical use planning, designing, constructing projects.

Engines of War. Catapult, Crossbow, missiles sling-shot, middle ages warfare, military engineer derivative from maker of engines of war.

Entrenchment. An earth breastwork or ditch for protection against enemy fire. Also intrenchment.

Fascine Fort. A long bundle of sticks bound together, used in building earthworks and batteries and in strengthening ramparts.

Fortification. Military work constructed for purpose of strengthening a position.

Fraise Fort. A defense consisting of pointed stakes from ramparts in a horizontal position, supported by abatis, chevaux-de-frise, and gabions.

Gabion. A cylinder of wickerwork filled with earth, used as military defense.

Line of Communications. A means or process of sending messages, orders, establishing routes and transportation for moving troops and supplies from a base, headquarters railhead to an area of operations. A part of the theater of operations which adjoins the combat zone, and establishes communications, supply and other activities for the support of field forces.

Linchpin. A pin inserted through the end of an axle to keep the wheel on.

Mine. A subterranean passage made to extend under an enemy's works or position, as for the purpose of securing access or of depositing explosives for blowing up a military position. Land Mine. A device containing a charge of explosive in a casing used on land against personnel or vehicles.

Palisade. A fence of poles or stakes set firmly in the ground as for enclosure or defense. Any of a number of poles or stakes pointed at the top and set firmly in the ground in a close row with others to form a defense.

Parallel. Fort. A trench cut in the ground before a fortress, parallel to its defense, for the purpose of covering a besieging force.

Parapet. Fort. A defensive wall or elevation as of earth or stone, in a fortification. An elevation raised above the main wall or rampart of a permanent fortification. Lateral parapet. Projecting sidewise; parapet in a protective line.

Parole. Mil. The promise, usually written, of a prisoner of war that he/she (the captured person) is released if he/she will return to custody at a specified time or will not again take up arms against his/her captors.

Pioneer. A foot soldier detailed to make roads, dig intrenchments, etc., in advance of main body. Performs battlefield engineering tasks.

Ponton. Mil. 1. Army nomenclature for basic component of ponton (floating) bridge. 2. Support for ponton (floating) bridge roadway. 3. French ponton, a wooden bateau, flat, double-ended. 4. Russian ponton, flat ended made of sail cloth or canvas, stretched over a framework of wood. The thwarts (transverse members) that spread the gunwales, when with side frames removed, the whole could be packed in a small space on a wagon. The canvas was well tarred or covered with a strong varnish.

Pontonier. Mil. An officer or soldier in charge of bridge equipment or construction of ponton bridges.

Pontoon. Mil. A flat boat, cylinder, or some other floating structure used as one of the supports for a roadway of a temporary (floating) bridge. Also ponton.

Prolonge. Mil. A rope having a hook at one end and a toggle at the other used for various purposes as to draw a gun carriage. Toggle. Pin placed transversely through chain eye, loop in rope to bind to another chain loop.

Redoubt. Fort. An isolated work forming a complete enclosure of any form, used to defend a prominent point. An independent earthwork built within a permanent fortification to reinforce it.

Revetment. A facing of masonry or the like, especially for protecting an embankment.

Rifle Pit. A pit or short trench affording shelter to riflemen in firing at an enemy.

Salient. A salient angle or point, as the central outward projecting angle of a bastion or an outward projection in a battle line.

Sap. Fort. n. A deep narrow trench constructed so as to form an approach to a besieged place or an enemy's position. v.t. Fort. To approach a besieged place or enemy position with deep, narrow trenches protected by gabions or parapets.

Sapper. One who digs a sap.

Saproller. Soldier who rolls a gabion in front of him while digging or moving through a sap.

Savoir faire. Knowledge of what action to take; tact; knowing how to do a specific action.

Siege. The act or process of surrounding and attacking a fortified place in such a way as to isolate it from help and supplies, for the purpose of lessening the resistance of the defenders and thereby making capture possible. Any prolonged or persistent effort to overcome resistance. Lay siege to, to besiege.

Strake. n. A continuous course of planks or plates forming a hull, shell, deck, the side of a deckhouse.

Stringer. A long horizontal timber connecting upright posts. A longitudinal bridge girder for supporting part of a deck or railroad track between bents or piers.

Technology. n. Study of practical use of industrial arts; progress in machinery; applied science; system to fill society's needs.

Topographical Engineer. A specialist in topography. One who describes the surface features of a place or region; prepares map showing topographic features, usually by means of contour lines.

Topography. The detailed mapping or charting of the features of a relatively small area, district, or localities. The detailed description, especially by means of surveying of particular localities as cities, towns, etc.

Transom. A cross piece.

Traverse. Fort. A defensive barrier, parapet or the like placed transversely. A defensive barrier thrown across the terreplein (the top platform or horizontal surface of a rampart, used as a support for a cannon), or the covered way of a fortification to protect it from enfilade fire.

Trestle. One of a number of bents having sloping sides of framework or piling for supporting the deck or stringers of a bridge. Trestle Bridge. Bridge made of trestles. Trestle Bridge Bent. A transverse frame of a bridge designed to support either vertical or horizontal loads.

Trestle Bridge Cross Beam. A transverse beam in a structure, as a joist.

Truss. Any of various structural frames based on the geometric rigidity of the triangle and composed of straight members subject only to longitudinal compression, tension, or both, and so disposed as to make the frame rigid under anticipated loads; functions as a beam or cantilever to support bridges. Any rigid construction extending horizontally well beyond vertical support, used as a structural element of a bridge.

Work. A building, wall, trench, or the like, constructed or made as a means of fortification.

Bibliography

Printed Works

Barnard, J. G. and W. F. Barry. *Report of the Engineer and Artillery Operations of the Army of the Potomac.* New York: D. Van Nostrand, 1863.

Billings, John D. *Hardtack and Coffee.* Boston: George M. Smith & Company, 1887.

Bond, Paul S. *The Engineers in War.* New York: McGraw-Hill, 1916.

Boniface, Jno. J. *The Cavalry Horse and His Pack.* Kansas City, Mo.: Hudson Kimberly Publishing Company, 1903.

Brown, Ida C. *Michigan in the Civil War.* Lansing: The University of Michigan, 1960.

Cullum, George W. *Description of a System of Military Bridges with India Rubber Pontoons in Use by the United States Army.* New York: D. Appleton & Company, 1849.

Dinkins, Captain James. *Personal Recollections and Experiences in Confederate Army.* Cincinnati: Self-published, 1897.

Dyer, Frederick H. *A Compendium of the War of the Rebellion.* 3 volumes. New York: Thomas Yoseloff, 1959.

Floyd, Dale E., editor. *Dear Friends at Home. The Letters and Diary of Thomas James Owen, 50th New York Volunteer Engineer Regiment.* Washington, GPO, 1985.

Gates, Arnold, editor. *The Rough Side of War. The Civil War Journal of Chesley A. Mosman, First Lieutenant, Company D, 59th Illinois Volunteer Infantry Regiment.* Garden City, N.Y.: The Basin Publishing Company, 1987.

Grant, U. S. *Personal Memoirs*. New York: Webster and Company, 1894.

Guernsey, Alfred H. *Harper's Pictorial History of the Great Rebellion*. 2 volumes. Chicago: McDonnell Bros., 1866, 1894.

Haupt, Herman. *General Theory of Bridge Construction*. Philadelphia: D. Appleton & Company, 1851.

———. *Military Bridges: With Suggestions of New Expedients for Crossing Streams and Chasms*. New York: D. Van Nostrand, 1864.

———. *Reminiscences of General Herman Haupt*. Milwaukee: Wright and Jays Company, 1901.

———. *Reminiscences of General Herman Haupt*. New York: Arno Press, 1981.

Henry, Robert Selph. *First with the Most—Forrest*. Indianapolis: The Bobbs Merrill Company Publishers, 1944.

Howard, Oliver Otis. *Autobiography*. New York: The Baker & Taylor Company, 1907.

Hubbard, John Milton. *Notes of a Private*. Saint Louis: Self-published, 1909.

Humphreys, Andrew H. *From Gettysburg to the Rapidan*. New York: Charles Scribner's Sons, 1883.

Hunt, O. E. *Engineer Corps of the Federal Army*. The Photographic History of the Civil War. Volume 5. New York: The Review of Reviews Co., 1912.

Johnson, Robert Underwood, and Clarence Clough Buel. *Battles and Leaders of the Civil War*. 4 volumes. New York: The Century Co., 1887.

Johnson, Rossiter. *Campfire and Battleground*. New York: Henry W. Knight, 1900.

Krug, Mark M., editor. *Mrs. Hill's Journal—Civil War Reminiscences, Sarah Jane Full Hill*. Chicago: The Lakeside Press—R. R. Donnelley & Sons Company, 1980.

Lanman, Charles. *The Red Book of Michigan—A Civil, Military, and Biographical History*. Detroit: Smith & Co., 1871.

Lord, Francis A. *Lincoln's Railroad Man: Herman Haupt*. Rutherford, N.J.: Fairleigh Dickinson University Press, 1969.

McKinney, Francis F. "The First Regiment of Michigan Engineers and Mechanics," *Michigan Alumni Quarterly Review*, 62 (1956).

Military Order of the Loyal Legion of the United States. *Illinois Commandery, Michigan Commandery, Minnesota Commandery, Ohio Commandery*.

Miller, Francis T. *The Photographic History of the Civil War*. 10 volumes. New York: The Review of Reviews Co., 1912.

Mottelay, Paul F., and T. Campbell Copeland. *The Soldier in Our Civil War*. New York: Bradley Publishing Company, 1890.

Neal, William A. *An Illustrated History of the Missouri Engineer and 25th Infantry Regiment*. Saint Louis: Donohue and Henneberry, Printers, 1889.

Nichols, James L. *Confederate Engineers*. Tuscaloosa, Ala.: Confederate Publishing Company, Inc., 1957.

Porter, Horace. *Campaigning with Grant*. New York: The Century Co., 1897.

Reminisco, Don Pedro Quaerendo. *Life in the Union Army or Notings and Reminiscences of a Two Year's Volunteer*. New York: 1864.

Starr, Stephen Z. *The Union Cavalry in the Civil War*. 3 volumes. Baton Rouge: Louisiana State University Press, 1979–1985.

State of Indiana. *Reports of the Adjutant General*, 1861–1865.

State of Kentucky. *Reports of the Adjutant General*, 1861–1865.

State of Michigan. *Reports of the Adjutant General*, 1861–1865.

State of Missouri. *Reports of the Adjutant General*, 1861–1865.

State of New York. *Reports of the Adjutant General*, 1861–1865.

State of Pennsylvania. *Reports of the Adjutant General*, 1861–1865.

Sumner, Merlin E., editor. *The Diary of Cyrus B. Comstock*. Dayton, Ohio: Morningside House, Inc., 1987.

Von den Steinen, Karl A. "Military Bridging in the American Civil War," *Mines Magazine* (November-December 1938).

Ward, James A. *That Man Haupt.—A Biography of Herman Haupt*. Baton Rouge: Louisiana State University Press, 1973.

Wiley, Bell Irwin. *The Life of Billy Yank*. Indianapolis: The Bobbs-Merrill Company, 1952.

Williams, Kenneth P. *Lincoln Finds A General*. New York: Macmillan and Company, 1964.

Wilson, James H. *Under the Old Flag*. New York: D. Appleton and Company, 1912.

Military and Government Works

Barnard, J. G. *The Peninsular Campaign and its Antecedents as Developed by the Report of Major General Geo. B. McClellan, and Other Published Documents*. New York: 1864.

Cullum, George W. *Biographical Register of Officers and Graduates United States Military Academy.* 7 volumes. Boston: Houghton-Mifflin and Company, 1891–1930.

Duane, J. C. *History of Bridge Equipage in the United States Army.* Printed Papers of the Essayons Club of the Corps of Engineers, U.S. Army, volume 1, 1868–1872.

Hannum, Warren T. "The Crossing of the James River in 1864," *The Military Engineer,* volume 15 (May–June 1923).

Hickenlooper, A. "Our Volunteer Engineers," *Sketches of War History 1861–1865.* Military Order of the Loyal Legion of the United States, Ohio Commandery. Volume 3 (1890).

Hodges, F. H. "Roster of Service with Engineer Troops and Brief Historical Sketch of their Organization," *Occasional Papers, Engineer School, U.S. Army,* n.d.

Humphreys, A. A. "Historical Sketch of the Corps of Engineers and Remarks Upon its Organization and Duties," *Occasional Papers, Engineer School, U.S. Army,* No. 16 (October 20, 1876).

Huston, James A. "Grant's Crossing of the James with the Longest Ponton Bridge Ever Built," *The Military Engineer,* volume 45 (January–February 1953).

Noxon, J. A. "The Battle of Fredericksburg," *The Military Engineer,* volume 25 (March–April 1933).

Patterson, William F. *Letters and Papers,* Manuscript Division, Library of Congress, Washington, D.C.

Rees, Thomas H., and G. A. Youngberg. "History of Engineer Troops in the U.S. Army 1775–1901," *Occasional Papers, Engineer School, U.S. Army,* No. 37 (1905).

Robinson, William H. "The Engineer Soldiers in the Mexican War," *The Military Engineer,* volume 24, 133 (January–February 1932).

Spencer, Ivor D. "Rubber Ponton Bridges—in 1846," *The Military Engineer,* volume 37, 231 (January 1945).

Thompson, Gilbert. "The Engineer Battalion in the Civil War," *Occasional Papers,* Engineer School, U.S. Army, No. 44 (1910).

———. "Military Bridges Over the Chickahominy, 1862," *Source Book Peninsular Campaign, 1862,* U.S. Army Command and General Staff College, n.d.

Traas, Adrian G. *From the Golden Gate to Mexico City: The U.S. Army Topographical Engineers in the Mexican War, 1846–1848.* Office of History, Corps of Engineers, and Center of Military History United States Army, Washington, D.C.: GPO, 1993.

Turtle, Thomas. "History of the Engineer Battalion," *Occasional Papers, Engineer School, U.S. Army*, No. 16 (December 21, 1868).

U.S. Army (War Department). *Annual Report of the Chief of Engineers, U.S. Army*, Washington, D.C.: GPO (1861–1865).

U.S. Army (Department of the Army). *ROTC Manual No. 145–20: American Military History—1607–1953*. Washington, D.C.: GPO, 1956.

U.S. Army (War Department). *The War of the Rebellion: A Compilation of the Official Records*. 130 volumes including 1 volume index and 3 volumes of atlases. Washington: GPO (1880–1901).

U.S. National Archives and Records Administration. *Civil War Records: History of 1st Engineers Battalion During Civil War*, Unpublished Manuscript, File 391, Entry 100, RG 77, National Archives, Washington, D.C.

U.S. National Archives and Records Administration. *Civil War Records: Civil War Book Records*, 1st Michigan Engineers and Mechanics Regiment; 1st Missouri Volunteer Engineer Regiment; 1st, 15th, 50th New York Volunteer Engineer Regiment. RG 94. National Archives, Washington, D.C.

U.S. National Archives and Records Administration. *Civil War Microform Muster-Event* Cards, Kentucky Company of Mechanics and Engineers, M397, Roll 472, National Archives, Washington, D.C.

U.S. Navy (Navy Department). *Official Records of the Union and Confederate Navies in the War of the Rebellion*. 10 volumes. Washington, D.C.: GPO, 1900.

U.S. Quartermaster General's Department, U.S. Army. *Instructions for Transport and Erection of Military Wire Suspension Bridge Equipage* Washington: GPO, 1862.

Newspapers and Periodicals

The American Historical Review

Atlantic Monthly

The Century Illustrated Monthly Magazine

Civil War History

Confederate Veteran

Harper's Weekly

Frank Leslie's Illustrated Newspaper

Michigan Alumni Quarterly Review

The Military Engineer
The New York Times
Scientific American Supplement
United Service Magazine

Index

First names are included where known.

269

DEMCO